# HOW
# CAN AFRICA
# SURVIVE?

# HOW
# CAN AFRICA
# SURVIVE?

Jennifer Seymour Whitaker

COUNCIL ON FOREIGN RELATIONS PRESS
NEW YORK

*For Craig*

Copyright © 1988 by the Council on Foreign Relations and the Overseas Development Council
All rights reserved.
Printed in the United States of America
Published by arrangement with Harper & Row, Publishers, Inc.

FIRST EDITION
This book may not be reproduced, in whole or in part, in any form (beyond that copying permitted by Sections 107 and 108 of the U.S. copyright Law and excerpts by reviewers for the public press), without written permission from the publishers. For information, write Publications Office, Council on Foreign Relations, 58 East 68th Street, New York, NY 10021.

Library of Congress Cataloguing-in-Publication Data
Whitaker, Jennifer Seymour, 1938–
    How can Africa survive? / by Jennifer Seymour Whitaker.
       p.    cm.
     Bibliography: p.
     Includes index.
     ISBN 0-87609-054-4 : $12.95
       1. Africa—Economic conditions—1960–
2. Africa—Social conditions—1960–    3. Africa—Politics and government—1960–   I. Title.
HC800.W48  1989  960'.328—dc19  89-670 CIP

88  89  90  91  92  PB  10  9  8  7  6  5  4  3  2  1

# Contents

*Acknowledgments*     vi

*Introduction*     1

1. Pre-Modern States in a Post-Modern World     13

2. What Went Wrong     29

3. The Wages of Altruism     57

4. The Blessings of Children     87

5. Eden Eroding     126

6. A Learning Society     167

7. "Seeing Is Different from Being Told"     197

8. A Future in Shadow     218

*Notes on Sources*     233

*Index*     253

# Acknowledgments

For their help, support, and forbearance during my time of total immersion in this book, I owe my friends and family much gratitude and reciprocal understanding. Among colleagues at the Council on Foreign Relations, David Kellogg deserves special thanks: as my chief critic and editorial advisor, his clear vision and wide-ranging imagination were invaluable in moving the book forward, and his professional sagacity was key in our efforts to reach a wider audience. Paul Kreisberg's consistent backing, careful reading and convincing deadlines were also essential in pushing me onward, while Peter Tarnoff's forthright support was highly gratifying. Alison Loeb, always the first and also unfailingly upbeat reader and facilitator, helped a great deal in putting it all together. At an earlier stage, Andrea Gilles sensitively and graciously undertook the preliminary research which provided the foundation for important sections of the book when I began writing several years later, and Alice McLoughlin's assistance bolstered my own initial research. Catherine Fant's sleuthing in the files here also enriched my store of illustrative material and Ned Farrar was of real assistance in tying up loose ends. Jeremy Brenner skillfully coordinated the transformation of parts into whole during the production. My general debts to colleagues are at least partially accounted for in the notes on sources at the end of this book, but I want to express particular appreciation to Crawford Young, Tom Callaghy, Steve Lewis and Carol Lancaster, for their encouragement and generosity with ideas and information. Special thanks are due to Frank Wisner, Mark Edelman, Carl Eicher and Niles Helmboldt for gracious assistance on my research trip to Africa in the winter of 1985. In Kenya, David Leonard was particularly helpful, and in Zimbabwe, David Rohrbach's field work proved especially illuminating. Colleagues at the Overseas Development Council also played an important role, in supporting this book as part of the work of the Committee on African Development Strategies: over several years of collaboration as my co-director on that project, Bob Berg shared with me generously his great knowledge of development and development assistance in Africa; John Sewell also provided professional and moral support throughout our joint efforts. All along the way, African colleagues, friends, and informants provided the most basic resources. I will not try to name them individually, for they should not be held accountable for what is essentially a Westerner's view of their dilemmas. To my editor, Cornelia Bessie, many thanks are due for her enthusiastic commitment and sage guidance throughout the process of making raw manuscript into a book. And, during that period, Colleen Gorove and Maria Tilves provided skilled and supportive assistance in revising, refining, and getting the book to press in one piece in due time. Finally, I want to thank my husband, Craig, to whom this book is dedicated, for his firm faith in my talents and for his unceasing efforts to keep my head above the typewriter.

# Introduction

When I was a teacher in Nigeria in the early 1960s, I used to ponder how Africans would put their stamp on the British institutions that had been bequeathed to them wholesale. Clearly, it would not work for Africans to slavishly imitate their Western mentors, nor to obediently follow their direction. I remember well a British bank manager I knew venting his frustration at the seeming inability of his "native employees" to "get it right" by following the rules and regulations minted in London. Obviously the bank would not run unless the ledgers were kept meticulously. But, on the other hand, the country could not run until Nigerians themselves took responsibility for how the ledgers would be kept. Africans, I concluded, would not do it exactly as Westerners had told them but would invent a way that would be a synthesis of the two cultures.

With this recognition, I had, even in those early days, begun to grasp how important culture would prove to Africa's economic development, how crucial the fit between how Africans lived and how Western institutions worked. What I did not foresee was how difficult it would be to move toward a synthesis that would serve economic progress. What I envisioned was a kind of happy layering, or adding on, as when the students I was teaching donned raffia skirts and wooden masks for a display of tribal dancing on Nigeria's Independence Day. After the dances were over, and the students had dressed again in their immaculate white shorts and shirts, the glimpse of tribal culture receded into the background, remaining, in memory, a gorgeous bit of decoration on our school-day reality.

In fact, as I will show repeatedly throughout this book, melding the two cultures would be much more painful than that: before it could take place, elements in both the African and Western patterns would have to break down. Once

1

started, the process would take a long time and the continent would probably look a lot worse before it looked any better. While the outcome is still too uncertain to justify any optimism, this melding process is now underway in Africa.

Today, Western observers are very well aware that African economies are in a terrible mess, as famine and disorder dominate the images that come our way. For understandable reasons, however, few people have more than a vague idea why this may be so. Since the early 1980s, the dark continent has fallen into increasingly heavy shadow. Now the casual observers who have always gravitated toward its mystery are beginning to locate the heart of Africa's darkness, not in the nighttime spirit world that so fascinated Joseph Conrad, but rather in an immense incapacity to cope. Beneath the extremes of hunger, on the one hand, and the peculiar local obstacles to "getting anything done" on the other, recent mass media coverage of Africa's economic crises has focused on a fairly simple story: Africans have made a dreadful tangle of their economic affairs since Independence, as a consequence of the well-nigh universal corruption and ineptitude of those in power.

This book grew from my reaction against this simplistic explanation. Although the prevailing images were not *wrong*, they were no more than half right. The continent's Western interpreters were giving short shrift to the rationality, and indeed the values, underlying the economic and political choices of Africans. In terms of the traditions that still rule African society almost everywhere, much of what we see as corrupt behavior looks sensible and even virtuous. To sum up profound differences in a few words, our view of what is happening in Africa is clouded by the distance between the Western and the African locus of loyalties.

By and large, Africans draw their community boundaries much more tightly than we do. Their overwhelming investment in tribe, village or family makes it difficult for them to manage larger, Western-style, institutions. It is often remarked that when Africans go to the city they don't leave their village—they take it with them. In town, no matter how "big" a man, how successful they become, they spend most of their time, on and off the job, boosting the fortunes of their own communal group.

And why not? The problem is that helping "brothers" and "sisters" often costs the nation dearly in the diversion of very scarce resources. And the waste of time—in a setting where people threaten to overrun existing structures before new ones can be created—may be equally urgent. While drought and international decline have erased local margins for economic error, the energies and talents of Africa's people have drained away into local institutions that no longer serve the common good, and national institutions that have not yet taken effective hold. Grasping all this, recognizing how far African countries must go before they can compete in the international marketplace, does not lead to optimism about the pace of progress. However, understanding Africans' choices better does help demystify the behavior of African people and heighten our sense of their struggle.

∽

Why does it matter whether or not we see clearly what is happening in Africa? What are these people to us? The importance of almost everything in Africa—particularly its largely untapped markets—remains potential. In any ordering of geopolitical and economic interests, most of the continent must rank pretty far down on the list. Rumors of a coup in Nigeria trouble oil brokers briefly; news of Cuban troops or anti-communist insurgencies provide conservative congressmen with pretexts for low risk ideological parrying; East African ports offer depots for U.S. naval maneuvers in the Indian Ocean. In our flickering concern about the continent, it is the potential risks in ignoring Africa's problems that undoubtedly have the most potency.

Right now African bankruptcy threatens to forge an unwanted link between Western and African interests. The

3

stratagems that have kept several African countries from default—though just barely—are fraying noticeably. Though as a weapon default would inflict fatal damage on those wielding it, the first to flee Pandora's Box will inevitably embolden others to follow. Thus the drag of African weakness on the international financial system may be considerable. Similarly, as we have seen in Central America, persistent economic chaos can bring interventions, insurgencies, and dependencies that may weaken existing ties to the West.

The main reason that we care about Africa's economic crisis, however, is both simpler and harder to define. Biologist Lewis Thomas has argued eloquently that we ultimately have to take responsibility for our fellow human inhabitants of this planet simply because people are genetically designed to do so: all human beings are part of a species programmed for "social living" with one other. One out of every eight of those human beings lives in Africa. These people are very far away from us, in miles and in circumstances—but not so far, in this world of instantaneous electronic images, that we can entirely ignore what they are going through.

Although Africa is four times larger than the United States and has twice as many people, the total gross national product of all forty-six states of sub-Saharan Africa amounts to less than 6 percent of the U.S. gross national product. As a nation, we staunchly resist guilt about inequity, but a gap of this magnitude insidiously invades our consciousness. The question for Americans is not whether to accept responsibility for Africa's problems but whether to feel the problems of Africans' as in some way part of our own.

During the late 1960s, the Nigerian civil war—and the military blockade of rebel Biafra—provoked a political furor in the United States and Europe over the failure of Western governments to take sides with the beseiged and starving Biafran rebels. Again, from 1984 to 1986, millions of Americans and Europeans were galvanized to intervene personally against famine in Ethiopia and other African countries. Here the Western publics evidently hoped by individual effort to allay sufferings they could not bear to witness. The discomfort of many Westerners, often vaguely felt but sometimes quite sharp, at the plight of hundreds of millions of people lacking most of the basic necessities of a decent existence, is likely to provide the West's most enduring link with the continent.

⌇

Throughout this book the main character, "Africa," finds its destiny played off against the secondary actor, that is, "the West." "The West" sometimes means the developed world as a whole but more often refers to the countries of Europe, the United States, and now, though much less so, Japan as well, which have provided most of Africa's foreign investment and trade. For these countries hold a cultural as well as economic monopoly in Africa. Even in African states where the Soviet Union is the chief military and political patron, both the lingua franca and the main models for modern life-styles and organization originate in the former colonial powers and the United States. Colonial styles in Africa did of course vary from metropole to metropole. With French "direct" and British "indirect" rule, as well as Belgian and Portuguese varieties of subjugation, the different national manners of the colonial powers shaped and colored the prevailing autocratic systems. Yet parallel forms of European psychological, intellectual, technological, and physical dominance have left remarkably similar marks on Africans throughout the continent.

Readers may have more questions about the extent to which the entity "Africa" becomes identified with a variety of trends evidently found within forty-six separate states. The extraordinary diversity of African languages and contiguous ethnic groups is well known. The existence almost side by side of people who have different gods, hierarchies, sexual and marriage customs, as well as languages, often amazed early explorers. Colonial history, post-Independence leadership, policy and resources have, over the past quarter-century, also taken African states on different paths. Through numerous specific examples, these differences and some of the reasons for them are marked and explained here.

Yet as we consider African economies in relation to the larger world they must inhabit—that is, the international marketplace—African states find themselves at very similar stages of development, with similar institutions and patterns of trade to sustain people and shape their efforts. Admittedly, the economic profiles of African states and of the whole continent sketched here will sound much more solid than the data actually available to support them: statistics on African economies are often compiled with great difficulty and recorded with widely varying degrees of accuracy. Thus the picture we can paint with them, though sometimes precise, is often merely suggestive. For example, estimates of food production from the U.N., the U.S. Department of Agriculture and African ministries may vary by a factor of four.

But the broad outlines are clear: all African countries depend on exports of minerals or agricultural commodities, and none can compete in manufacturing. For virtually all, ethnicity has played a key role in shaping economic decisions, both of individuals and government officials, by fragmenting political loyalties and narrowing economic cooperation and trust.

Because the way it works is linked so closely to economic culture, the area considered includes only the countries that share that culture, that is, sub-Saharan Africa. The countries of the Mediterranean littoral (Tunisia, Libya, Algeria, and Egypt) and South Africa are explicitly excluded. Though part of the OAU (Organization of African Unity), the North African countries are cut off from the rest of the continent by more than the Sahara. In language, culture, and history, they belong to the Arab world and in political concerns are essentially part of the Middle East.

Nor does South Africa itself play a major role in this book. Unlike the Arab North, South Africa will be a key part of Africa's economic future. With its apartheid system of racial separation, however, the country is set apart from the rest of Africa by a unique set of political problems and economic patterns enforced under that system. After apartheid, South Africa could become a strong catalyst for growth in the region. For now, though, it figures in this story mainly as an an impediment to the well-being of its neighbors. South Africa's aggressive pursuit of apartheid may well decimate the economies of Angola and Mozambique, and could seriously disrupt those of Zimbabwe, Botswana, and Zambia. In its regional assaults, South Africa is now abetted by the United States, whose aid to the UNITA (National Union for the Total Independence of Angola) insurgents in Angola and flirtation with the South African sponsored RENAMO (Mozambique National Resistance) rebels in Mozambique prolong civil chaos in those countries.

Domestically, the Republic of South Africa has built a modern industrial economy, drawing on what is in effect the coerced labor of blacks as well as the skills of its well trained white work force. Although the color line between skilled and unskilled workers is now becoming blurred, the duality of the country's economy is still pronounced. Because of apartheid, more than half of South Africa's blacks are confined to grossly overpopulated rural "homelands" areas (occupying 13 percent of the country's land area). Perhaps a million more live on white-owned farms and the rest are crammed into black "townships" around the cities. Although out of sight to most whites, apartheid has undoubtedly heightened fundamental population and environmental problems that afflict all African countries. Population growth among South Africa's blacks has soared to the level (around 3 percent) common to the continent. In the black "homelands," unemployment is the common condition, and the dumping of black population not needed in the cities has placed such extreme pressures on the land that even subsistence farming in many places has been crowded out.

When apartheid ends, South Africa's seemingly endless conflict is likely to figure as a particularly clear cut and decisive event within the larger African institutional struggle. For the rest of the continent, satisfactory "progress" may be perceived only if economic evolution is plotted over a very long period. Viewed through the lens of the late twentieth-century Western world, caught in the most accelerated era of technological change this planet has yet seen, Africa's pace will doubtless seem unbearably slow.

Beyond the general platonic injunction to cultivate understanding as the basis for right conduct, recognizing how difficult development will be in Africa won't solve the continent's problems. It may, however, bring realism about what needs to be done and patience about the outcomes of African actions and our advice. I offer no roadmap for Africa's route to economic success: anyone who says they have a blueprint is either a fool or a dreamer. What *is* clear to me falls far short of a master plan: that is, one way or another African governments must create larger wholes from many separate communities. As in politics, economic life generally begins to flourish as the boundaries of trust expand beyond kin, clan, neighborhood.

Some notions about what Africans, and to a much lesser extent, Western donors can do to make this happen are sketched throughout this book. Like many other Westerners (and Africans) seeking remedies for Africa's problems, I see the need to "free up" economies by paring away costly and unwieldly state controls. I also believe that increasing private initiative can help break down incentives for corruption arising from communal ties and feeding upon state regulatory systems.

8

Thus social change is essential to economic progress; it will, however, further disrupt the order also essential to progress. These themes will recur throughout the book, for they are the dominant threads in the tapestry of Africa's difficult future. Would that these themes were our only focus: the tale would then be much simpler and probably more satisfying. But, in fact, Africans will have so many other things to contend with at the same time, as they try to build human, physical, and technological infrastructures that do not now exist.

In this book, I want to tell the whole story, as far as that is possible, of how African economies got stuck. Although Africa's problems seem unique to us now, or perhaps uniquely intractable, it helps our understanding to look at them in a larger perspective: to speculate a bit on how Africa's dilemmas compare with those of the European nation builders several hundred years ago, and with the Latin American and Asian countries currently outstripping those of Africa by several lengths, to sketch an historical context for the continent's current plight. Africa's situation did not always seem so bleak.

∾

After eighty or ninety years of autocratic rule, at the end of the colonial period, many of the European powers began to shower blessings—roads, bridges, schools, clinics, even Western-style politics—on their African subjects. Even the weather smiled, with unwonted constancy, for almost two decades. At Independence, in the early 1960s, Africans rose up full of elation to grasp the deed to power handed over by their former rulers. Modern times had arrived.

After gaining political control, Africans began to stage campaigns to secure its economic fruits. In the "developmental revolutions" they launched, they enjoyed a good deal of assistance from the governments of the former colonial nations. This complaisant good will on the part of

9

those ceding power—stemming from the confidence of the "haves" during the postwar era that they were still very much in control—fostered an illusory sense of how easy it would all be. Only after a decade had passed, when the OPEC oil embargo and the accompanying recessions had hit the continent hard, did Africans and others begin to realize what they were up against.

In the first place, Africans were coming to recognize how far real economic control still eluded them. More importantly, it was becoming clear that within African countries the hybrid systems left from colonial days no longer worked very well. The strongest institutions were still the local ethnic and family groups that for the most part set and enforced the rules before the Europeans arrived: tribal councils judged disputes, distributed land, regulated markets, and mediated with the spirit world; and families apportioned work loads, arranged marriages, shared food, built shelters, and cared for the aged. In the capital, on the other hand, the government's power to tax and bureaucrats' discretion over the proceeds did create fortunes for some while limiting opportunities for others. Yet although many officials worked diligently at desks, telephones, telexes, and eventually computers doing government business, very little of what they did seemed to touch people's lives.

While Africans were exploring the uses of the systems they had inherited, they were also learning a lot: in schools, the vocabulary of the modern world; in offices, the rules and strategems for managing within it. African officials learned to spar effectively with would-be foreign investors and aid officers; they cut their teeth on comprehensive national plans covering every conceivable aspect of production and social welfare. Yet the massive plans and growing skein of regulation were not accompanied by a commensurate increase in control. Nor did a solid injection of economic aid and plentiful advice pay off in commensurate growth. Over time, as the systems grew in size and complexity, African entrepreneurs became increasingly ingenious at devising schemes for profit without productivity. Farmers, who were the main victims of governments' power to tax and inability to deliver, slowed their output.

Amid the complexities that characterize Africa's relationship to the West, the role of economic aid particularly eludes easy assessment. While recent critiques of aid have caught a good deal of attention because of their satisfying iconoclasm, in fact, aid has both increased African capabilities and encouraged dependency. In a word, Africans cannot live with it and they cannot live without it. Africans must "develop" their own societies, but they will need extensive—and expensive—infusions of Western expertise as well as debt relief if their best efforts to do so are to succeed.

By the mid-1980s, when it was very clear that the bubble had burst, the outsiders who had helped lay Africa's modern foundations and then confidently stayed on to help their former charges "develop," evolved a new line suitable for tougher times. As aid money dwindled, Western advisers counseled Africans to develop on the cheap by "privatizing" their state-controlled enterprises. Some form of this new Western prescription seemed to make sense even to many Africans. But it was also apparent that new economic strategies alone would not be enough. Clearly, African countries also would need strong governments to create the infrastructure and institutions that could cope with the continent's problems. For, in addition to the policies that had cut the output of farmers, two mutually reinforcing physical pressures threatened the long-term prospects of African agriculture. The fickle climate withdrew the blessings of rain from much of the continent, and at the same time populations soared: as the earth dried up, human fecundity increased dramatically. Thus people were pressing at the limits of arable land.

Africa's burgeoning human fertility reflects both the poverty of its people and their attachment to local roots, to the family. In fact, family bonds may now be gradually loosening. Though that may give hope for an eventual fall in birth rates, the slackening of these ties will also bring wrenching social dislocations to Africans. As communal land diminishes, village-centered family life will lose its hold. As more and more university graduates absorb Western ideas about social organization, old loyalties will get shorter shrift. The result, in our eyes as well as in those of Africans, will often be unlovely. African fiction in the post-Independence period has become obsessed with the theme, "things fall apart; what replaces them is jerry-built."

Short of a major natural calamity, it is also true that extreme pressures on food supplies, jobs, and incomes are likely to ease only with an infusion of new technology. Only Africans themselves can engineer the changes in their own societies and economies that must underpin the use of new technologies. To obtain such an infusion, however, and bring about a resulting African "green revolution" in agriculture, the continent must depend heavily on the West.

It's not a neat equation. Ingrained tradition is stubborn, but change is inevitable. Tradition impedes progress and change unleashes social chaos. A lot more change is needed before things can get better but for some time to come change will often make things look a lot worse. My unwillingness in this book to chart the outcome of these tensions or resolve the oppositions may leave some readers frustrated. Satisfaction, where it is found, must accommodate great uncertainty.

Mao Zedong's view of history, as recounted in a story told by Edgar Snow, would serve us well in thinking about Africa. Snow once asked Mao what he thought was the significance of the French Revolution. After musing a bit, Mao replied, "I would think it's a little too early to tell." In Africa too, we will not know what is happening now for a long time to come.

# 1

# Pre-Modern States in a Post-Modern World

*[A] cumulative increase in the rate of change has been the decisive factor in the making of the modern world, [whereas] the static societies that consumed most of human history perceived no great difference between present and past . . . tradition was sacred and controlling.*

Arthur M. Schlesinger, Jr.
*The Cycles of American History*

*While the United States is trying to reach the moon, Tanzania is trying to reach its villages.*

Julius Nyerere

On Africa's northwestern coast, in Mauritania's desert margin, even the vultures have fled. Throughout the parched waste, sand blows over abandoned mud-hut villages, shrouding the carcasses of emaciated cattle. The nomadic tribesmen straggling in from the dying land to cities swollen by refugees cannot go back without the herds that gave them life.

On the other side of the continent, farmers in eastern Zambia sit in the doorways of their huts, gazing at a November downpour, and then at their dark clay fields, as they wait for the delivery of seed corn that should have been planted before the first rain. Watching for government trucks now almost a month late, they ponder the chances for the harvest and how they will feed their families for the next year.

Far from the desert and farmland, Nigeria's capital, Lagos, runs down slowly, shedding layers of modernity it can no longer afford. Overseas telephone service fades out

13

without warning, perhaps for days; air conditioning and refrigeration flickers off as the equatorial sun blazes; cars fall to scrap and potholes widen; factories idle and shut down; clinics dispense advice but little medicine; at the nearby University of Ibadan, long Africa's finest, salaries of professors arrive late or not at all.

Throughout the continent roads and bridges are wearing out and rotting away; elementary schools are jammed with children but have no blackboards, books, or paper; villagers crowd into festering shantytowns around the cities, joining the growing numbers of unemployed who scrape out a bare survival. In many places, the average citizen is worse off than he was twenty years ago.

What's gone wrong in Africa?

This question has innumerable different answers—most plausible—but one simple statement sums up most of them: Africa is out of phase with the times. Before they have even begun their own industrial revolutions, the countries of sub-Saharan Africa find themselves hurtling toward the high-tech world of the twenty-first century. They have neither the money nor the skill to play with the others around the table, yet there is no other game in town. It's as if Rip Van Winkle's whole village woke up to find itself right outside present-day Manhattan. But where Van Winkle's compatriots might be expected fairly soon to don pin-striped suits and join their neighbors aboard commuter trains, Africans do not have that option. In Africa today there is no way to escape the modern world, but no easy way to join it either.

Images of wealth—shopping malls, swimming pools, and limousines—come from the West via television; role models for material achievement—astronauts, ad executives, neurosurgeons—wear Western uniforms. But modern aspirations live side-by-side with traditional capabilities, often unhappily; modern technologies penetrate traditional systems, often disruptively. On the land, populations swollen by the success of Western epidemiology push against available acreage. In cities, more and more people struggle to share in an economy where rewards flow mainly from ties to the outside world.

Although the exchange is unequal in virtually all respects, African countries have become hooked on it. Since Independence in the early 1960s, Africa has continued exporting agricultural commodities and minerals while importing everything required for modernization, complete with infant industries. Over the years, this has resulted in an increasingly lopsided balance sheet. And the gap will not diminish soon. In fact it is widening further as the international marketplace becomes glutted with farm products, and as robots in the industrialized countries compete with cheap Third-World labor in producing consumer goods.

African states face an extraordinary set of pressures as they struggle for viability. Like the European contenders for statehood four centuries ago, they still must establish the legitimacy of government and the responsibilities of citizen and state toward one another. They must weld political and economic entities from scattered ethnic fragments. At the same time, leaders and people watch highly evolved political systems elsewhere—democratic and socialist—delivering the goods for their societies. In the two decades since Independence, Africans have lost the illusion that sovereignty would bring all that, but now they may be equally mesmerized by the staggering distance they themselves must go. If famine and plague do not overtake more mundane problems, coping with their disparate dilemmas will surely involve as much pain as progress.

At such a moment the past may look more promising than the present or future. A tribal elder in Nigerian novelist Chinua Achebe's *Things Fall Apart* looks back longingly to a time when kinship was strong and men spoke "with one voice," lamenting that now a man "curse[s] the gods of his fathers and ancestors." The notion of "African autonomy" exercises a continuing strong appeal. Its promise to shield African traditions from Western cultural imperialism while

15

bringing self-reliant growth is particularly important to people who are relinquishing old values without any surety of what will replace them.

For some of the same reasons, many thoughtful Africans advocate increasing economic ties among African countries. On a continental level, fragmentation again blocks progress: industries cannot grow in tiny, protected national markets. African countries lagging behind the rest of the world may not be able to build manufacturing unless they close ranks in an African common market shielded from outside competition.

Neither self-reliance nor growth will be possible, however, without skills and technologies that must, for some time, be imported. If it can be tapped, the reservoir of Western expertise probably constitutes the continent's main lifeline to the future.

Throughout Africa, people are struggling to survive. For years nature has scourged the continent with particular fury. The searing drought of the early 1980s—the most severe in over a century—came on the heels of another dramatic and prolonged rainless period in the 1970s. During 1984 and 1985 people in half the countries of Africa either starved or survived on handouts. In 1987 rains slowed again in Ethiopia and much of Southern Africa. Half a million people may have died. Millions more left their dessicated farmlands for the bare lifeline of a refugee camp. When those who have fled political turmoil are counted with the victims of famine and drought, more than 5 million people (some estimate as many as 10 million) now live as refugees in Africa. For many, loss of traditional lands and livelihoods may be permanent. In some places the fragile soils have been worked to death, or the climate itself may have turned inhospitable. As with refugees elsewhere, the trauma of uprooting often seems to erase the hopes, aspirations, and habits of the old life.

Flimsy and sprawling, encampments in Sudan, Ethiopia, Somalia have become small cities whose populations scrounge for work or try to grow food in the surrounding countryside. As international concern with African famine ebbs and flows, medicines, books, and supplies fall like occasional manna on clinics and schools run mostly on the zeal of a few selfless individuals.

Yet Africa's troubles only begin with the drought. In the mid-1970s, OPEC and international recession dealt the continent several more gratuitous blows, suddenly changing trade balances and draining monetary reserves. Until then, African economies had enjoyed per capita growth averaging about 1.5 percent a year, and the lives of most people had been improving. Average national incomes rose; schools greatly increased enrollments; newly trained doctors and nurses delivered modern health care to more and more people. Though a decade had exposed often serious cracks in the new structures, most people believed that things were moving forward and that the learning essential to further progress was happening.

After the first oil shock of 1973, however, Africa lost 10 percent of its income and again in 1979 sustained the same sort of blow—suffering altogether about five times the loss taken by the industrialized countries. Between 1980 and 1982 alone, the prices of non-oil commodities that most of Africa sells declined by 27 percent. In addition, almost before anyone realized, soaring population growth had placed huge demands on food, land, and welfare. Probably most worrisome, however, was the growing gap between problems and institutions for handling them. African ability to cope lagged so far behind the combination of crises that systems basic to economic survival began to run down almost everywhere. As the paint peeled away, the flimsy structures underneath were exposed.

Africa's mainstay, farming, was the most important casualty. Given little encouragement, the soil itself seemed increasingly reluctant to yield its fruits. In 1960, Africa was a net food exporter, and as recently as 1970 it was essentially self-sufficient in food. But in the 1970s and 80s, while food production per person in Asia and Latin America rose steadily, in Africa it increased at only half the rate of population growth. Just to stay even, many African countries applied for food aid and began importing increasing quantities of wheat and rice. Food imports rose from 4 million to 24 million tons during the 1970s. By 1985 the continent was importing two-fifths of its food supply and about a third of its people depended wholly or partly on imported food. What was not food aid represented a particularly appalling drain on poor agrarian economies. In many cities, people stopped eating domestically grown grains as they developed a taste for wheat bread. While local production lags behind, this dependence will be hard to break: African governments cannot afford to let city dwellers starve. Neither, however, can they afford to have American and European farms fill the growing gaps in local harvests.

Africa's traditional source of revenue—export crops—also lagged. In places like Kenya and the Côte d'Ivoire, tea and coffee flourished and brought occasional windfalls. However, African countries began to find themselves edged out even in markets for many of their traditional commodities—like palm oil, rubber, and cocoa—by Asian and Latin American countries that came late to the game but worked to improve plant stock that was deteriorating in Africa. While the trade of other Third-World areas was growing, Africa's share of international trade dropped from 3 percent in 1960 to 1 percent in 1985. At the same time, prices for Africa's main farm and minerals exports fell, while costs of oil, food, and manufactures escalated. In 1986, as Africa's terms of trade plunged an astronomical 29 percent, the region experienced its largest drop in export revenues ever—from $60 billion to around $44 billion. The erosion of agricultural competitiveness left most African countries with limited means for paying their own way.

That African economies were caught in a long-term squeeze was not apparent at first. For a while it could be viewed as a series of crises. Aid helped, and African governments borrowed to fill the gaps. For a few years, everyone tried to look the other way. Thus the growth of Africa's debt caught both debtors and creditors almost unaware as it rose from $14 billion in 1973 to perhaps $125 billion in 1987.

When the banks and governments turned off the spigot at that time, Africa's debt still looked small compared with those of Latin America and Asia. In terms of ability to repay, however, Africa was the worst off: payments on its loans consumed about half of the continent's export revenue in 1985—greater than that of the major Latin American debtors and about twice the proportion paid on average by the countries of Asia. The thin margin for survival of African states came into clear public focus at the Paris Club, the forum for negotiation and renegotiation of terms of official debt terms by finance ministry officials. Between 1980 and 1984, out of 31 reschedulings, 23 were for African countries, some of whom came back more than once. The line between rollover and default often seemed very thin. As debt mounted, the flow of capital into Africa slowed sharply, with commercial bank loans falling to $1.1 billion in 1986, down from $3.5 billion in 1981. Not surprisingly, import volumes per capita for low-income Africa also declined sharply—more than 30 percent—from the end of the 1970s to 1985: the money to shop, even for essentials, was fast dwindling.

On world scales of wealth and development, Africa has always come last, behind Asia and Latin America, as well as the industrialized world. But now it is difficult to see the end of a slide that will take it farther backward. By 1990, African incomes may fall to the levels of 1960. By 1984, average national growth rates were declining at a rate of 1.2 percent, and by 4.2 percent per capita.

With so many more people trying to eat a pie that has expanded only slightly, the measure of "per capita" has now become the controlling factor in the equation. While population growth was falling in the rest of the Third World, it was escalating sharply in Africa. Rising from 2.4 in 1960 to

19

about 3.2 percent today, Africa's rate of population growth is the highest seen anywhere, anytime, throughout human history. At a similar level Africa's numbers could quadruple in the next 40 years. With this explosion of people, African countries would have to run very fast to stay even. In the long run, more people might mean more work and talent to build economies, but for now, with around 50 percent of populations under 15, they threaten to swamp fragile systems before they have a chance to adapt.

What this means can be grasped physically in Africa's sprawling cities, where paved streets, piped water, and electricity work at the center but peter out in the surrounding shantytowns. Crowding into shacks made of boards and boxes set in the mud, people leave the settled patterns of the village to scramble among strangers. Yet they keep coming. Twice as many people live in cities now than at the time of Independence, and urban areas may increase another five times by the end of the century. In Kenya, where population is growing faster than anywhere else on the continent or the world, migration into the city could bring the equivalent of 15 more Nairobis in the next 30 years.

Even with the exodus, people press against the limits of the land. Farmers have relied on opening new fields to expand harvests, and it is now apparent that they cannot go much farther in many places without money and technology not now available. Farmers have already cleared vast forest areas whose soils are ill suited to agriculture, and without roots to hold them, these soils are blowing away. As forests disappear, fuel can become scarce rather suddenly. Then all trees become potential firewood. In the northern Sahel region, fuelwood is being used 30 percent faster than it can be replaced by new growth.

Another threat to their land lies in growing herds of cattle. As a result of stock raising programs, livestock in Africa has expanded nearly as fast as human population, without a corresponding increase in fodder. Even before the drought, the great herds were denuding foraging areas

20

of grass and trees. Thus, human and animal life are beginning to overwhelm the plant life that has sustained them for centuries. With overcultivation, overgrazing, and deforestation, vast areas have been surrendered to the advancing Sahara. While the desert holds sway over 20 percent of the continent now, it is expanding—often by more than 90 miles a year.

~

Ironically, one of Africa's greatest problems—its exploding populations—has resulted directly from its most demonstrable success: health care. African mortality rates are still the highest in the world: 5 million of the 7 million infant deaths in the world each year occur in Africa. But, while the numbers of children born to each woman have stayed the same, infant mortality has dropped from 167 per thousand in 1960 to 145 in 1970 to 122 at current estimates. Thus the successful intervention of Western science has knocked Africa's material cosmos askew. It is difficult to see how the balance can be restored without further interventions on a similar scale.

However, technology cannot be applied in a vacuum. Africa's political and economic institutions have faltered considerably, wasting national wealth or investing it badly. Some of the responsibility for this institutional weakness undoubtedly lies with the colonialists. They started the process of integrating Africa into the world, but a poor start it was indeed. By and large, the British, French, Belgians and Portuguese imposed relatively shallow central control on clusters of separate tribal entities. When they departed at Independence, they left African countries with what looked on the surface like twentieth-century parliamentary democracies, plus a deed of sovereignty. For the time being, at least, most African states would not have to fight off challengers at their borders, as the European kingdoms did throughout the fifteenth to nineteenth centuries.

21

But this is a mixed blessing. On a continental level, as well as within most states, Africa is deeply fragmented. Three-quarters of Africa's people live in countries numbering under 10 million in population. More than a thousand ethnic groups, speaking approximately 2000 separate languages, inhabit the continent. Unity and control have to be fought for, and African leaders must engage in that battle now, even as they try to confront overwhelming economic odds.

The quest for control moved most of them very quickly toward authoritarian forms of government—often directly under the military—with little formal popular participation. This was most often the pattern followed in the evolution of Western Europe as well, with sovereigns wresting power from the nobles or people before it was wrested from them in turn with the emergence of democracy. But the efforts of African governments to gather the economic reins firmly within their own grasp have not fostered development.

In the first place, to make things work from the top down you need a whole class of skilled and experienced managers that clearly does not yet exist in Africa. At every level you also need the sort of commitment to a job well done that is rare in most societies. And this commitment will seldom flourish where labyrinthine regulations on trade and investment can slow operations to a virtual standstill.

Where centrally controlled economies have succeeded in galvanizing masses of the population to revamp the economy, (as in the Soviet Union and China), well-organized and stringent coercion has driven the program. Thus effective state economic control is also likely to have high human costs. Although most African regimes have plumped for wide-ranging state controls, they have been both unable and unwilling to pay the price—either in obsessive management or repressive governance—for making them work.

Secondly, the institutions supposed to run things are only rarely African in origin. Imports started with the ministries inherited from colonial governments, complete with sacrosanct titles and grades that clearly established the equivalence between African officials and their colonial predecessors. After Independence, large state corporations (commonly known as "parastatals") that produced everything from banking and insurance to vegetable oil were put together with advice from the World Bank and hired foreign consultants bringing blueprints from East, West, and everywhere else. Aid donors like the United States have also put their oars in, often creating new bureaus or agencies within African governments to run their projects.

As a result, while growing vigorously, African bureaucracies too often have become ends in themselves. Of course this happens the world over in both public and private enterprises: bureaucratic life seems to dictate that participants will feather their own nests, protect their turf, build internal empires. But in Africa the gap between the job to be done and what institutions actually effect is often so wide that stated goals progressively lose their meaning. Famous white elephants—cement plants, paper mills, glass factories that produce little at great cost before shutting down in a very short time—represent most visibly the gap between complex plans and what organizations actually do. It is less obvious when agencies formed to foster, say, the technical knowledge of small farmers quickly lose sight of that mandate as they realize how little they have to deliver, and more importantly, how seldom anyone notices whether they deliver or not.

The problem is compounded in Africa by the prevailing economic culture, where ties to tribe and family still rule most economic exchange. Because of this, people put the good of local and ethnic communities before whatever the government may declare as national goals: a job is probably not worth doing well unless you're doing it for your family or ethnic group. When everybody feels this way, there will not be a lot of pressure from below for good government. Moreover, it puts the national treasury itself up for grabs.

President Mobutu Sese Seko of Zaïre (formerly the Congo) described the situation regretfully (without explaining his own central role in creating it), when he said, "everything is for sale, everything is bought in our country. And in this traffic, holding any slice of public power constitutes a veritable exchange instrument." In these circumstances, public accountability becomes a very weak reed with which to chastise errant officials. The result is a major hemorrhage of scarce African resources.

In a setting where margins for survival are exceedingly narrow, where litter vanishes because paper is used and reused, where a trader may live for days on the sale of half-cigarettes from one pack, where people ransack anthills for stray grains, the waste engendered by the system seems intolerable. Outsiders and Africans agree that if African nations are to survive—in some shape to feed, educate and employ their people—things will have to change drastically. Profound revolutions in political culture will have to accompany explicit reform programs. Agreement is less clear on what form these must take. Westerners, as always, have a hard time visualizing the future except in their own image. Africans, while also imbued with that image, may often overtly reject it.

Whatever their form, however, these revolutions will inevitably hasten social upheaval. How much order and how much change may be "good" for Africa cannot of course be calculated. While growth will probably continue to falter unless tradition recedes, a frontal assault on traditional authority will only make the social stresses more painful.

∽

As the crisis has deepened, Africa's economic isolation has intensified. Since the early 1970s, foreign investment has slowed to a virtual standstill. The specter of foreign control over Africa's industrial plant no longer evokes outrage now that even the carpetbaggers who once swarmed across the continent have pulled up stakes. With commercial bank loans drying up, almost any opportunist with a little money would in most places be welcome.

Nor will aid fill the gap.

Apart from emergency food doles triggered by periodic media coverage of famine, locusts, or plague, aid to Africa is leveling off. In the wake of budget cuts, U.S. aid has fallen sharply. Thus, after debts are serviced, net flows of money into Africa are way down. By the end of 1986, the interest on debt equaled two-thirds of all new aid. Since the North-South dialogue of the mid-70s, and the Brandt Report of 1978, which pushed for a more equitable distribution of international resources, the atmosphere has chilled and sharpened. The notion that the West must assume major responsibility for narrowing the gap between rich and poor has lost most of its grip on Western liberals, and its credibility now looks frayed even to Third-World officials who refuse to abandon it. Although Africa is clearly the number-one international welfare problem, most donors have entered a period of retrenchment that seems likely to endure until the next major technological or managerial revolution expands perceived wealth again. No outside powers will come riding to the rescue. No matter how difficult it may be, Africans will have to do it mostly themselves.

African culture, history, and nearly total technological dependence on industrialized countries have made it hard for Africans to accept that idea. In exchange for service and homage, throughout much of Africa rich men are expected to take care of less well-off kin. Analogously, in the last 20 years the obligation to help poorer African states has flowed to the rich nations, and they have partially accepted it. Until now, however, they have not worked out an exchange like that between the rich African and his kin. Thus the gift may seem to have dropped from heaven—and like any miracle. ultimately call into question mere human effort.

The colonialists, of course, acted as godlike as they were able, evoking submission through minimal force but with maximum awe of their guns, ships, language, books, religion, and ways of managing. A character in the Kenyan novelist Ngugi wa Thiong'o's *A Grain of Wheat* gives an African's-eye-view of white men as species of demigod: "unmovable like a rock, a power that had built the bomb and transformed a country from wild bush and forest into modern cities, with tarmac highways, motor vehicles on two or four legs, railways, trains, aeroplanes and buildings whose towers scraped the sky." White men had a monopoly on the knowledge and information essential for dealing with the world outside Africa, or anywhere outside the bush. They held that knowledge close, and when they left, it seemed to Africans that they had taken most of it with them.

Now most African countries have many times the number of university graduates as they did at Independence, but this has not yet really narrowed the gap. Without working institutions, trained people find themselves pulling levers in the air. To compensate for the lack of institutions, ingenious and skilled people are forced to engage in highly creative administrative gymnastics to accomplish the simplest tasks. With no good way to sort and store information, for example, data collection is an inexact and sometime science: Africa's statistical profile is often available in Washington, D.C. (through the World Bank) long before it trickles back to the economic officers of African governments. Manufacturing and farming equipment dubbed by Western development specialists "appropriate technology" for Africa is peddled by aid donors. Prices for African exports are set by Western brokers. African art treasures are saved for posterity by Western collectors in museums located in Europe and America.

It would be surprising if this unequal interaction had not fostered the conviction that others should solve Africa's problems, and the expectation that they would. The way in which these illusions are now being dispelled can be cause for both discouragement and hope. The learning process has been painfully accelerated by the contraction of the international economy, which while hitting Africa hard has also aroused the fears of Western nations about their own economic development. Even the donors who believed firmly in their own omniscience now are facing the fact that only Africans can build African institutions. And the African leaders who customarily structured their five-year plans around capital investment from abroad are now pocketing their wish lists. Without major debt relief and transitional help in rehabilitating deteriorated systems, no one's hopes for Africa are likely to be fulfilled. Yet, for the future, unpalatable as it may be to some Africans, it is becoming evident that most new investment monies must be found within the continent itself.

Perhaps because this realization has been sinking in, African leaders have recently been talking about basic policy changes—and even trying some. Crisis has galvanized them. To find the resources they need within their own societies, Africans will have to change the way their systems work to get much more out of people and money invested. Whether they can do this—either by seizing the reins more firmly or spurring private initiative more sharply—remains to be seen.

Political leaders are only rarely able to step back and take the long view of systems they head. For African leaders, presiding over this sort of far-reaching and disruptive change will be like riding a whirlwind. Understandably, they may be reluctant to embark. Yet if they refuse to do so events will very likely roll them over anyway.

◡◠

It is important for onlookers to realize what Africa's leaders are up against. More than anywhere else in the world today they should be viewed as not merely governing their states well or badly but as creating the systems they run. What the leaders must do to save their economies may rub harshly against the grain of their societies. Even the wisest leaders and the most courageous will not be able to insulate their people from the widespread upheaval that profound changes will inevitably bring. (The fact that failure to change will lead to even worse upheaval probably will provide small consolation for the time being.)

Judging themselves, and being judged, by the standards of the advanced countries that colonized them makes their task more difficult. Before the current post-colonial era, no other fledgling states in history had the world looking over their shoulders via satellite transmission.

But for the African countries, the lopsided relationship can also yield benefits which they must now grasp if they are to survive. Western aid has sometimes deepened African dependence, but it is doubtful that African states can cope with the crises they now face without Western technical help. In purely material terms this lien on the West gives Africans an advantage over earlier peoples involved in similar struggles. When the Europeans in the Middle Ages periodically overran the land and fuel supplies, they had nowhere to turn; thus they could do little more than just sit and watch things die. Africa's Malthusian crunch is unparalleled, but the continent's relationship with nations inhabiting a different technological era gives Africans a chance to arrest and reverse their decline.

Ironically, the depth of Africa's crisis may offer the best hope for change. Economic issues have always been at the top of the rhetorical agendas of African leaders. The real and desperate concern many are showing now, however, represents a watershed. A realistic appraisal of where they stand is, at least, a beginning.

# 2

# What Went Wrong

*Seek ye first the political kingdom and all else shall be added to you.*

Kwame Nkrumah

At exactly midnight on March 6, 1957, the Union Jack made its last stately descent down the flagpole in Accra's Parliament Square, and the red, green and gold flag of the new Republic of Ghana ran up in its place. As shouting and fireworks erupted outside Parliament, the new prime minister, Kwame Nkrumah, cut short his inaugural speech and dashed out to address his compatriots, who had been massed in the adjoining soccer field for most of the day. He was followed by the Duchess of Kent, Vice President Richard M. Nixon, and dignitaries of some 65 other countries. In that moment, African colonialism was ending, African sovereignty beginning.

Speaking in English and in the Fanti language, the leader of the first African nation to receive its independence in the great colonial exodus told his people that they were no longer slaves and that they must throw their chests out when they walked. Earlier in Parliament he had laid out his plan for a Pan-African confederation, insisting that Africa must establish its own "personality in international affairs." He also called for a language all Africans could understand. In the streets the people chanted: "Freedom, freedom, freedom!," and, lovingly, their country's name: *"Ghana, Ghana."* Many in the crowds wore cotton prints bearing life-size images of their prime minister, whom they called *"Osageyfo,"* or "Redeemer."

It was a heady time. Though not one of Africa's largest countries, the world's newest state had the most highly educated population in the sub-Saharan region, (starting with Nkrumah, who earned several bachelors and masters degrees during 10 years in the United States). Though not the most richly endowed in natural resources, Ghana started its independent existence with a hefty stash of £480 million in its treasury and strong potential earning power with its monopoly of half the world's cocoa exports. The country's political future was in the hands of elected leaders, and its agriculture was solidly based in the holdings of small peasant farmers.

Looking back, Ghanaians have a right to feel particularly chagrinned at how quickly and completely their golden age disappeared. Three years after Independence, their democracy had become a one-party dictatorship, and much of their national treasure had been spent on prestige projects like the national "Black Star" steamship line, or in lining the pockets of politicians. In 1966, with the country now heavily in debt, Nkrumah was deposed by a military coup, which was followed during the next decade and a half by eight changes of government, including three more coups and the execution of three former heads of state accused of corruption. During the same period, cocoa production plummetted, and the country dropped from first to eighth among exporters.

In hindsight, Ghana's history is virtually a parable on how to decimate an African economy. Like Uganda on the other side of the continent (an African garden spot despoiled by its mad despot, Idi Amin), Ghana stands out as an example of early promise betrayed.

In many African countries, however, the early elan of Independence was followed by an optimism shared by their friends abroad and borne out by initial results. Although rosy hopes of the pre-Independence period about African democracy faded soon after the champagne corks stopped popping, Africa still seemed to be starting out free of many

30

problems that plagued Asia and Latin America. In Asia, food shortages—largely caused by misplaced development strategies—plagued India and China, while throughout the 60s most African countries were feeding themselves. Unlike Latin America, where the monopoly of land ownership by the wealthy bred class warfare, African farmlands were frequently communally owned and most often in the hands of the small farmers who worked them.

With almost no industry of any scale in place at Independence, a virtual tabula rasa offered open-ended possibilities to African governments and foreign investors: each new brewery or textile factory was hailed as an opening shot in Africa's industrial revolution. As many countries, spurred by historically high commodity prices, continued to grow modestly but steadily, people could, in fact, see the emergence of modern Africa, in the highrise office buildings, hotels, and conference centers that created new skylines in Africa's cities. Construction of roads, schools, hospitals, and clinics accelerated, bringing change within reach of great numbers. To the Peace Corps and other Western volunteers who swarmed over the continent in the early days, anything seemed possible: just drop a seed on the ground and it would probably grow.

African confidence was bolstered by forays into the international arena, where the expanding group of African nations began to carry increasing weight in the Commonwealth, the United Nations, and the nonaligned movement. With their numbers, Africans felt very comfortable at the U.N., and began to use that body as the main forum for communication among themselves and with the rest of the world. After the mid-60s, Africans made apartheid—Africa's burning racial issue—the main major continuing item on the world organization's political agenda. The prospect of 40-odd new nations undoubtedly was one spur to India's Prime Minister Nehru, Indonesia's President Sukarno, and Egypt's General Nasser, who brought in Nkrumah to help set up the nonaligned movement of countries now seen as forming a "Third World." At that time the fruits of sovereignty seemed bounteous indeed.

Even when the first major external blow to African prosperity fell—in OPEC's successful oil price escalation of 1973—most Africans and many others saw it instead as a harbinger of increased leverage for all the Third World. A drive to create a New International Economic Order grew out of the elation of Third-World nations at seeing their fellows seize control of the oil industry from the West. With visions of commodities cartels down the road—and some windfall price hikes for their minerals exports along with oil—Africans were slow to realize the full impact the oil price rise would have on them. Few of course could foresee the depth of the international recession that followed, or the technological revolution that spurred production of commodities everywhere and substituted synthetics for many of Africa's raw material exports.

In the upshot, the adverse effects of both these developments on Africa's traditional commodity exports and economic growth were profound. Over time, the prices of Africa's minerals and agricultural exports deteriorated sharply, while oil prices rose sevenfold, grain imports rose fivefold, and manufactures rose proportionately to Western inflation. The average loss of income as a result of skyrocketing energy costs was 10 percent, and in some countries it was as high as 25 percent. The purchasing power of Africa's exports fell 30 percent. Investment was drying up. At the beginning, OPEC and a number of Western donors tried hard to help fill the gap with concessional aid, and the World Bank created a special loan window for those "most seriously affected." Foreign zeal to help had slackened by the second oil shock of 1979, however, by which time African countries were borrowing as heavily as they were able.

At the same time they could not avoid cutting imports, at first somewhat gradually, and then in many cases, drastically. Small poor economies have less range for choice, and in their desperation less ability to choose, than those better off. Thus the shocks of the 1970s hit Africa with particular force. Opportunities for a better life declined visibly.

In Senegal, for example, as prices for their main exports—peanuts and cotton—fell, the government tried to keep its share of export revenues by dropping the farmers' take; it also increased both grants and loans from foreign donors. Nonetheless, work eventually stopped on new food processing plants and production dropped, as spare parts dwindled, at currently going concerns. Elementary school construction slowed, new roads were scrapped, and potholes scarred the old ones. In the capital city, Dakar, an oceanfront jewel, paint peeled, shutters sagged on stately stucco buildings, highrise office buildings were flanked by empty lots filled with debris. Cereals crops shrank as farmers withdrew from the market.

In Zambia, happy under a decade of benign rule by Prime Minister Kenneth Kaunda and the upward mobility guaranteed by its rich lode of copper for all those energetic enough to seize it, the steep drop in copper prices in 1974 tore the bottom out of the country's slow but seemingly steady progress. As copper went from a high of $1.40 a pound in 1974 to less than half that for many of the years thereafter, the country first tried to bridge the gap to better days by borrowing more than $4 billion from foreign banks and governments. When things failed to improve, Zambian belts had to be notched in—at first gradually, then sharply. Inflation caused the buying power of salaries to evaporate; livelihoods disappeared, and the numbers of petty traders hawking meager wares to their fellows on the streets of Lusaka swelled. Newly imposed school fees kept the children of many secondary school graduates from following in their parents' footsteps. From 1980 to 1986 most people's incomes dropped by around 50 percent, and the country was visibly straining at the seams.

The mineral wealth of Zaïre (also mainly from copper, but also diamonds, tin, zinc, and oil) has never gone to better the lot of the ordinary people but to line the pockets of President Mobutu Sese Seko and his henchmen. With the shocks of the seventies, however, the razor-thin margin of survival of the Zaïrean peasant sharpened, as the country's infrastructure deteriorated and the exactions of government officials increased. With only about 12,000 miles of usable road remaining of some 85,000 miles laid by the Belgian colonists, and with steamers rusting beside silted riverside quays, deliveries of seeds and fertilizer to farms became more and more sporadic. Farmers dropped back into subsistence cultivation and tried to hide from the ubiquitous "taxes" levied by local officials, ruling party stalwarts, or unpaid soldiers living off the land.

Like the price of oil, many of the blows that struck Africa were beyond the ability of most countries to deflect or even anticipate. And like the four horsemen of the Apocalypse, they all seemed to arrive at once. Exploding populations and contracting rainfall both began to take a major toll of lives and well-being in the early seventies (though the first was only dimly perceived while the second was suffered acutely). After several decades of fine weather, drought abruptly changed the conditions of life for a quarter of the continent's farmers early in the 1970s and close to a third in the first part of the 1980s.

Unfortunately, the prices of their commodities exports—as much as of their manufactured and food imports—proved as far out of their control as the elements. Commodity prices, which had doubled during the postwar era, began to fall in the late 1960s, and the downward trend accelerated with the post–OPEC recession in the industrialized nations, where the prices were set. Moving with the market, as Adam Smith might have advocated, into more profitable exports was not an option Africa's small poor economies could readily pick up on. In the early 1980s, U.S. monetary and fiscal policy added greatly to Africa's woes. The steep climb in interest rates and in the value of the dollar inflated African debt, denominated, as it is, in dollars, and compounded in periodic rescheduling.

∽

How African governments responded to these crises also depended partly on past experiences shaped largely by foreigners. For some 80 years the institutions governing African political and economic life were imported from the West and tailored to the needs of the small groups of white Europeans who had the notion of taking over Africa. In hindsight, the scramble for Africa appears to have originated not in quest of treasure but simply because the continent was there and the European powers figured that their strategic positions must therefore be affected by it. In any case the Europeans really didn't want to go to war with one another over rival claims. So in 1884–85 the group huddled over a drawing board at the Berlin Conference, carving up faraway and unknown lands quite amicably into what looked like bite-size pieces.

In taking their slices, the colonizers paid scrupulous attention to their own balances of force and alliance in Europe and none to the political patterns already existing in the territories they would rule. Thus in some places they split apart kindred peoples like the Ewe in Ghana and Togo; the Somali in Kenya, Italian Somalia and French Somalia; the Hausa in Nigeria and Niger; while in other places they threw together disparate and sometimes bitterly antagonistic tribes. Apart from enduring border disputes, the arbitrary divisions left legacies of linguistic and cultural discord that bring to mind the Tower of Babel.

In precolonial Africa large empires had arisen in the west, center and south to bind separate groups under one prevailing hegemony. In many places, however, political units were much smaller, comprised of tribal groups like the Yoruba, with their sprawling towns scattered through western Nigeria; or, more commonly, like eastern Nigeria's Ibo, with their linked villages. Often the smaller entities were governed quite democratically, through village councils charged with finding a consensus. In others, hereditary rulers and their aides fulfilled the same charge, or as hap-

pened not infrequently, were deposed if they didn't. Whatever the form, local government fused politics, religion, and
economic custom. Literally and figuratively, everybody
spoke the same language. Answering to the same gods, they
accepted without thinking their responsibility to the group
and to one another.

When they arrived in Africa, many colonial governors
were not blind to tribal government; they used existing
hierarchies—or when they proved intractable, their own
substitute chiefs—to support their rule. But still they saw
themselves as creating government where, essentially, none
had existed. As an early British settler in Kenya put it,
"There was no law, so we made it. *We* were the law." Thus
confident, as another Kenyan settler expressed it, that they
were helping the Africans "to move away from barbarism
towards civilization and a better way of life," the colonialists
were able to throw a mantle of control over their subject
populations with seeming ease. In the brief six to eight
decades they were in place, however, the new central governments never acquired moral legitimacy in the eyes of the
people. That legitimacy continued to reside in the tribe or
clan. With Independence, the colonial institutions were
turned over almost in toto to the new African regimes—but
legitimacy continued to elude them.

Therein lies the crux of the problem. By their coming,
the Europeans interrupted the local processes of consolidation—the struggle for power among groups that took place
in Europe over six centuries before modern states
emerged—and that must take place in some form before
political power can be securely installed. African borders
ride roughshod over ethnic patterns; they were arbitrarily
imposed. But the main problem is that the borders were
imposed by *mapmakers* more than by conquest, alliance,
trading. Most importantly, they weren't imposed by Africans. Nor did the colonial governors stay long enough to
solidify their legacy. Turning over power eight decades
later, after only fleeting struggles in most places, the de-

36

parting viceroys gave the African nationalist leaders a gift they couldn't refuse—newly minted states with borders guaranteed by international writ and a set of modern institutions seemingly in running order. It soon became clear, however, that these turnkey governments lacked the power to sustain themselves, or any real roots in the populace.

What the Independence era regimes inherited were authoritarian systems with a last-minute graft of parliamentary democracy applied by the departing colonists as the approved form for the transfer of power. While there were significant differences among the colonial powers in style and type of repression, for most of the colonial period, the British, French, Portuguese and Belgians ruled autocratically, with control exerted from the center, and orders and exactions extending down and out to local areas through hierarchies of officialdom. Supported by African clerks and laborers, the European civil servants lived lordly lives, secure in their innate superiority as members of the white race, a preeminence confirmed, for the British, by the explicit exclusion of "natives" from the "official classes".

The Europeans were paid handsomely, with wage scales equivalent to those in Europe, extended home leave—a week for every month of work in British West Africa, for example—and numerous "perks," an array of special allowances laid on at the behest of successive administrations. Top civil servants earned at least 40 and sometimes up to 100 times the average income of salaried Africans. The enormous gap between senior service salaries and those paid to Africans in the "junior service" became one of the main targets of nationalist grievance in the drive for Independence.

For Africa's colonial governments, legitimacy was derived not from the relationship between themselves and the people they ruled but from the support of regimes and public opinion in the metropole. Their constituents were in the foreign and colonial offices and sometimes the parliament and press of their home countries. Among their indig-

37

enous subjects on the other hand, they assumed and took total authority, with their own sense of justice rather than the reaction of their subjects determining the limits. Within these, they disposed of land, resources and people as they saw fit.

They did so for two primary objectives: control and revenue. Required by the mother countries to be at least self-supporting, the colonies had to be run on the cheap. After the initial forays—and particularly after the development of the maxim gun in 1889—military force could be kept to a minimum. The missionaries were a great help in selling the benefits of the white man's culture and training indigenous people to serve in the colonial system. The white man's God showered clear and visible blessings on those trained in Christian schools, as catechists, teachers, clerks, court messengers, and policemen joined the wage economy. To a great extent, after hegemony was initially established, the vast distance maintained between whites and blacks served to uphold it.

Yet salaries still had to be paid. Without, in most cases, the treasures of King Solomon's mines to draw on, or much existing commerce to be taxed, revenues had to be extracted from the main available resources—African labor and land. Arguably, the easiest taxes to administer are those on exports and imports. Thus the colonial administrators pressed Africans to switch from subsistence farming to export crops. In each colony, a few crops or minerals were selected for a major effort—gold or diamonds, coffee, cocoa, rubber, sisal, cotton—and one or several main exports were developed. Sometimes grown by settlers with cheap African labor, and sometimes by peasants, the harvests were marketed by the government, which took a sizable cut along the way. At the same time, cheap consumer goods imported from Europe drew more Africans into the money economy.

Clearly, African states would continue to benefit from the creation of this earning potential. Nonetheless, a number of productive African systems were undermined.

First of all, the colonial pattern ensured the future depend-ence of African economies in several ways. The heavy in-vestment in a few main crops made African exporters very vulnerable to fluctuations in prices set abroad. Moreover, the export orientation eroded the ability of Africans to produce the food they needed. The speeded-up expansion of agriculture in the export sector also began to change traditional methods of cultivation that had nourished peas-ant families and sustained farmland for many centuries. At the same time, inter-African trading systems were discour-aged in favor of trade with the metropole, and local African artisans found their village sales shrinking, as cheap foreign pots, tools, cloth and ornaments flooded into local markets. The unequal and virtually exclusive trade between African countries and their metropoles had begun.

For most of the colonial period, welfare was not a state but a private concern, with the missionaries and sometimes the settlers bringing schooling and medical care to a fortu-nate few. At Independence the group of people trained to fill the shoes of departing Europeans was pitifully small. Among its 25 million people Zaïre had only about a dozen people with the equivalent of a Belgian university degree. Congo-Brazzaville (now called Congo) had only one African senior civil servant. With all its copper wealth, Zambia had only 100 university graduates and a thousand secondary school graduates. In 1961 the universities of Kenya, Tan-zania, and Uganda turned out a total of only 99 graduates (within a combined population area of 23 million). Ninety percent of Mozambicans were illiterate.

In the final few years before Independence, however, the colonial governments rushed in with last minute pro-grams to deliver elementary education, clinics, and local "amenities" more broadly. Seeking to control what they saw as a lengthy transition to "native" rule, they tried to upstage the new nationalist leaders who were promising a cornu-copia of wealth and privilege to flow once the Europeans left. The last colonial governors were able to pay for this

39

expansion out of overflowing treasuries. In the final decade of their tenure commodity prices reached record highs and the weather maintained a nearly unbroken perfection. With all these blessings falling on them in one season—and with Independence just ahead—it is not surprising that many Africans now look back on those years of the 1950s as a golden era.

African leaders thus came to power in the early 1960s with national expectations aflame. As Nigeria's former head of state General Olusegun Obasanjo has noted, his compatriots happily leavened their nationalism with the slogan "life more abundant," and after Independence seemed to believe that development meant "consumption rather than production." In addition, the historical bind in which Africa is caught created particular popular pressures on African governments. Though existing in a different economic and political cosmos from the advanced countries, for African people Western and communist governments provide the models by which they judge their own welfare. International mass communications give them a good idea of what they ought to be entitled to. Apart from the military, only a few groups—principally students, labor unions, and civil servants' guilds—have actively mobilized to apply the sorts of pressures on government characteristic in modern pluralistic societies. Yet even when people appear quiescent and apolitical, the standard by which they measure the legitimacy of government is immeasurably higher than that, say, held up for European rulers during the period of their national consolidation. While European and American governments did not begin to act like "welfare states" until the mid-twentieth century, when their "development" was far advanced, African states were held to the contemporary standard immediately.

∽

Once they actually had the power African leaders could not fail to realize there was much less to it than met the eye. Awe of white expertise and the majesty of the metropole had bolstered the imported order. When they left, the colonial governors took with them the set of mirrors by which they had magnified their own stature and that of their administrations. The new African leaders lost this layer of insulation from their populace at the same time that their campaign promises of wealth and happiness for all on a European scale were coming due. Very soon it became evident that the first order of business was to maintain control, at least at the center, over fragmented polities. How they coped—or not—with the consolidation of their own power gravely affected the economic productivity of their countries.

Looking at the record of various African regimes over the past quarter-century, it is clear that economic development is closely linked to political stability. The countries enjoying the most solid growth have all been fortunate in strong and continuous leadership or relatively smooth successions and virtual freedom from rending civil upheaval. West Africa's Côte d'Ivoire and Cameroon, East Africa's Kenya and southern Africa's Malawi and Botswana are each examples of particularly successful economic management. Côte d'Ivoire, where President Felix Houphouet-Boigny has led his compatriots for over three decades with a patriarchal majesty even his former French mentors could not rival, had averaged a 5.9 percent increase in its gross domestic product by 1983 and achieved a national income of over $700 per person in 1986. Malawi's President Hastings Banda, certain for over two decades that he knows what's best for his people, has combined tight political control with substantial economic benefits to build a solid base for both food production and farm exports, with gross domestic product growing on average 4.9 percent a year during the late 1970s and early 1980s. In Cameroon, former President Ahmadou Ahidjo and his chosen successor Paul Biya steered a firm course for 25 years; husbanding much of the country's oil revenue and investing heavily in agriculture, they achieved for their country a 5.5 percent rate of growth by 1983, and their compatriots' incomes rose to about $700 a year. In Botswana, Africa's only example of democracy sustained since Independence, President Seretse Khama and his successor, Quett Masire, carefully managed the desert-like country's considerable mineral wealth, raising national income from about $60 per person in 1960 to around $1,000 in 1984, and at the same time working to parley that revenue base into diversified development of their cattle industry. In Kenya, whose Independence leader, President Jomo Kenyatta, ruled for 15 years until his death in 1978, followed by his Vice President, Daniel arap Moi, who has held office since then, the economy has grown at an impressive 6.3 percent since 1965; income has risen from $85 at Independence to around $300 in 1986 and literacy and life expectancy have increased markedly.

Regrettably, Kenya may soon provide an obverse example: if corruption and repression continue to grow under Moi, Kenya's blessings may fade fast. For it is also true that endemic instability—particularly coups, civil wars and other forms of violent upheaval—have left economic disaster in their wake. Central Africa's Chad, a continuous battlefield for competing tribal factions and their French, U.S., and Libyan patrons over the last decade, has seen per capita income sink to about $65 per person, while growth has dropped over 5 percent a year during the last decade. Ghana and Uganda also registered negative growth rates of 1.1 and 3.0 respectively in that period. Although only a handful of African countries today are fighting with their neighbors or with organized insurgent movements, most have been prey since Independence to abrupt regime changes, usually via military coup. Only twelve countries in sub-Saharan Africa have not succumbed to military coups, and at least half of the countries of Africa today live under military rule.

These coups have often been mounted in the name of very real economic failures and grievances. Despite im-

42

mense pride in their painstakingly constructed American-style democratic system, which had survived two fiercely contested presidential elections, most Nigerians cheered the 1984 New Year's Eve coup that ended five years of free-wheeling electoral politics—and promised to end rampant corruption. In each of Ghana's coups, the generals or colonels or majors have vowed to right economic wrongs and clean out bribery and graft; so did Sergeant Samuel Doe when he wiped out Liberia's political oligarchs in 1980. "Now you have seen the last of the fat politicians with their Mercedes and Swiss bank accounts: we are here to insure that the common man will have his day." That refrain almost invariably follows the strains of martial music on the national radio station that customarily signal a military take-over.

The trouble is that even when their intentions are as high-minded as their oratory the morning after, the military are prey to exactly the same pressures and seductions as their civilian counterparts. And they are not notably better at resisting them. With extremely strong and upright leadership at the top, military discipline can keep subalterns on a relatively straighter and narrower path; but on the other hand, internal service pressures may divert additional resources both into private pockets and into military spending. The proportion of African funds going to equip and pay the military has been steadily rising, reaching for example, over 40 percent in Ethiopia, and 25 and 20 percent respectively, in drought-ravaged Mauritania and Mali.

In fact, the civil servants who run the economy under a military government are usually the same sorts of people who would do so in a civilian regime. Therefore it is difficult to pinpoint differences in performance. What has declined under the repressive regimes often characteristic of military rule is the ability to offer alternatives, to debate the necessity for change in policies. Thus has civic education—probably the most important spur to better government—been set back significantly.

Where coups become endemic, the atmosphere of uncertainty can paralyze commerce and investment. Government officials, wary of sticking their heads up, slow action to a virtual halt. The turnover of personnel that often accompanies regime changes can also decimate the meager ranks of trained technocrats. After Nigeria's 1975 military coup, the government of General Muritala Mohammed, pledging with great zeal to "clean out" the civil service, purged some ten thousand officials who had served since Independence. Because the fundamental weaknesses lay not in individuals but in the way the system worked, however, their successors—many of them less competent—soon settled down to business as usual.

Unfortunately, African states are likely to have coups for some long time to come. Except in southern Africa, only a few of their armies face an external threat, and thus they focus their energies inward. After the first African coup, against Togo's Sylvanus Olympio in 1963, the genie was out of the bottle: with no other effective source of power, the takeover was a walkaway. So it will be until African societies form the basis of African governments and demand accountability from them.

Serious civil wars, often fought with external support, have hampered development in both the northern and southern extremities of the continent. With its continuing struggle between Arab-Muslim north and black animist south, the Sudan staggers under the heaviest load of debt of any African country except Nigeria—at $9 to 10 billion. Insurgents in the country's south have forced the Chevron Oil Company, which has invested $1 billion prospecting for oil there, to suspend exploitation of highly promising areas. Despite Soviet aid, Sudan's neighbor Ethiopia will probably remain one of the five poorest countries in the world while its long-running conflict with insurgents in Eritrea on the Indian Ocean as well as in Tigre province in the country's north continue.

At the other end of the continent, South Africa—occasionally in league with the United States—is actively engaged in disrupting the economies of most of its neighbors. Richly endowed with oil and fertile land, Angola has been shredded economically by the civil war it has been waging since Independence against a South African and American protégé—the UNITA insurgent group—with the help of Soviet and Cuban troops. Although its considerable oil resources, strategically located near its capital Luanda, have been protected by Cuban troops, the war has destroyed Angola's roads and railroads, nearly wiped out its once thriving agriculture, and virtually made its capital a military bivouac for the struggle.

With far fewer resources, Angola's neighbor Mozambique is, if possible, in even worse shape, after a seven-year battle against South African-supported rebel bandits who have cut transport and communications and terrorized a large portion of the farm population. Mozambique's capital, Maputo, now has only a tenuous connection with its hinterland, and the country can barely be said to have a functioning economy at all. Although no reliable statistics are available on their growth or decline, both countries are worse off in many ways than they were at the end of their wars of Independence against Portugal over a decade ago.

These wars show most starkly how conflict and instability can push African economies backward. As the struggle over apartheid heightens, and international sanctions bite more deeply, South African attacks and possible counter-sanctions will probably place the other countries of the region increasingly at risk. While South Africa continues at odds with its neighbors, two productive economies, Zimbabwe and Botswana, will undoubtedly pay a steep price. Both depend heavily on the white-ruled country for trade, investment, and transport; the cities and infrastructure of both are an easy shot for the South African air force.

If conflict and upheaval inevitably obstruct economic development and stability is a necessary condition for it, strong leadership by itself unfortunately is in no way sufficient to assure progress. Zaïre, Tanzania, and Guinea were

45

all firmly led by the same head of state for several decades but have at the same time run their economies into the ground. While President Mobutu Sese Seko has held the unruly pieces of Zaïre together since the U.S.-led U.N. intervention there in the early 1960s, his style of government has been most aptly characterized as "kleptocratic" rule; with diversion rather than development of resources the name of the game, the standard of living of ordinary Zaïreans has fallen steadily since the mid-70s, with overall growth dropping over the last decade and a half at a rate of more than 1 percent a year, per capita incomes have come down from $140 in 1974 to about $70 today and real wages have dropped to about 10 percent of their pre-Independence levels. Tanzania, on the other hand, has suffered not from corruption but from the misplaced zeal of its idealistic former head of state, Julius Nyerere; his attempt to achieve perfect equity and self-reliance under rigid state control contributed to a sharp decline in production of his country's major exports—cotton, sisal, cashew nuts, and coffee—and steeply increased dependence on aid grants. In Guinea, Independence leader Sékou Touré, pursuing a more repressive form of socialism for almost a quarter-century, turned bauxite wealth into universal poverty.

In fact, in the pursuit of political control and order, African leaders have made some fairly bad economic mistakes. In the beginning, however, political and economic strategies seemed to mesh very nicely. Bright young economic advisers to African ministries, fresh out of the London School of Economics and the Sorbonne, turned their Fabian and other forms of socialism into an African development doctrine that promised to serve everybody's best interests: strong state control over the economy was necessary to insure an equitable share for everyone. Thus the absolute discretion of politicians over the country's wealth was not only morally justified but also imperative.

This stance was supported by the World Bank and the major donors, including the United States, on the eminently sensible ground that the state would have to take the lead if small, poor countries virtually devoid of private domestic wealth were ever to put together the capital and skills needed in larger enterprises. Development theorists in the mid-1960s, including those with strong capitalist credentials like Walt Whitman Rostow, shared a kind of consensus on the need for state-led industrialization as the main path to development for the newly independent nations in Africa and elsewhere. The fact that the Soviet Union had succeeded in moving its people into the twentieth century by forced march also played some part, at least in the calculations of their Third-World counterparts. To reverse the Marxist order, socialism would, perhaps, be a stage enroute to capitalism.

A decade or so later, however, it became apparent that these policies were not working as predicted. Ravenous states were themselves gobbling up national resources, and pervasive economic controls were stifling the ability to reproduce those resources. Moreover, the enormous economic discretion wielded by African leaders created its own set of problems. Personalized decision-making led to colossal miscalculations about the viability and cost of pet projects. In addition, individual officials were exposed to venal solicitations from buccaneering capitalists peddling turnkey factories and assorted white elephants. Too often investments were designed to load longer-term risk onto the African state while showering immediate profit on both expatriate developers and African officials. Too few African governments appeared able—and many did not even seem disposed—to use their economic power effectively and for the benefit of all their people.

The problem was not just one of corruption or inept administration—though both were a serious drain on African resources—but also of economic culture. As an engine of development the state was breaking down; perhaps more seriously, it stood as a massive obstruction in the way of individual effort. Paradoxically, it became questionable at the same time whether the state's resources in many African countries actually could be considered the common property of all citizens when they appeared to be the private fiefdom of a few powerful individuals or groups.

After Independence, few African governments could or did resist the slide toward increasing reliance on patronage to shore up their power. Apart from the dubious protection of their armies' guns, and an occasional assist from former colonial powers (to spike those guns), the new regimes had very little to draw on. Their nations had been seen as alien constructs by most of their inhabitants until the very end of the colonial period, when nationalist agitation drew people together more in protest than commitment. Without a tradition of patriotism or membership in a larger nation, people regarded the government—as they had the colonial regimes—principally as a provider of benefits or taxes and not as an expression of themselves. Their patriotism centered on local ties to ethnic group, village, and family. So African leaders looking for support were thrown back on the purchasing power of the state treasury or on their own ethnic groups.

∽

"Tribalism" is a bad word in Africa, an epithet hurled at your opponents and hotly abjured for yourself. Divided by the British into three regions corresponding to the three main ethnic groups—Hausa, Yoruba, and Ibo—Nigeria's national slogan, "One Nigeria," continued as a rallying cry while politics organized itself around ethnic alliances and a civil war was fought from 1967 to 1970 over sectional hostilities. In present-day Kenya, charges of "tribalism" accompany a redistribution of spoils: what they seem to mean is that the largest tribe, the Kikuyu, got more than their share under former president Jomo Kenyatta, and other groups should have a chance now. The passions engendered by this pulling and hauling flared up quite literally in January

1986 when Nairobi's City Hall burst into flames, allegedly torched by Kikuyus enraged at the appointment of 680 non-Kikuyus to municipal jobs.

In fact, tribalism arguably is stronger now than it was under colonial rule or before the whites arrived. Sharpening insecurities and conflict over resources have heightened the need to band together with people you can trust. In Africa today that means kin. Relatives speak the tongue you learned as a child, before English, French, the East African lingua franca Swahili, or any other half-assimilated second language came to bedevil all your lessons at school. They will without question give you a bed and food for indefinite periods, help pay your school fees, lend you money if they happen to have some, work to bring in your harvest—and expect the same of you. You will marry their children, nephews and nieces, or cousins. No matter how distant the blood relationship you will call them "brother," "sister," "uncle." The protagonist of Achebe's novel *No Longer at Ease* puts it very strongly, when he says that kin who do not stick together are like snakes: they would be invulnerable if they lived together in one place, but if "they live every one unto himself" so they "fall easy prey to man."

Kinship provides the only sense of security most Africans feel today. It also makes it very difficult to carry on the business of a modern nation-state and economy. Power struggles among ethnic groups pose continuing and often grave threats to civil order: Nigeria's civil war, Uganda's decade of unending bloodletting, Rwanda and Burundi's genocidal massacres all provide glaring instances of their destructive force. Analogous struggles taking place more quietly within armies, cabinets, and state corporations elsewhere consume enormous energy even when they do not threaten the peace.

Apart from actual conflict, ethnic loyalties also perpetuate the fragmentation that blocks development throughout Africa, as well as within each country. To a great extent it's a question of trust. Institutionalizing political behavior and extending private commercial transactions depend on broadening the basis for trust beyond family and ethnic group. Political alliances based on common interests—among, for example, small farmers—have seldom gotten off the ground. Class issues have been appropriated by populist leaders in the name of "equity," but at the grass roots most people do not seem very stirred by abstract class connections but rather by whether their tribal brothers and sisters up and down the economic scale are getting a fair share.

While ethnic ties supersede national allegiance, many, probably most, Africans, see the state's resources not primarily as the common property of all citizens, but rather as fair game for ethnic groups building their own bases of support. They regard the state, in fact, as the primary source of available resources. This attitude leads to deep public ambivalence about government accountability for national monies. Insofar as they think of themselves as citizens of a nation-state, everyone is opposed to corruption, but on the deeper level where they identify with family and tribe, they do not question the legitimacy of taking their share.

Their share comes mainly in the forms of outright graft or patronage. These are, of course, common to politics everywhere. But where institutions are weak and accountability is porous as in Africa, they can become the main engine driving economic policy. As the Nigerian proverb has it: "When a wall cracks, the lizards can find a place to hide."

Often remarkably open, the outright plunder of state resources in Africa is well known. Some of it is, arguably, invested in people and projects that increase productivity. Schooling for your relatives, a generator or a television for your village—like the good works of local bosses in American cities a few decades ago—cannot be considered a total loss. In earlier, more optimistic days, development economists sometimes argued that corruption was a necessary cost of production, or alternatively, a way of capital formation. Overall, however, the diversion of national wealth has clearly become a severe drain on poor African economies.

The flight of ill-gotten gains to Swiss bank accounts has sometimes reached legendary proportions. Giving new meaning to the Zaïrean proverb, "No matter how full the river, it still wants to grow," that country's President Mobutu reportedly has stashed away overseas assets sometimes estimated to equal his country's national debt of $4.5 billion. Nigeria's former transport minister, Umaru Dikko, the object of an unsuccessful attempt by his government to kidnap him trussed in diplomatic baggage to be sent home from London, got away with an estimated $600 million, probably the record even for the notorious assemblage of "opportunists" who stole their country blind during the regime of deposed President Shehu Shagari. Others feathered their nests less flamboyantly, like Cameroon's former president Ahmadou Ahidjo, who lives well in exile on the French Riviera. One culprit caught in the act, former Upper Volta (now Burkina Faso) minister Pale Walde, explained the hundreds of thousands of dollars found under his bed in nonchalant court testimony, saying "I like to look at money. Doesn't everyone?"

Conspicuous consumption on the part of high government officials accounts for another slice of national wealth. In good times—as in Nigeria's oil boom of the 1970s—this is usually accepted, often jocularly, as a sign of rank. The Mercedes-Benz automobile has become such a ubiquitous status symbol among the "big men" of East Africa that they are known as "WaBenzi." Inevitably the prevailing tolerance can extend a license to go pretty far. Tales abound of king-size beds wrought of 24-karat gold and presidential wives commandeering the national airline for shopping sprees to Paris. It is hard to raise eyebrows with stories about Nigeria's plutocrats—their exploits are too well known— but a new high for sartorial extravagance reportedly was set by a former leader of Nigeria's federal legislature, whose custom-made $25,000 suit sported pin stripes of solid gold. Official trappings of power have legalized acquisition for those at the top. From former Liberian President Tubman's presidential yacht, whose running expenses amounted to 1 percent of the country's budget, to the stately capital city erected in the home village of Côte d'Ivoire's President Houphouet-Boigny, Africa's leaders have not suppressed their instincts for grandeur.

As far as the workings of government are concerned, various forms of patronage probably do more damage than the more blatant graft. The power to allocate jobs and projects—as well as to redistribute resources through fiscal and monetary policy—offers African leaders the main instrument of control they have to wield. On slender means they have to secure the loyalty of the military and the upper-level bureaucrats and to buy off potentially volatile city dwellers. At the same time ethnic pressures are working throughout the system. As a result, all too often the cart gets shoved before the horse, and the economy is, in effect, run *for* patronage. Where this happens economic viability assumes a very low priority: witness steel mills where there is no iron ore, no coal, and no transport for inputs or finished product; irrigation where the soil at best can support light grazing; eight-lane highways leading to small villages.

～

As several studies by political scientist David Abernethy show, these systemic problems have come to roost most visibly in expensive and inefficient government bureaucracies. Since Independence, government employment has increased greatly in most African countries—by an estimated 160 percent over two decades. Parastatal organizations—public sector corporations that dominate both manufacturing and services in every country—have grown particularly rapidly. In Senegal, for example, 70 new parastatal agencies were created between 1970 and 1975. After Kwame Nkrumah's eight years at the helm, Ghana possessed 53 state enterprises, 12 joint state/private enterprises, and 23 public boards. Between 1964 and 1975, Tanzania created nearly 400 state corporations. By 1986, the percentage of African domestic product accounted for by state-owned enterprises (almost 20 percent) was about double the average for developed and developing countries worldwide.

The success of governments in expanding secondary and university education forces them into the role of employer of last resort. For some time it was assumed in many places that a school certificate or a degree automatically entitled the bearer to a job. And governments have felt obliged to fulfill these expectations. This pressure has been reinforced by responsibilities of office holders to vast networks of kin. In the upshot, job creation often became an end in itself, the desk preceding the task.

The effect was to undermine the importance of doing a job, in relation to having it. The sense that certain sectors were ethnic preserves further eroded the idea that competence would play an important part in your record of achievement. The story is told in many African settings of the young man who went to apply for the job of clerk advertised in the newspaper. When he got to the office he waited in line all morning for the application forms. Reaching the front, he asked the receptionist for the name of the boss. On his way out he dropped the forms in the gutter. The boss was from the wrong ethnic group.

Many of these problems originated in institutions preserved from colonial days. What Africans saw in those days were European civil servants who worked much less hard than African farmers and earned much more. And hierarchy was crucial. One criterion was quite arbitrary: race, which effectively barred Africans from the heights. But for the African junior staff strict educational qualifications were the prerequisite to entry: the colonial officers needed clerks who could read and write, interpreters and constabulary who commanded the European language well enough to transmit their directives. Thus certification through education could supply the essential ticket to a good life.

Before Independence Africans agitated for equity with Europeans. And they got it. What this meant was that the colonial hierarchies—and wage scales—were transferred nearly intact to the new African governments. The gaps between the incomes of senior government officials and average citizens are still enormous: whereas the average government wage is 1.74 times the average per capita share of gross domestic product in the Western industrialized countries, 2.9 times that in Asia, and 2.94 times that in Latin America, in Africa it is 6.05 times GDP per capita. Further, the secure wages even of lower-level positions are a mighty attraction in an environment where most people's livelihood depends on the vagaries of nature. It is understandable that many would decide to invest all they have to get that position—and money. So they will educate their brightest children to get the certificate or diploma that will give them a place on the ladder. The young scholar's great achievement is in securing that place. After that, his or her most important role will be to act as a conduit back to the family.

Clearly, one effect of these systems is to distort the relationship between jobs and work for government bureaucrats. Beyond that, the wage bills have consumed increasing portions of African resources. These bills include the cost of numerous perks like automobiles, housing, "home leave," and allowances, which often have been retained nearly intact from colonial times. With the rapid expansion of the public sector after Independence and pressures from lower ranks for more equity, the costs have increased astronomically. In Congo-Brazzaville (now the Congo), for example, the expenditures for wages and salaries jumped nearly 90 percent in four years after

Independence; in the Côte d'Ivoire, they climbed more than 16 percent a year between 1966 and 1975; in Nigeria, costs for public administration and the military rose from 4.5 percent of GDP in 1972 to 12.1 percent of a greatly expanded GDP in 1977.

Finally, the proportion of government budgets going for wages and salaries in Africa is very high in comparison with those in the rest of the world: twice that of Asia, and about 50 percent higher than that of Latin America and the Caribbean. From 1974 onward, the African figure stayed at about 30 percent while the industrialized countries and Asia slowly reduced their ratios about 4 percentage points to 12 and 14 percent respectively and Latin America hovered around 20 percent. While austerity brought cutbacks in almost every category of African budgets, in many places bureaucratic salaries have remained sacrosanct.

～

Western influence on African bureaucracies did not in fact end with colonialism. In some measure, the opportunities for African bureaucrats have been shaped by their international connections. The revenues from aid and the premiums flowing from trade and investment transactions have helped sustain African elites and undoubtedly absorbed much of their energy.

With a fair amount of turf to guard, African bureaucracies have not been laggard in doing so. Apart from the military, the bureaucracy can exert the most direct threat to government—to slow it down or stop it altogether. Pay-related protests by civil servants brought down the presidents of the Central African Republic and Upper Volta (now Burkina Faso), and sharply threatened that of Ghana. While Tanzania has succeeded in reducing disparities between top- and lower-level bureaucrats to about 4 to 1, in the prevailing circumstances most other regimes have been reluctant to follow that example.

In addition to protecting their own salaries, bureaucrats are well placed to shape overall economic policy. Not surprisingly, their decisions have favored urban dwellers and helped undermine agriculture. Looking toward "modern development" in the cities and through industries, many African countries opted for import-export regimes and exchange rates that made it harder to sell their farm products in world markets. At the same time, they tried to keep the prices of food low to keep city dwellers happy.

Because they have the most money to spend and to invest, the bureaucrats gain directly when the national currency is overvalued and imports are cheap. It would be unfair, however, to assign sole responsibility for unproductive policy to the new African elites. As we have seen, the colonial governors originally determined that agriculture should support the administration and reorganized farming to provide that support. And later on, the best and brightest international development gurus quite reasonably advised that real progress would require African economies to cut their dependence on one or two commodities exports by launching their own industries.

For some time little heed was paid by anyone to the goose that was supposed to keep on supplying the golden eggs. Wholly unorganized as a group in most countries, farmers have close links to their ethnic city kin profiting from the system. Thus they have remained mute politically. However, when macroeconomic policies decreased their rewards, farm production showed it. The main engine of African development had slowed to a halt.

# 3

# The Wages of Altruism

*There is a new mood of realism in Africa—a willingness to enter into a tough analysis of past mistakes and present confusion, a sobriety that verges on humiliation. Africans are looking, frequently Westward, for new ideas.*

"Compact for African Development"
Report of the Committee on African Development Strategies

*The humble pay for the mistakes of their betters.*

Chadian proverb

In testimony before a congressional subcommittee in September 1986, an official of the U.S. Treasury delivered the verdict on Africa's malaise tersely, saying "the principal factor underlying this performance was poor economic policies." Specifically, "maintenance of overvalued exchange rates, non-remunerative agricultural prices, establishment of inefficient public sector firms, and ill-advised investments" were all culprits. However, he sounded downright bullish on problem-solving in Africa: "African leaders themselves," he said, "have been candid and forthright in admitting to past policy failures and the need for a better policy environment." In fact they see eye to eye with us.

After a quarter-century of African Independence, the continent's doldrums have evoked a loud and clear Western response. From the Reagan administration, the World Bank, the European Community, and even the Scandinavians comes the message: free up those economies! Let the marketplace spur individual effort and galvanize productive energies that have been held in check by stifling state controls.

57

The new orthodoxy cuts sharply athwart African ide-
ologies and interests now entrenched for two decades. African leaders holding the keys to money and jobs in all the
nooks and crannies of their economies are understandably
loath to give up any of them. Are U.S. Treasury and State
Department officials merely deceiving themselves when
they claim to see a meeting of the minds?

For Africans, swallowing Western prescriptions is
hardly a new experience. In good times and bad, African
governments have never lacked for advice. This came at
first mainly from their former colonial mentors, some of
whose nationals stayed on to teach school, counsel (and
sometimes direct) government ministries, and run their
own businesses. In many former colonies of France, the
French population grew after Independence. The Côte
d'Ivoire in particular has made its former governors very
welcome, relying on French personnel to staff key official
positions. With the teachers, military advisers, and free-
lance entrepreneurs, the number of French nationals in the
Côte d'Ivoire's seaside capital city of Abidjan has swollen to
four times that in the colonial period. The only comparable
case in English-speaking Africa is Kenya, where the white
settlers have been doubly replaced by an influx of development experts, private voluntary aid organizations, journalists, and others who are happy to make the temperate and
modern city of Nairobi their headquarters.

Americans had never been much involved in Africa,
except in several movements to resettle freed slaves, in
Liberia and Sierra Leone, and Washington generally followed the lead of the Europeans on the welfare of their
colonies, dealing with Africa from the State Department's
European Desk until 1958. But the United States played the
dominant role in the international directorate that created
the postwar economic world and established the place of the
so-called "underdeveloped" nations within it. During the
war, President Roosevelt had proclaimed among the "four
freedoms" sought as Allied goals the "freedom from want-

... everywhere in the world." Then the United Nations Charter in 1946 decreed that the promotion of "higher standards of living, full employment, and conditions of economic and social progress and development" was an objective of the community of nations. In 1948 Congress enacted the Marshall Plan, the prototypical aid program, though directed first and foremost at Europe (with aid to the colonies to be channeled through the metropoles). And President Harry S. Truman promised U.S. technical assistance to backward nations as a safeguard to world peace in his Point Four Program of 1949.

The Bretton Woods Conference of 1944, which set up the International Monetary Fund and the World Bank, ignored these concerns for the most part, concentrating on the overriding interest of the United States and Europe in establishing a stable relationship among their own currencies, meeting balance of payment needs, and creating cooperative mechanisms for international finance. Most of the developing countries, which were still colonies, were not invited to what was clearly an American and British show. Those who were—mainly Latin Americans—came on sufferance. The British economist and architect of the conference, Lord Maynard Keynes, pronounced beforehand that they would "have nothing to contribute" and would "merely encumber the proceedings," helping create "the most monstrous monkey house assembled for years." When the World Bank—more formally titled the International Bank for Reconstruction and Development—got underway in 1955, the emphasis was definitely on "reconstruction" rather than "development." Decolonization was not expected to come right away nor to sweep all the way through the former imperium. But all this while, the development economists were beginning to stir their new brew.

The term "economic development" was seldom used before the 1940s, but by the end of the 1940s and early 1950s a whole new subdiscipline aimed at curing the economic ills of the underdeveloped had come into being. In the idealism of that moment, this new venture must have seemed particularly promising: because "we" had arrived and "they" were struggling to catch up, it shouldn't be too difficult to plot out the steps in between. The early practitioners enthusiastically plumbed the analogues they had, which were depression survival strategies, Soviet planning, wartime mobilization, and the Marshall Plan. Culminating in the optimism of the early Kennedy period, the confidence of that time comes through clearly in a 1965 discussion by Harold Lasswell of "The Policy Sciences of Development," when he declares: "the goals of development are gaining clarity; the historical perspective deepens; the interdependence of conditioning factors is better understood; the probable lines of future growth are more fully projected; and the invention and evaluation of policies designed to maximize or at least to achieve minimum results are forging ahead." As now, the pioneers' theories showed a strong degree of consensus. What was different was that Western notions then accorded closely with key interests of political leaders in the new nations.

The prevailing wisdom was shaped in the euphoria of the postwar period, when it seemed that the United States, and then the Europeans as well, would and *could* afford to keep the world peaceful by helping keep its people happy. The accelerated growth that would bring prosperity to the underdeveloped was seen to depend on large infusions of capital—most of which could not be generated by domestic savings in the poor countries and would therefore have to come from the industrialized nations. Since world demand for the farm and minerals exports of the underdeveloped countries was likely to fluctuate widely, they should get on with building industry—first of all to supply their own markets. Pulling together the capital and holding the international market at bay until infant industries could compete would call for energetic government activity within a national plan.

Because industry worldwide was more productive than agriculture, it seemed clear at the time that if you shifted people from farms to factories the gross national product would rise. The argument made sense, for in the longer run developing countries would have to supply more of their own needs, and expanding prosperity would depend on creating new sources of wealth. It assumed, however, that the new industries would pay their way, and that productivity in agriculture would not be jeopardized but rather would rise, as new farm technologies replaced workers pulled into industry.

Africa, to be sure, hardly figured in the formation of this theory—development economists were looking mainly at the early industrialization in Latin America, on the one hand, and the Asian giants, China and India, on the other. By their sheer numbers, Africa's new nations forced themselves on the world's political consciousness in the early 1960s. It is doubtful, though, whether the prototypical African economy, a commodities exporter with a very small internal market and no industrial base, played much of a role in shaping the nostrums dispensed to their new clients by experts at the World Bank, the United Nations, or the aid-giving nations.

The main ideas, however, were absorbed by the young Africans who made it to universities in their mother countries and who would become ministers in their governments. Because the prevailing theory implied swift modernization, economic independence, and increasing control, African policymakers found these ideas very congenial. At the same time, the notion that much of the investment capital they needed would come from abroad seemed a particularly desirable extension of their new sovereignty.

And the aid did come. Even in 1965 almost 20 percent of the Western countries' development assistance went to Africa. In the 1980s, Africans, who are about 12 percent of the developing world's population, were receiving about 22 percent of the total, and the share per person was higher than anywhere else in the Third World—amounting to about $20, versus about $7 for Latin America, and $5 for

Asia. As it became clear that the continent's access to other sources of finance—investment, trade and commercial loans—was comparatively meager, the World Bank and the United Nations earmarked more money for Africa. In 1986, twenty-five of the 46 countries in Africa depended on aid for more than two-thirds of their externally provided finance. Of these, 15 depended on aid for more than 90 percent.

Where did all that money go? That's a hard question to answer—not because someone took it and ran (although in some cases they did)—but because our understanding of the effects of aid is pretty rudimentary. Clearly in Africa the very weight of aid within the continent's diminutive economies exerted a distinctive pull. The pull, however, sometimes went in several different directions at the same time. What seems clear is that aid helped African countries to build material and social welfare infrastructures, in some cases almost from scratch. At times, less happily, it also added to the confusion and distortion often characteristic of African governments' economic management.

✆

Talking about "aid to Africa" means generalizing broadly about a bewildering spectrum of operations in which most of Western and Eastern Europe, the United States, several dozen international organizations, and numerous private philanthropies are represented. For much of the postwar period, France's effort to bind her former colonies to her through a massive Peace Corps-type *coopérant* program and extensive commercial subsidies pushed Paris out front as the largest national donor. In the early 1970s, responding to pressures from their former colonies for more say in mutual economic transactions, the Europeans as a group also worked out a deal (the Lomé Agreements) offering trade guarantees as well as grants to a group of African, Pacific, and Caribbean nations.

From the early 1960s, the World Bank and its soft-loan window, the International Development Association, supplied the lion's share, at least 25 percent on average. Over the years, U.S. aid fluctuated widely, doubling during both the Kennedy and Carter presidencies, and falling back in the mid-1980s as the United States itself became a major world debtor. Although its share continued to grow until 1985, the United States never played the primary role in Africa it has taken on in Latin America, Asia, and the Middle East.

However, the American program was always a bellwether. Not only because it was so much larger worldwide than other national programs, but also because the U.S. approach was noisily thrashed out in Congress, U.S. aid-giving made waves that set the other boats rocking. Despite considerable congressional and administration hostility to the World Bank, this country continued to channel about 40 percent of its aid money through that institution. As its congressional critics pointed out, the Bank was not merely an extension of U.S. foreign policy, and like other U.N. bodies, the proportion of its American and European staff has declined, while the Third World component has risen. But the Bank has hardly been immune from Washington's influence. With a professional staff of about 3,000, and annual commitments now about $12 billion, the Bank carried more weight than any individual donor—even the United States, whose total allocation worldwide (about half of which went to Israel and Egypt) ranged around $9 billion by 1986. Because the United States contributed 25 percent of its working capital, however, the Bank's president was always an American, and each in turn has watched his congressional flank warily.

In Africa, over the years, the Bank and the U.S. followed roughly parallel paths. These swerved markedly at several points. Probably because of wide swings in America's international mood over the last two decades, abrupt changes in direction characterized the U.S. aid program.

This country's ongoing involvement with Africa's development started in the presidency of John F. Kennedy. Coin-
ciding with the wave of nationalist elation during the Independence era, Kennedy's bouyant idealism set the tone for a
new embrace of the Third World, in which the aid program
would, in his words, "help make a historical demonstration
that in the twentieth century as in the nineteenth—in the
southern half of the globe as in the north—economic
growth and political democracy can develop hand in hand."
As a senator in the late 1950s, Kennedy's attention was
drawn to the wave of Independence movements cresting
throughout the continent by the violent struggle of the
North African country of Algeria to free itself from France.
When he took office in 1960, Kennedy swiftly followed
President Eisenhower to the Congo (now called Zaïre) to
fight the communists—triggering a considerable flow of
U.S. aid into that country.

Zaïre's lien on U.S. assistance, which continues to the
present day, illustrates the strong drag of security concerns
on what is ostensibly a humanitarian program. Because its
leader, President Mobutu, was considered "our man," and,
much later, because he had been attacked by insurgent
forces based in "Marxist" Angola, we allocated around $800
million between 1965 and 1987 to develop Zaïre. The min-
eral-rich country could be one of the wealthiest in Africa,
but while the United States poured money into programs
for agriculture, education, and infrastructure, the people
grew poorer and poorer and the leaders richer and richer.
From Independence onward, the support of the United
States and other Western countries has played a considerable part in maintaining Mobutu in power.

During the Korean War, again with Vietnam, and with
the advent of the "Reagan Doctrine," the pendulum has
swung markedly toward security. Other African aid recipients whose purported strategic salience loosened U.S.
purse strings include: our longtime stepchild, Liberia, the
most "American" though also one of the poorest African

countries and location of a satellite tracking station; the Sudan, like Zaïre a potentially rich African basketcase and a former ally of Egypt against Libya; and Somalia, a two-thousand-square-mile desert enclave locked in enmity with "Marxist" Ethiopia (formerly an unofficial U.S. protectorate and location of a U.S. tracking station but now the Soviet Union's main African client). Whether or not some economic progress resulted from allocations to these countries, they usually accounted for roughly half and sometimes two-thirds of U.S. aid to Africa.

Granting that politics will always rule the day, even where development goals held sway U.S. priorities shifted widely: between growth and equity, poverty and policy, "privatization" and the "poorest of the poor." In the beginning it seemed much simpler.

Our first big commitment for development in Africa was a hefty $225-million Independence gift to Nigeria in 1961. The innocence of those early days, and the relaxed spirit of giving and receiving, is reflected in the remarks of Nigeria's first head of state, Sir Abubakar Tafawa Balewa, in 1962, when he wrote: "we welcome aid whether in the form of foreign investment, loan or grant. So long as this assistance is given in a spirit of genuine desire to make life happier for the people, we would gladly accept and welcome it."

That first grant to Nigeria went for capital investment in roads, water supplies, and education. Three new universities, Ahmadu Bello in the north, the University of Nigeria at Nsukka in the east, and Ife in the west were started at that time in collaboration with American land-grant colleges on which they were modeled, including Kansas State, Michigan State, and Colorado. Other similar programs with close U.S. friends, Liberia and Ethiopia, as well as with Tanzania, Kenya, Sudan, and Zaïre followed. In Ghana, an early favorite, the United States supported World Bank involvement in the massive Volta Dam and hydroelectric plant and guaranteed the U.S. investment (by Kaiser Aluminum) in the nearby Valco aluminum smelter.

Like the World Bank, the United States saw the development process in those days the way most Africans did: governments would expand and diversify the economy by creating industries and services, moving into areas where Europeans and sometimes Asians now held a near monopoly. In West Africa, Lebanese family combines had long controlled much of the import-export business, and the British and French were also on the scene eyeing commercial opportunities in the new states; in much of East Africa, Indians monopolized internal trade and the British settlers and their kin were looking for larger possibilities. The only African money that could compete was in government treasuries.

So the United States and the World Bank actively supported national planning to provide the basis for both government activity and their own projects. Ghana proved an apt student of this new science, pioneering the multi-year comprehensive development plan, and Nigeria's independence gift was based on a blueprint for its first five years. The plans grew increasingly sophisticated as economists invented new techniques, including input-output analysis, growth simulation models, and dynamic programming. Development programs, national planning boards, and industrial development corporations sprang up everywhere.

Looking at what actually happened in this period, the early focus on relatively concrete capital projects and education had the great advantage of simplicity. Everyone was starting with a clean slate, and the needs seemed more basic. Many African countries did not have road systems for internal marketing, water systems extending beyond the margins of one or several major cities, universities, teacher training institutes, or even many secondary schools. There was no place to go but up, and aid helped African states to provide more education, better health, and more opportunities for many more people.

In time, however, problems emerged. Many of these stemmed from failures in maintenance. Grants had been made on the understanding that once infrastructure was built African governments would shoulder the costs of keeping it going. In practice, the responsibility often seemed to fall between the central and local governments. And as roads, for example, deteriorated, the value of the aid investment eroded sharply, and recouping it often meant starting again almost from scratch. In addition, too great a share of project budgets were in effect invested in the life-styles of middlemen and bureaucrats whose interest dropped off abruptly after the contracts were signed. The illusion was fading that the business of development would be easy. Yet what came next was a demand for sure-fire solutions—to new questions.

In the late 1960s and early 1970s in the United States, the Vietnam War cast a heavy shadow over the aid landscape. By the end of the sixties, about a third of the aid budget was earmarked for the "economic development," and later for the "reconstruction" of South Vietnam, Laos, and Cambodia. The U.S. Agency for International Development's contingent in Vietnam grew to more than 4,000 at the height of the conflict. In Congress, aid became a political football, with Nixon supporters fighting to enlarge security assistance and kill amendments that would "tie the President's hands," and opponents attempting to do just that through restrictive amendments and budget cuts.

In the wake of the war, Senator William Fulbright launched a campaign against foreign aid on the grounds that any involvement at all could be the first step into another quagmire. With that argument, he succeeded for a few years in limiting to forty the number of countries that would receive aid, out of which Africa's quota was 10—spurring aid planners to turn out regional development schemes that would include many more. (It also spurred African lobbying, during which at least one Washington ambassador of a concerned African microstate reportedly called in at the State Department to inquire who the other nine recipients might be.)

In 1972 conservative opponents of aid, disillusioned liberals and a pro-war faction combined to defeat the foreign assistance bill, which contained an end-the-war amendment by Senator Mike Mansfield. When President Nixon sent his foreign aid proposals to Congress, with $632 million in new money for Indochina Postwar Reconstruction and the lowest level in years for bilateral development, Congressman Zablocki called it "more of the same." If economic aid were to survive at all, new directions appeared in order. Shoving the pendulum back again, a new coalition of liberals and moderates emerged to argue that aid should aim not at fighting the communists but at reducing poverty. The target of aid should be "basic human needs." As Senator George Aiken of Vermont put it: "Let's help people and let's not make our objective getting control of as many governments of small countries as we can."

Along with the humanitarian impulse, Congress was seized with the imperative that comes upon that body periodically, to Take Control of National Affairs, or in this case, to regain the constitutional prerogatives given up during Vietnam. Senator Lawton Chiles of Florida expressed it pungently: "The Constitution is like the Bible. It is overlooked because it was written so long ago . . . the Senate is looking for a new direction . . . on war powers and economic matters, completely across the front, and I think now is the time if the iron is hot to move."

What Congress wanted to do was to start with a clean slate. In order to avoid involvement with privileged and perhaps corrupt elites (as in Vietnam), the program would be redirected toward the millions of very poor Asians, Latin Americans, and Africans. Large, expensive projects like ports and electric power would be left to the World Bank. According to the Foreign Assistance Act of 1973, future U.S. bilateral support would "focus on critical problems in those functional sectors which affect the lives of the majority of the people in the developing countries: food production, rural development and nutrition; population planning and health; education, public administration, and human resource development." In emphasizing the participation of the poor, the new directions partially echoed Kennedy's earlier emphasis on political participation; it also paralleled a key aim of domestic poverty programs, which were then at their zenith.

While Congress was rescuing aid, a former architect of Vietnam, Robert S. McNamara, was steering the World Bank into its own assault on international poverty. The former Secretary of Defense, now President of the Bank, turned his formidable managerial skills and new zeal into an enormous expansion and redirection. From 1968, when McNamara took over, until 1981, when he left, the Bank raised its total lending commitments from $13 billion to $92 billion. The new strategy was laid out in September 1973 at a Board of Governors' meeting in Nairobi. From then on, within the limits of its charter, the Bank would venture beyond its clients in finance ministries and central banks, aiming to reach the countless millions who lie beyond the margins of "traditional market forces and present public services." Most Africans undoubtedly fall into this category.

What was envisioned by Congress and U.S. AID, however, went further: they saw U.S. assistance going in a direct infusion to the grassroots. Down a new dirt road into the village, aid would deliver modest options for improving people's lives directly into the hands of the poor themselves. Villagers would help build primary schools, and low-cost clinics staffed from among their own ranks; they would assist technicians in designing communal water systems and improved farming methods for local fields. As the quality of life improved, the peasants' well-being would "trickle up" into the entire economy. While the health and education of urban dwellers could not be ignored, small-holder agriculture, and particularly the food crops consumed in the villages, came to head the list of U.S. priorities. Population planning also acquired new impetus: there would never be enough food, health care, or education to go around if existing land and available services had to support so many more every year.

What the new approach would mean in practice was difficult at first for everyone—the AID staff and the African recipients—to understand fully. Large capital investments in railroads, highways, large dams, telecommunications, and manufacturing, were of course out. And with Congress looking over its shoulder, the aid agency interpreted its new mandate as excluding technical assistance or institution-building at higher levels, for example, sophisticated agri-cultural research, university education, or advanced train-ing programs in the United States. Governments could not be bypassed entirely. However, if they wanted any assistance they had to take what was on offer.

For all those who had given any thought to the material lives of the Third-World poor, never quite free of the tug of hunger or the ache of illness, the idea of all those villagers feeling better, seeing further, working harder, living longer, was very appealing. More than that, the basic hu-man needs approach rightly identified the need for action at the grass roots on food production, irrigation and conser-vation and population limitation. Little headway had been made at local levels when the poor were not enlisted.

∽

The problem with the frontal attack on poverty was that it ignored the overall growth of the economy. Trying to avoid the bureaucratic traps in the capital city, aid planners overlooked the ways that state controls shaped the oppor-tunities of the peasants. Whether or not they were literate and well versed in the latest agricultural methods, farmers would not grow more unless they got a good price and received seeds and fertilizer on time; whether or not the village had a clinic and the clinic had medicine, they would not stay healthy unless they had enough food. In the cities, no one would eat unless they had work.

Making local programs stick also proved much more costly than anyone had foreseen. In debating the basic human needs legislation, congressional proponents had argued that the U.S. could have more impact for less money by foregoing massive projects and going straight to the poor. Starting local clinics, literacy classes, credit unions and keeping them going, however, in most cases meant continued visits and support by committed professional workers—an extremely labor-intensive proposition. In Africa, the scarcity of trained personnel and lack of institutional structures meant extensive training efforts and elaborately designed institution-building programs. AID personnel in the field began to proliferate. In the Sahel—object of a crash program during the 1970s—technical assistance personnel absorbed 25 to 40 percent of around $13 billion in international aid revenues from 1974 to 1983. This essentially populist approach was, in effect, highly interventionist. As a result, overhead was high and delivery slow.

Even when things went well, dealing with donors could place heavy burdens on governments. Too often, when donors brought in expatriate staff, these experts moved into ministries and formed foreign enclaves there that answered not to the host government but to the aid agency back home. Because it was easier than trying to teach African "counterparts" to take over, the expatriates continued to run the project themselves, and when their time was up it is no surprise that the work they were doing did not survive their departure for very long. Confusing and blurring lines of authority, donor enclaves could not help but sap the confidence of host country officials in their ability to take charge of their own affairs. And in the event that the cost of staffing and equipping them was supposed to be passed on to the government, the effect of these programs was to saddle African budgets with heavy recurrent expenditures.

Much of the problem lay with Congress itself: over time, congressional interpretation of the new program grew progressively narrow and its oversight increasingly fussy. With the appropriations process in the hands of conservatives not very sensitive to aid and decidedly unsympathetic to Third-World governments, Congress set standards almost impossible to attain and thus put limits on the money AID could disburse. As one insider has characterized what was called the "direct" approach to helping the poor, it meant that AID "almost had to get out in the poorest farmer's field, hand him the seeds, and watch the food produced being eaten from his family's table."

It is difficult now to assess what might have been achieved through this approach if U.S. and other donors had stayed committed to it and Africans had been able or willing to follow through. In fact everyone walked away. Like the American domestic poverty program, it was launched at the end of good times and the beginning of a downward slide. As the 1970s wore on, Africa's combined crises made it difficult to sustain even well-established institutions like national universities.

As African economic growth dried up at the end of the seventies, Western donors took a harder look at the continent's difficulties. And, yet again they switched gears. With Congress now on the sidelines as aid's fortunes declined, the U.S. administration and the World Bank began to argue that the magnitude of Africa's problems called for fundamental solutions. The key, they now concluded, lay in changing the macroeconomic policies that encourage or discourage people's private efforts.

Not surprisingly, this new tack fit very closely within ideological currents running strongly in U.S. and European domestic politics by the beginning of the 1980s. The resurgent humanitarianism that had spurred Jimmy Carter's human rights policy was eclipsed both by Ronald Reagan's focus on security and the strong pressure to cut costs that started under Carter and continued throughout the 1980s. With the Western countries in a mood of prolonged pessimism about their own ability to sustain growth, the Third-World program for a new international economic order faded from public discussion, and the claims of the less developed were heard more faintly.

Although the backwash from the Western downturn hit Africa (and other Third World regions) very hard, as time went on the external dimension of Africa's problems evoked progressively less sympathy. Since the adverse trends afflicting the international economy seemed in some senses beyond the control even of the advanced industrial states themselves, the feeling grew that Africans would do best to focus on solving their internal economic problems in order to lay a more solid groundwork for future progress. Whatever supply-side economics may have wrought within its parent context, the United States, a broad range of Western observers came to agree that for Africa the malfunctioning of overblown state controls called for a corrective dose of streamlining, rationalizing, and private competition.

Inevitably, it did not take very long for the new approach to acquire the status of dogma, particularly for ideological stalwarts in the U.S. Treasury and the International Monetary Fund. Through continuing debate, however, starting in the early 1980s, Western economists of varying ideological stripes and many African officials with economic responsibility bought into much of the program. Whatever the merit of this new consensus, the abrupt shifts in fashion that preceded it dictate a certain wariness. Over the past two decades, how much have we learned about African economies—and about how our assistance actually works within them?

༄

Aid these days has even more critics than clients. And, in Africa, it has sometimes been part of the problem. The eagerness of African countries to get foreign exchange often fed the desire of donors to get projects established and to disburse their revenue allocations—frequently in competition with other donors. The joint interest of donors and recipients in spending the money led to hasty planning and diminished concern about what happens once a project actually gets going. As one of the main projected beneficiaries of a mid-70s scheme to combine Arab petro-dollars and Western technology, the Sudan, for example, was the object of inordinate donor attention. Partly in consequence, its landscape was strewn with the carcasses of more failed foreign aid projects than any other African country. These included a plant for making tomato paste in an area where the farmers cultivate date palms, not tomatoes. A milk dehydration plant was built in an area where there are no dairy cows. A massive sugar refinery, whose output should not go to waste in a country that takes its sugar with only a dash of tea, had to be totally disassembled for cleaning every year, and it took a computer to sort out orders for the 32,000 spare parts needed from abroad to keep it and the machinery of the adjacent sugar plantations running.

In addition, as they looked around at what needed to be done, donors have piled on multiple objectives. "Integrated rural development" projects, spawned during the heyday of basic human needs, brought rising complexity and some confusion. In addition, design flaws were compounded by ignorance of the African cultural and material environment. In the desert of northern Kenya, for example, efforts to improve the lives of the Turkana nomads seriously misfired. A pastoral people who survive by raising cattle, goats and camels, the Turkana were taken in hand by Norwegian aid officials who planned for them a future as fishermen and even built them a fish-freezing plant adjacent to a nearby lake. Once built, it became clear that in daily 100-degree temperatures freezing the fish would take more electricity than was available in the entire Turkana district; so the plant shut down after two days. Next, the part of the lake where most of the fish had been caught dried up, and the Turkana who had taken up fishing (like their fellow tribesmen who had been persuaded to try their hand at another failed venture in irrigated farming) found themselves totally dependent on handouts from their would-be benefactors.

Again, in the rice paddies of western Nigeria, visiting experts surveying the local crop offered the villagers some simple advice: why not increase the yield by planting the rice closer together? The local farmers did so—once. When the rice came up they discovered that their hoes were too big to cultivate between the plants; lacking money for new tools they shrugged and went back to their old ways.

More costly was AID's effort to create a barrier forest of eucalyptus trees in Senegal that would stop the encroaching desert and supply 10 percent of the firewood for the city of Dakar. Five years later the 14,800-acre Bandia forest was a field of scrub; lacking moisture, over half its trees died and the rest were the size of twigs. Its designers used rainfall statistics from the colonial period and apparently did not realize that since 1966 rainfall there had been about half as plentiful. Reforestation through planting eucalyptus trees was popular with donors because the trees are suited to relatively sandy soils, but the majority of efforts fared almost as badly as Senegal's: establishing the trees required quite a lot of water as well as cultivation, and management skills that the local people often did not possess.

Tanzania's experience illustrated serious donor and government miscalculations about capacities of national institutions and markets. Long a favorite with donors due to the high-minded egalitarianism of former President Julius Nyerere, the country attracted more enthusiasm than judgment on the part of would-be benefactors. The country received more aid per person than any other African country, approximately $600 million a year over 20 years, but fell progressively behind in per capita income and growth (its per capita gross national product was 14th lowest in the world in 1982). Its heavy government controls sometimes choked off vital raw materials and spare parts almost before the new donor-funded enterprises could open their doors, but an alarming number were never remotely feasible to start with.

The World Bank, for example, lent Tanzania more than $10 million to finance the expansion of the country's cashew industry, creating, by 1982, processing plants with a capacity three times the size of the country's annual cashew crop and vastly more expensive than factories in India offering similar services. And a Swedish-financed $600-million pulp and paper mill, opened in October 1985, used the latest technology but relied totally on imported spare parts, fuel, and chemicals; operating at a fraction of its 60,000-ton capacity, it produced paper costing three to four times as much as comparable imports. (Also overlooked by planners, acid rain from the mill threatened to damage nearby tea estates that are one of Tanzania's largest hard-currency earners.)

In some instances, recipient countries were in danger of drowning in a proliferation of donor projects. In 1981, an estimated 340 separate aid missions, official and private, visited the small northern African country of Upper Volta (now Burkina Faso: some wags speculate that it subsequently changed its name to make it difficult for these missions to find their way back). Each of these delegations asked for high-level attention from the finance and other economic ministries—and many received it. Talking with them, helping plan their projects, traveling with them to the field, writing out grant applications, keeping accounts ate heavily into the scarce time of senior officials. What it meant was that the demands of foreign donors superseded their own planning: often they simply did not have time to establish their own priorities and implement them.

One major obstacle to effective coordination of donor efforts was built into the process at its earliest stages by the parliaments of all Western countries—through the "tying" of aid to exports. A hefty chunk of U.S. bilateral assistance to Africa always goes for equipment imported from the United States and the salaries of U.S. aid personnel. The share of British, French, and German aid tied to recipients' purchase of their exports is much higher. As a result, African procurement policies have often focused on the supply side rather than on end use, assembling a hodgepodge of vehicles and machines that did not work well in local conditions or could not be serviced easily. An adequate inventory of spare parts for, say, tube wells in Tanzania would include items from 16 countries. In the upshot, shared goals for long-term development lost a lot of their credibility for Africans and much of their reality for donors.

Surveying this graveyard of mostly good intentions, some observers were happy to conclude that in Africa aid did more harm than good: if Africans weren't so hooked on international welfare payments they would have pulled up their socks and turned things around. This conviction numbed concern about the fact that aid levels were falling anyway. Conveniently, aid bore the brunt of donors' frustration at their inability to solve—sometimes even to understand—very basic problems in the countries they were trying to assist.

The equation, however, was not so simple. In fact, a number of aid programs succeeded: without them African countries would have been decidedly worse off. Clearly, the foundations laid for African university education right after Independence bore fruit in a generation of African-trained professionals. Twenty years later, Nigeria's universities teemed with students. At campuses in Zambia, Senegal, Ghana, Congo, students earned degrees in engineering, computer science, and agronomy. Without these new educated Africans, their countries would have had little chance of seizing real control of their own economic destinies.

Further, despite the well-known pitfalls of aid in Tanzania, World Bank support there helped bring real gains in primary and adult education. The expansion of primary education in that country brought the national literacy rate up to 80 percent. For the first time young Tanzanians absorbed and used information that had never touched their parents—about weather, for example, or atoms, or Egypt's pyramids, or mass production, or the U.N. Without this knowledge they could not have hoped to make the modern world work for them. With it they at least had a start.

On the village scale, U.S. AID showed that new technologies could work. Efforts to increase grain yields with new hybrid seeds in the semidesert Sahel region of Niger, for example, paid off. There a growing population must depend on the 10 percent of the land that is arable. With supervision by government extension workers, peasants learned to mix animal droppings with chemical fertilizers and to plow them all into their fields with ox-drawn plows. One farmer amazed his family when he harvested twice as much on his ten acres as they did on twenty. Again, in Zaïre, a Peace Corps fish-farming project helped increase production 300 percent between 1974 and 1980, enriching some five thousand farmers and improving protein intake in their communities considerably.

It also seems clear that further prospects for progress in Africa will depend on infusions of technical assistance and training from the advanced nations. During 1986, two Africa-wide donor programs showed how much well-timed and precisely targeted technical aid can achieve. In the fall of that year, the U.N.'s Food and Agriculture Organization succeeded in eradicating a plague of locusts, which had threatened to wipe out harvests in West and East Africa, through systematic spraying starting early the previous spring. Again, a UNICEF program combining breathtaking simplicity and scope promised to save the lives of countless African children through vaccinating infants and teaching mothers a basic remedy for diarrhea. Since 40 percent of Africa's babies now die before the age of five, snatching all those infants from an early death could change people's minds about fertility and health care profoundly.

Looking again at the farmers in Niger, the leap in their output was only possible with imported fertilizer, which they could not afford without a U.S.-supported subsidy. Perpetuating the new methods and abundant harvests will depend in great part on developing high-yielding seeds and fertilizers within the means of farmers. Asia's Green Revolution could not have happened without lavish international effort. Similarly, an African breakthrough would have to depend heavily on the expertise of its friends.

Thus the record looked decidedly mixed. By the mid-1980s, however, Western confidence in prescribing for Africa seemed entirely undiminished. Justifying what was in effect a new prescription of unadulterated free enterprise, a number of experts pointed to the evidence of economic success and failure on the part of "capitalist" and "socialist" regime within the continent. To American eyes, the terms "socialist" and "capitalist" as they are commonly used hardly seem to apply to what is happening within Africa: all African economies look heavily state-controlled; yet most of Africa's people—subsistence farmers, traders, and purveyors of small services—lie beyond government's arm.

Considering the African countries that have done notably better so far—including the Côte d'Ivoire, Kenya, Malawi, Zimbabwe, Botswana, and Cameroon—what distinguishes them from others? Apart from effective political leadership, they do, in fact, share several modus operandi: they have all consistently supported agriculture; they have all made extensive use of expatriate experts; and they have all encouraged market forces.

The economies and the policies of these countries vary considerably. The Côte d'Ivoire has bolstered its coffee and cocoa farmers consistently through high prices and a strong infrastructure, reaping rich export revenues from its farm products. Kenya, which has paid its way through exports of coffee and tea as well as through tourism, has built one of the strongest groups of infant industries in Africa. Malawi, very small and very poor at Independence, has put in place an efficient system of support for both large and small cotton, peanut, and tobacco farmers, greatly increased farm output by doubling the price of corn (known in Africa as maize) and other crops between 1982 and 1986, and created a complex of market-oriented though state-run agribusinesses. With a group of light industries (developed in response to economic sanctions) that is the envy of all sub-Saharan Africa and a thriving agriculture, Zimbabwe is still following an economic course that belies its socialist rhetoric—giving free rein to a private sector that competes with government enterprise. Botswana is a unique case: firmly entrenched in South Africa's economic orbit, the country has used its diamonds and other precious minerals to enlarge opportunities for its population of about a million farmers and cattle herders, building an efficient export-oriented meat-packing industry and investing in agricultural research in the hope of someday making its desert landscape bloom. Finally, Nigeria's next-door neighbor, Cameroon, has resisted the distortions that almost inevitably go along with oil wealth and continued to support small farmers who grow cotton, peanuts, and coffee for export, as well as abundant foodstuffs, while investing its oil revenues in capital projects for longer term development.

All these economies have problems: except for Botswana the whole group has borrowed heavily to keep up levels of investment and consumption during the past decade and, for the foreseeable future, they all will have to race to stay even with swelling population growth. Yet their output has grown consistently, and they have put in place physical and human infrastructure that they can build on. In each country a fair share of the national wealth has been reinvested in its own economy mostly because governments have fostered private business and maintained sound money.

Looking at these cases, it is clear that each is dependent on widely varying leadership and resources as well as economic strategy. Yet by the mid-1980s many Western analysts—and many Africans—agreed that some lessons could be found in these experiences. For most countries in Africa basic changes were in order. With investment from abroad falling sharply, most new monies had to be found within Africa's own economies. And African economies were unlikely to produce the resources they needed without either highly organized coercion over land and labor or much more opportunity and security for individual initiative.

For obvious reasons, the alternative of much more rigid control struck most Western observers as distinctly undesirable. Moreover, during the past decade socialism in Africa had appeared to recede as a viable option for African states. The first sustained African socialist experiment, Sékou Touré's Guinea, emerged from two decades of virtual isolation in West Africa in 1978, when Touré turned to the West to rescue his bankrupt economy from the ministrations of the Soviet Union and its East European allies. As early as the mid-1970s, however, it had already become clear that the economic lines of force from Africa to the advanced industrialized economies almost entirely bypassed the Soviet Union. Except to Ethiopia, Soviet economic aid was miniscule, and trade with the Soviets and the Eastern bloc constituted only a small portion of Africa's commerce. During the U.N. debate on the New International Economic Order, the Soviet Union explicitly absolved itself of responsibility for Third-World economic welfare: the Soviets pointed out that the problems clearly originated with the colonial powers, and they pleaded their own relative poverty on the remedies.

As Africa's crisis intensified, left-leaning regimes in Mali, Benin, and Congo began to eye structural adjustment with wary interest as they grappled with precipitate economic decline. Rebuffed by the Eastern bloc's economic combine, COMECON, the Marxist leadership of Mozambique sought Western aid and counsel. By the mid-1980s both Mozambique and its fellow revolutionary regime Angola were so decimated by South Africa-supported civil insurgencies that they could hardly claim any surviving economic structures—socialist or otherwise.

Quite apart from the fluctuations of superpower politics, the appeal of socialist strategies declined because they didn't work economically. In effect, they put the cart before the horse. The highly effective control necessary to run centrally planned economies demanded managerial skills that would not be available until Africans acquired much more experience running modern institutions.

The second alternative, involving less state control (though not necessarily less active state effort) became a kind of panacea for many Western donors. Admitting that this strategy posed its own set of problems in countries where weakly rooted governments hoard all means of control and where the private sector consists largely of peasant farmers, the donors asserted that less state control still provided the most affordable way for virtually destitute countries to use the resources they had more efficiently. The idea was that the profit motive would channel effort and money that until then had been spent on status and accumulation of property into productive enterprise. Until policies changed, it was unlikely that the private wealth of Africans would be invested in their own economies. African countries needed to create a new economic world for their people to live in, a place where the rules of the game were constant, uncomplicated, and supportive of productivity.

Western donors were proffering several main prescriptions. First, government investment must give priority to agriculture as the chief form of production and source of income in all African countries except the mineral exporters. Viable industries will have to be built on a healthy farm economy. Second, policy should be redirected toward building agriculture and generally increasing output; reforms should include higher prices to farmers, currencies pegged to international markets, and tariff and tax structures geared to export rather than import substitution. Third, scarce available resources should be invested to maximum effect; this can happen only if governments curb state controls that dampen private initiatives and cut government bureaucracies way back.

Whether or not African leaders would, in the long run, regard the prescription as a real alternative or as an unpalatable dose of Western ideology, few observers could side-step a harsh reality—that policy reform and institutional change were the main means for fostering growth within African control. History indicated how risky it was for donors to draw up blueprints for institutions that Africans must build and run. Yet, it was clear enough that whatever the balance between state and private control, enterprises charged with productive use of African resources simply did not have the means to ignore the bottom line.

⌒

How committed the *donors* actually were to the reforms they launched also remained to be shown. One litmus test would be found in their response to the debt crisis. All debates on policies and programs could run aground on this issue. Increasing at 24 percent a year between 1973 and 1984, by 1987 Africa's debt threatened to siphon off a major share of future investible resources.

By the end of 1987, sub-Saharan Africa's external debt had risen to an estimated $125 billion. Given Africa's stagnating export earnings, the rising cost of debt service in many cases virtually precluded continuing growth. During the 1980s debt service consumed increasing shares of revenues, rising to over 100 percent of earnings for many individual countries. Comparing Africa's situation with that of low-income Asian countries, Africa was paying seven times as much interest on its debts in relation to the size of its gross national product.

A major problem for Africa was the change in the form of its debt over the last decade: from long-term flows at low, "aid-type" interest rates, to shorter-term flows at high commercial interest rates. Much of the recent escalation came with the spate of rescheduling and rollovers, which added unpaid interest payments to the stock of debt, or extended new loans—at much higher interest rates—to cover arrears due. Interest payments rose from 25 percent of the total debt service in 1973, to 30 percent in 1978, 43 percent in 1982, and 49.3 percent in 1984. With government and private long-term lending to Africa declining sharply, the outcome should have surprised no one: in addition to their plunge into short-term debt, African governments depleted reserves, borrowed from the IMF, and ran up payments arrears as high as they were able.

Debt rescheduling itself became a major drain for Africa, both in usurping the energies of African finance ministries—which often had to undergo three or more major bouts with their creditors over a five-year period—as well as in increasing the debt burden. While some payments on principal were deferred, interest charges on debts incurred at original interest rates of 6 percent increased to an average 10 percent. As a result the interest bill rose from $429 million in 1973 to an estimated $11.6 billion in 1985.

During the 1980s the power of the International Monetary Fund in Africa grew enormously, and, at the same time, its shortcomings as an arbitrator of Africa's economic adjustment became more and more obvious. Routinely, rescheduling required debtors' agreement to an IMF stabilization program. While IMF lending to Africa increased more than threefold from the mid-1970s to the latter part of the 1980s, the nature of that lending changed. As time went on, the IMF placed increasingly strict conditions on its lending to Africa. Though inducing discipline in Africa's financial transactions seemed all to the good, IMF prescriptions to achieve that were increasingly unsuitable for Africa, stressing expenditure cuts rather than increased growth in economies which had very little margin for either spending or growth. The Fund also required countries to improve their financial balances in three to five years and sometimes within one year—usually far too short a period for real progress.

Nor did IMF agreements ease the liquidity problems of African countries. While the Fund's programs for major debtors in Asia and Latin America had been accompanied by IMF pressure for new lending from their main creditors, that sort of pressure was rarely applied on behalf of small African countries. Finally, the use of Fund resources became increasingly costly for Africa. In 1984, the Fund was owed 50-75 percent of the debt-service bill. By 1986, African countries paid the IMF about a billion dollars more than they received from it. Looking ahead, African countries appeared likely to pay out some $200 million more to the IMF than they would receive each year after 1987.

By the late 1980s, concerted revolts by groups of African debtors and quiet nonpayment by individuals were growing increasingly likely. In order to forestall financial chaos and relieve some of the pressure on African economies, donors considered a number of actions, including debt forgiveness, moratoria, and conversion of costly short-term debt into long-term loans at low interest rates. Definitive action was stalled, however, at successive Western summits and IMF ministerial confabs. The precedental link between easing up on Africa and letting the major Latin American debtors off the hook was one roadblock; the other was the reluctance of the U.S. Congress and the Reagan administration, in the era of Gramm-Rudman, to use new aid money to ease African debt burdens directly.

For the future, sympathetic observers agreed that African leaders confronted nearly impossible choices. Though long-term survival demanded changes in the way the system worked, direct reductions in governments' control over economic benefits and in revenues from tariffs and taxes threatened regime power. If the current drive to reform their economies was to survive the latter 1980s, African leaders would have to deal with a number of separate problems almost simultaneously. They would need to

create much stronger human, physical and technical infrastructures; they would have to confront strong popular
beliefs to sell the idea that fewer children would mean more
of life's blessings for everyone; they would have to save the
land. The next chapters in this book will take a longer look
at three main keys to Africa's future: people, land and
learning.

# 4

# The Blessings of Children

*Every man here knew that he was watched from above by his
ancestors, living forever in a higher sphere, their passage on
earth not forgotten, but essentially preserved, part of the
presence of the forest.*

V.S. Naipaul
*A Bend in the River*

*So people are now the enemy.*

Ngugi wa Thiong'o
*Petals of Blood*

An African child blesses his family's past as well as their
future. He comes into this world as a gift from God and a
direct link with his ancestors. As he grows, he comes to see
himself as one twig on a vast tree. His parents, brothers and
sisters are the closest supporting limbs, but aunts and uncles
and cousins twine together almost as closely. All are rooted
in the spirit of dead forebears, buried in the village. While
he grows up in the village, as most Africans still do, the
family order shapes his relationship to the world. Even
when he lives in the city, some distance away, ties to family,
near and far, ultimately determine most of his choices.

In the city, of course, other orders compete. Since the
advent of the European explorers, and the missionaries
who trod quickly on their heels, Christian values have followed Western power into Africa. Formal education was
created by the missionaries to transmit their view of the
cosmos, and those who went to school began to live at least
some of the time in two worlds.

Technology led the way. The potency of the Christian
God flared first of all from the muskets of the European

87

soldiers. Then some of the missionaries crowned their churches and houses with shiny tin, and astonished the rural people by riding about on bicycles (or, as Kenyan villagers called them, "the metal which walks on legs"). Some Africans were drawn into the new religion. For those converts, Western material civilization was not only a lure but also a strong philosophical argument for Christianity: a God who could so reward his adherents must be one to reckon with. It was not lost on the villagers in Achebe's *Things Fall Apart* that in the wake of the white man's religion came a trading store, "and for the first time palm-oil and kernel became things of great price, and much money flowed into Umuofia." Few of the new Christians, however, broke entirely with tradition. Like English or French, the white man's religion became a kind of second language for use in the new moral realm.

Subsequently the Europeans brought from the West technologies that in themselves would radically alter the African's world. First of all, they introduced crops that could be sold in Europe for cultivation by African farmers who previously had grown only food for their community's subsistence: thus African peasants were drawn into the international cash economy. Secondly, they began to treat African illness with Western medicines. As more and more children grew to adulthood, the traditional balance between people and nature came under severe threat.

In the 1970s the exploding growth of African populations began to puzzle experts. While in Asia and Latin America better health care, extension of education, and rising incomes were accompanied by falling population growth, in Africa the reverse was true. In Kenya, for example, a sharp drop in infant mortality and rapid spread of elementary and secondary school education paralleled a surge in fertility to an historically unprecedented 4 percent. In 1960, just before Independence, the average Kenyan woman had 6.2 children; in 1970, she had 7.2; by 1980, 8.3.

At the same time, many people wondered if the population explosion was really a problem. Most African governments said absolutely not. At the 1974 U.N. Conference on Population in Bucharest, Rumania, the African group passionately denounced Western conspiracies aimed at restricting the numbers of black inhabitants of this planet and keeping their countries small, poor and marginal. "You want us to go back to our villages and take your pill," one African delegate declared bitterly. "Why don't you listen to us for a change?" More broadly, they argued that their countries were in fact underpopulated, with unused land and such great distances between people that trade could not flourish. An Ethiopian proverb expresses very succinctly the traditional attitude toward people and land that still prevailed: "One is born; one dies; the land increases."

Whatever their own convictions, as politicians, African leaders could not ignore the reaction of their peoples to the notion of population limitation. The very idea of birth control was guaranteed to arouse nearly universal antipathy among Africans in every strata. In that period, many African governments were actively encouraging population growth.

Most Africans still do not see any reason that they should not have as many children as possible. Few people anywhere, of course, spend much time thinking about the connection between their own decisions and the economic health of their country as a whole—Africans are no different. What is different in Africa is the combination of pressures and supports for unprecedentedly high rates of fertility. In Europe before the Industrial Revolution, scarcity of land, a new calculus of costs and benefits coming with the growth of the urban money economy, and constantly high mortality rates kept population growth at about 1.0 percent. In Africa, on the other hand, the advent of modern life has brought better health but almost no visible change in the desire for even larger families. Unlike their counterparts in Asia and Latin America, many African women put no limit on the number of children they would like to bear.

As a study by Australian demographer John C. Caldwell powerfully demonstrates, for both men and women in traditional society many children have been the surest and strongest source of prestige. In African society, remaining unmarried is an extreme social aberration. It was considered central to man's nature to beget, and woman's to conceive and bear, children. To her mother, the heroine of Ghanaian novelist Asare Konadu's *A Woman in Her Prime* becomes "a woman" only at the age of thirty-five when she conceives her first child. For men of the Akamba tribe of eastern Kenya, in the same way, talk of unwanted pregnancy makes no sense: every pregnancy is desired. If they survive infancy, sons and daughters become valuable economic assets. But they have also been considered an essential link with the world of the spirits.

African traditional religion fuses the concerns of the living with those of the dead, and the patterns of nature with those of human society. A pantheon of gods, usually including one considered supreme and a number of lesser and more personal deities surveys human behavior. These gods dispense rewards and punishments for virtue and sin through their control of natural phenomena like rain or fertility in particular places, and through their intervention in human striving or conflict. Senegalese novelist Cheikh Hamidou Kane's *Ambiguous Adventure* tells how the protagonist, Samba Diallo, feels this fusion of physical and spiritual in his daily encounters: "I never open up the bosom of the earth, in search of my food, without demanding pardon, trembling, beforehand. I never strike a tree, coveting its body, without making fraternal supplication to it." Whether or not people can always understand how divine law works (often they cannot), they have understood that what happens to them flows directly from the fit between their actions and the pervasive moral order. The key to this order is fertility—both of land and of people. The Edo of Nigeria signified this priority of gods and men by calling their supreme god "the bringer of children." But gods can also deny offspring to the unworthy. So the birth of children can be seen as a direct mark of divine approbation and human

90

virtue, as wealth is for the Calvinist. Proudly signaling this, the Asaba of midwestern Nigeria often call their babies "God's verdict." Elsewhere, childlessness was thought to result from a perverse bargain with the spirits: among the Bera of Tanzania, successful people with few children were thought to have bargained away their offspring through witchcraft.

The most direct influence on human life, however, has traditionally been exerted by the ancestors. The spirits of the forebears, going back several generations, have been seen to play a continuing role in the welfare of the family. Until recently, children were widely believed to be reincarnated ancestors and were given the names of grandparents and great-grandparents. After the death of a father, the Yoruba of Nigeria used to compete to conceive children because with the first new son the departed parent would return to the world of the living. Moreover, the birth of children has always been crucial to the ancestral shades, for their immortality in the spirit world depends on the performance of the proper rites by their descendants.

Male children and grandchildren still continue to pour libations to ancestors going back several generations. The most significant tribute, however, that begins the immortal life of parents is their funeral. More than weddings, funerals are the most important—and expensive—gatherings of the entire family. The Abonnema people of eastern Nigeria decorate village houses with rich brocades brought from Portugal long ago and preserved in chests now for the supreme occasion of death. In many places, surviving children often spend the equivalent of several years' income on feasts and gifts shared by kin and villagers over weeks or months and then repeated in second-burial ceremonies some time later.

The funeral, however, is just the beginning of the new relationship with those who have died. Like the gods but more watchful, ancestors often make themselves felt through some misfortune inflicted on unwitting descendants for their sins or transgressions. Failure to pour the proper libations would be an obvious breach of the sacred order, but the ancestors also enforce a much broader spectrum of moral laws. Their disapproval can bring physical illness or injury, even death. In this milieu, no child can ever forget that parents will one day become ancestors, possessed of the same sort of power.

Therefore, the relationship between living and dead has insured the continued strength of family hierarchies. It has also tightened bonds between often complex networks of living descendants, linked to grandparents and great-grandparents over several generations. Like families everywhere, African kinship groups are bound by their common history, but for many Africans the past still lives, and indeed rules, in the present, like the unseen roots of a tree.

The traditional relationship between family and land also reinforces enduring ties. As Nigerian Yorubas express it, "the land belongs to a vast family of which many are dead, few are living, and countless numbers are unborn." Land, as the burial place of ancestors and sometimes still their dwelling, traditionally belongs not to individuals but to the community. Village or family elders or headmen apportion it as needed. Even as people have left the village for the city they have kept in close touch with their past and with one another through the land.

Until recently, land almost everywhere seemed very plentiful. In order to control more of it you only had to be able to work it. So the aid of family was all-important. For ambitious people, the implication was clear: the more children you have, the more land you can farm. Among Zambia's Gwembe Tonga, for example, more distant kin such as cousins offer sporadic help in exchange for reciprocal assistance, but the only reliable labor supply is in the immediate family: the wives and children of each compound.

The Sisala of northern Ghana are candid about child labor. It is good to have children because "they produce more than they eat." In fact, before elementary school became common, children were active participants in the labor force by age six. At that time they can start running errands and scaring birds away from the crops and domestic animals out of nearby gardens. As they get older they fetch water and firewood and begin to work at weeding the fields. Among the Nuer of southern Sudan children dry dung for use as fuel, help with fishing using spears in shallow water, collect wild fruits, and take part in cooking and brewing. Children everywhere also take on a major part of childcare: at about a year infants go from their mother's back to that of a five or six-year-old sister or brother who look after them lovingly and responsibly.

A West African proverb expresses it succinctly: "Each extra mouth comes attached to two extra hands." After children are weaned from breast feeding they also eat quite austerely, as the most and the best food customarily goes to the most senior adults, particularly fathers and other men. Thus many Africans say with reason, "children are cheap."

If they survive infancy, they are also the best possible investment for the future. Where in the Western world today wealth flows from parents to children, in Africa the reverse has always been true. Reinforced by the link with the ancestors, traditionally the authority of parents over their children has lasted all their lives. Not only are children responsible for taking care of their parents in their old age, but also fathers have often exercised total control over their sons' labor and surplus into adulthood. Among the Gonja of northern Ghana, for example, as long as sons live in the same village with their parents they will greet them both morning and evening and will send them a leg of every animal killed as well as regular bowls of food.

In a number of places, especially in the plains area of West Africa, sons continue after marriage to live in large extended family compounds with their parents. When the father lives in the same compound with his son he is always treated as the head of the house, and all decisions are made in his name, even when his son oversees the farming. Among the Ewe of Ghana, when the son establishes a separate compound, his father chooses the location and ritually lays out the groundwork. Sons and daughters who go to work in the town or city also send money home to their families regularly.

By the same token, fathers control the wealth their sons need in order to marry. Polygyny, which is still practiced by a third to a half of Africans today, depends on the older men's monopoly of wives while the younger ones wait their turn. A story is told among the Mossi of Burkina Faso of a son who sent home money from wage labor in the city to pay the fee for betrothal to a village girl. Instead of paying it to the family of his son's fiancée, the father took a new young bride for himself.

By the very nature of the kinship system, however, those disposing of wealth can also be called upon to share it. With the control they exercise, heads of households have responsibilities as well as prerogatives. Among Nigeria's Igbo people, for example, traditionally patriarchs apportioned the land, helped out those in trouble, organized sharing in times of shortage, paid the major part of wedding and funeral costs, gave a new mother cloth, food, and a goat for the celebratory feast, offered sacrifices to the gods for family members. In Kenya, those with wealth are expected to contribute generously to "Harambee" (community self-help) projects. With the advent of the cash economy, the obligations of the comparatively wealthy have come to include school fees for children of relatives, and often extended support for numerous kin who want to share in a modern life-style. Nowadays the well-to-do are also called upon to support a whole new class of dependent: the unemployed school graduate who is now overqualified for farming.

When they return home to their villages at harvest time or Christmas or for funerals, "big men" distribute largesse widely, as wealthy farmers do surplus grain during village festivals. If they do not, their wealth is no compensation for their loss of prestige. A story is told of a government minister who returned home for the holidays in his Mercedes bringing tales of his high life in the capital and excursions to Europe. Once installed in his village compound, however, he failed to lay out the cash gifts, beer and palm wine needed to swell the villagers' appreciation of his good fortune. Soon his neighbors began to shun his compound as they passed to and fro on their Christmas visits. In the New Year, the "big man's" senior uncle died. Calling him a miser, his family chose an illiterate brother as family head.

Because in most circumstances the obligation for redistribution is widely accepted, the burdens of children are minimized. When their parents cannot provide for them, or when they are needed by relatives, they can be sent to live away from their immediate family. A great many African children (in some places as many as 50 percent) have lived apart from their parents for considerable lengths of time. Some may work as house servants while others are sent to school. Others go to delight the days of doting grandmothers or of aunts with no children of their own. Responsibility for feeding children may shift quite fluidly as well. Even while living with their parents, hungry children may beg food from relatives nearby.

In the city, the calculus should seemingly be very different from that of the village. On one hand, urban families obviously do not need to add new hands to work communal fields. And, on the other, they have to pay for what in the village seem almost free goods: rent, food, entertainment. Beer, for example, which village folk brew at home, can take large chunks of urban salaries. They are also tempted by an insistent array of consumer goods that are not available in the rural area. First and foremost, proximity to the modern world increases pressures to secure education for one's children. Thus parents have many reasons for wanting fewer children.

However, fertility in the cities of Africa is still very high—given better water and health services, sometimes higher than in the rural areas. The main reason, apparently, is that strong family and kinship ties still skew economic choices. Most African city dwellers are still close to their village roots. Particularly in West Africa, many people travel back to their villages whenever they can, particularly on holidays and also on weekends. If they can afford it, they build a concrete multistory retirement home near their ancestral burial ground. Men often take additional wives in the village—probably plumper and less educated than urban mates—who live there and work the land.

In the city itself, bonds with relatives and ethnic kin shape social life. Away from the constant familiar exchange of the village, people try to recreate its warmth as best they can. In many places, rural neighbors cluster in the towns, and even where they are scattered widely, kin spend much of their leisure time together. On Saturdays and Sundays they move about town dropping in on one another casually as they would in the village, keeping up to date on the doings and whereabouts of mutual relatives and friends, and whatever good or bad fortune may have recently befallen them. At the time of death or other emergency, kin flock to support those in need, bringing food and money and the comforting presence of many people nearby. When a kinsman dies in the rural area, those who do not return home for the funeral gather to mourn, sometimes for several days, at the home of a close relative in the city.

As Africans move back and forth between village and city, they still draw their main sense of security from traditional ties. The burdens of children are still shared, even when their parents live in town. Since few people are able to save very much and Social Security is not widespread, children remain the best investment. If you have many children one of your sons may get enough education and be smart enough to land a lucrative job in the bureaucracy or one of your daughters may be beautiful or clever enough to marry a "big man," therefore assuring you a comfortable old age. And the more there are, the better your chances that some at least will turn out loyal and reliable.

If you have any money, the surest return will come from spending it on your children's education. If you start a business or buy a store, your relatives may lay claim to the payroll or the merchandise. If you have money to save, they can ask you to spend it on schooling for their children. A wealthy man with few children can find himself in a highly beleaguered position. A story is told of an army officer in Congo who decided to have only three children. Thereupon his parents sent him seven brothers to raise and educate. When he protested, they berated him for his mean spirit in having so few offspring of his own and said if he refused to assume the familial obligations he was well able to bear they would no longer take any responsiblity for him. Those who fail to accept the responsibilities that go with wealth lose the position of authority within their family that has traditionally been the richest reward of superior achievement for an African.

~

Not surprisingly, the pressures on African women to have many children are particularly intense. Marriage is chiefly a means to this end. The Banyankore of western Uganda say, "When a crop is ripe it is harvested; when food is cooked it is eaten"; meaning when a boy or girl matures marriage and children should follow.

For women, marriage traditionally brought a variety of economic responsibilities and often only one source of both honor and security: their children. In much of Africa even today a man pays the family of his betrothed a bride price to secure her in marriage. In many places the payment meant significant wealth to the bride's family, often enabling her brothers (or sometimes her father) to take wives themselves. The payment was given in exchange for the economic value of a woman to her husband—in her labor and her children. Thus, for the husband and wife marriage was as much as anything else an economic compact.

Customs governing division of labor, rights to land and to children varied widely. But while a woman was married her husband generally held her labor and its fruits firmly within his grasp. After the wedding gifts had been exchanged and both families had feasted lavishly and offered the gods and ancestors their share, the bride usually went to live with her husband's kin. Except in matrilineal societies (where husband and wife often started their marriage within her family compound but frequently moved to his thereafter), a wife found herself abruptly separated from the warm web of relationships she had been wrapped in since infancy and suddenly dependent on a group in which she was a virtual outsider. For this reason and others, among the Coniagui in Guinea, marriage reportedly is finalized only when a girl "is absolutely forced to." Similarly, the Senegalese heroine of Mariama Ba's novel *So Long a Letter* describes her wedding as a moment "dreaded by every Senegalese woman, the moment when she sacrifices her possessions as gifts to the family-in-law, and worse still . . . she gives up her personality, her dignity, becoming a thing in the service of the man who has married her. . . . "

Once ensconced in her new household, an African woman often lived a life quite separate economically from that of her husband, in which the basic unit was herself and her children. She was usually expected to cook her husband's food, to bear children regularly, and to feed and clothe the children as well. Her husband most often provided her with a hut and some land to farm. She sustained her family by working the land allotted to her and by trading. While her husband generally cleared her land and usually helped with the harvest, her children were the only ones who owed her their labor. Often her surplus was hers to keep; at other times she sold it to her husband; sometimes he kept it himself. While she helped with cultivation chores on her husband's land, she did not share in his income. Nor, when he died, did she inherit his property, which went to his sons—or, sometimes, in matrilineal societies, to the sons of his sisters.

Often she herself might be inherited by her husband's brother, who married her to give her a home and keep her procreative powers in the family. Ultimately, however, even more than men, women had to depend on their children for their economic well-being, and, in their old age, for their survival.

Between husband and wife, mutual respect was the most important personal bond. Intimate companionship or "love" in the Western sense of that word was rare; the closest ties for men were with other men of their own age-group, and for women with their own mothers and children. A majority of African women could expect to share their husbands with other wives, decreasing still further their individual power though perhaps spreading their responsibilities more comfortably. In the competition for their husband's regard, beauty undoubtedly counted, but respect flowed to the wife who performed her designated role with skill, energy, and good humor. Most of all, honor grew with the numbers of children she gave her husband and his family.

The custom of woman-woman marriage—not a sexual but an economic arrangement—which was at one time widespread in both West and East Africa, laid bare the utilitarian roots of the institution. Women who had acquired enough money to pay the bride price, through trading, and often through prostitution, married other women for pretty much the same reasons that men did. In West Africa widows who possessed oil-bearing palm trees took wives to expand their labor forces. In Western Kenya unmarried women took wives to found lineages, sometimes in their own name, and sometimes in that of their fathers and brothers. Commonly, in order to maintain their role within their dead husband's family, widows married women whose children would be considered those of their dead husbands or of their lineage.

Given the primacy of fertility, it is not surprising that in many African societies motherhood is endowed with a mystique of near-sacredness and freighted with strong emotion. Among Nigeria's Igbo today, many village women aspire above all to belong to the Society of Those Whom God Has Blessed. To join those ranks, you must have had ten pregnancies. At the initiation ceremony the husband of the new member wraps a living goat around her waist. The animal is then sacrificed and eaten to help assure that neither the fortunate mother nor the attendant deities will rest on their laurels, and that her fertility will not end prematurely.

In his novel *African Child* Guinean Camara Laye voices the feelings many African sons express for their image of the all-nurturing mother, saying:

> O my mother, you who bore me upon your back, you who gave me suck, you who watched over my first faltering steps . . . how I should love to be beside you once again, to be a little child beside you!
> Black woman, woman of Africa, O my mother, let me thank you; thank you for all that you have done for me, your son, who, though so far away, is still so close to you!

Throughout the continent women are happy to be identified not by their own names but as mother of their children.

Correspondingly, barrenness is dreaded. Traditionally, a woman would be sent back to her family, and the bride price returned, when she failed to give birth. Her husband's reaction could be cruel. In Buchi Emecheta's novel *The Joys Of Motherhood* the childless heroine's first husband tells her frankly why he no longer wants her, saying "I am a busy man. I have no time to waste my precious male seed on a woman who is infertile. I have to raise children for my line."

Often the man would take another wife whose off-spring provided proof of the barren one's own flawed womanhood. The story is commonly told of the woman slowly driven toward what we would describe as a mental breakdown by her failure to give birth. As beautiful as she is, she feels her husband's desire slowly turn to bitterness, as his family reproaches the couple for their transgression against the basic demand of spiritual and earthly survival. If she must return to her own family, her kin are often loath to take back a barren woman whose bride price may be forfeit forever. If she stays in her husband's compound, her status will be less than that of other wives. Eventually, her frustration comes out in anger or despair. Then she takes on the aura of a malignant presence in the compound and a scapegoat in times of trouble. If a child falls ill or another wife brings forth a stillborn infant, the barren wife is suspected of causing the misfortune by evil magic. At this point, she might be better off if she were indeed a witch: she is left with no acceptable role to play in the world she was reared to inhabit.

It was believed that a woman's barrenness, or a man's sterility, could be caused only by intervention of the spirits, the ancestors, or human magic. The ancestors most often would punish the woman or the couple for improperly performed marriage rites, failure to pay the full bride price, or insufficient sacrifices. The wrath of the gods might stem from evil in a woman's previous life or from a specific breach of conduct, which might not be known by the woman and man affected or by those close to them until the punishment was meted out. More mundane but no less serious, resentful in-laws on either side or jealous co-wives could invoke harmful charms. A difficult childbirth, for example, was often ascribed to a woman's adultery, and its successful termination required her to confess her sin on the spot.

Whatever the cause, the best way to find a remedy was to consult a diviner. He could trace the cause back into the spirit world or to human malevolence. If the gods or ancestors had to be propitiated he told the couple how to amend their conduct and what sacrifices they must bring; if human magic was interfering with fertility, he would try to counter it with stronger charms of his own. If he failed, the contrary forces clearly were just too powerful.

Although women almost invariably have borne the larger share of opprobrium for the childless marriage, many men felt the same pressures in almost equal measure. Without children, a man is a tree trunk bare of branches. And he often shares the onus for causing the fruitless union or the death of an infant: for example, by fighting with his in-laws or his own parents; by flouting customary sacrifices; or by sharing the guilt for sins of his ancestors. Traditionally, childless men as well as women had reason to fear that they would be dishonored in death as in life: few societies buried the childless, whose corpses were often thrown instead into the bush to be devoured by wild animals.

It is not surprising that people whose religious lives center on fertility find many forms of contraception immoral. When children are seen as an outpouring of divine providence it is regarded as sinful to interfere with that flow. Moreover, if children embody the spirits of dead ancestors it is sacreligious to prevent their return to life. When asked how many sons and daughters they desire, many Africans often refuse to set any limits on God's will and reply that they wish "as many as God sends." Therefore abortion is seen as directly thwarting the will of God or the ancestors. Similarly, both men and women hope to prolong the period of childbearing—that of their greatest honor and fulfillment—as long as possible. Sterilization, which would permanently impair fecundity, is viewed with horror.

Less radical methods of contraception do not carry the same odor of impiety unless they severely curtail numbers of children. Indeed, traditional African customs and taboos themselves served as a natural means of spacing births. In many places women were forbidden to have sex until their

102

infant was weaned from the breast. Therefore, if all went well each woman would give birth about every two-and-a-half to three years. For men, polygamy made possible a continuing sex life during one or another wife's periods of enforced abstinence.

However, this post-partum sexual taboo was weakened by the advent of new moral codes that did not include it—in Islam and Christianity—as well as by "modern" counsel against breast-feeding. As a result, babies came faster than before. Further, a modern trend away from polygamous marriage, particularly among Christians and in cities, also helped raise birth rates. Men in monogamous unions now sought to produce their desired quota of offspring with only one woman rather than sharing the procreative burden among several different wives.

❧

Looking at the present situation, it is very difficult to know how firmly fixed traditional beliefs remain. What is clear is that the desire of Africans to have many children remains much higher than that of peoples in any other region of the world. Africa now is the only part of the world that has not yet seen its rate of population growth drop from postwar highs. In 1960, African and South Asian rates hovered around 2.5 percent, while Latin America was pushing 2.9 percent. Today, however, the two other Third-World areas have fallen to 2.1 and 2.5 respectively, while Africa has risen above 3 percent.

Whereas in the rest of the world a classic demographic pattern has repeated itself—falling birth rates run parallel with better health and rising life expectancy—in Africa falling death rates have not led to falling birth rates. Better health care has brought down African death rates by around a third and infant mortality by even more in the past several decades; but while fertility rates in much of Asia have fallen from a peak of five to six to an average of four today, and those in Latin America from around six in 1960 to around four today, African fertility rates have stayed around seven to eight. If these trends were to continue, Africa's current population of over 500 million would double in the next several decades.

According to World Bank projections, sixty years from now the population of Africa may have grown from half the size of Europe's population in 1950 to more than twice that size (while Europe's population will have risen only about 6 percent). In some densely populated countries like Kenya and Nigeria, crowding is already visible: for the traveler returning after a decade or two, people seem to flow in one mass down provincial town streets where a few idlers used to meander. In Kenya, partly as a result of successful rural health efforts, the population of 19 million wiii probably double every 17 years, leading to further division and subdivision of farmland already cultivated to the limit of its fertility. At Kenyan Independence, a father could leave about two and a half acres to each of his sons; now that must be divided by four. With its moist equatorial climate, Nigeria still has not made strides comparable to Kenya's in bringing down death rates and thus has grown more slowly; yet its enormous current population of around 100 million may nearly triple by 2020.

Africa's population densities sound low: averaging from two and a half to one hundred persons per square mile in most countries and rarely rising above 500 even in the most densely settled places, compared with Asian densities ranging from 105 to 1500, and rising above 2500 in some places. But about a fifth of Africa's people live in countries that even now do not have sufficient arable land or rainfall to feed them.

Everywhere, but particularly in countries like Kenya where land is already scarce, people are elbowing their way into cities already swollen way beyond habitable limits. Between 1950 and 1980 African cities grew by almost 7 percent a year compared with 4.4 percent for Asia during that period. Future prospects are daunting. Whereas today 22 percent of Africa's people live in urban areas, by 2025 the World Bank projects that 54 percent of Africans will have moved from the country to the city. By 2000 the United Nations predicts that 60 African cities will exceed 500,000 inhabitants, compared with only 28 urban areas that large today. By that year Dakar and Nairobi will probably reach 5 million, up from one and 2 million today. Unless services are enormously extended, shantytowns will massively dwarf core cities. But where will the money come from to bring electricity, water, sewers, schools, and health care to five times as many city dwellers? Where, in fact, will the money come from to educate the children who will continue to arrive in ever-larger bumper crops for many decades, or to innoculate them, or help their parents save the dwindling land from exhaustion?

And what will they work at? In 1985 half of Africa's people were not yet 15 years of age. According to World Bank projections, the number of Africans of working age (15–65) was about 200 million in 1980; by the end of this century it will have almost doubled and by 2020 it will have tripled. Seventy percent of Africans now work in agriculture. Unlike Asia and Latin America, where absolute numbers of farm workers have been declining since the 1960s and 1970s, Africa's farm labor force will continue to grow until well into the next century. Despite massive shifts of people to the cities, the number of Africans working the land will probably double in the next several decades. By the end of this century, land per person in Africa, now higher than the world average, will fall below it. At the same time, nearly half of the world's farmers will live in Africa.

According to a U.N. study, about a third of the African work force now live in countries where there is unused land of comparable potential to that now being farmed, but the rest live in countries where expansion of agriculture must depend chiefly on heavier cultivation of the land now being farmed. Even if agriculture grew by 2.5 percent a year (as it did at its apogee during the 1960s), it would probably absorb only about 40 percent of new workers.

Industry, which now employs about 12 percent of Africans, is unlikely to take up much of the slack for some time to come. Large numbers thus will have to go into the rural or urban "informal" economies, employed or underemployed on the fringes of the modern sector, usually for very low wages. Pressure on already bloated government bureaucracies to open up more jobs is likely to intensify. Inevitably, large numbers of unemployed will lean heavily on better-off kin. Extended family bonds will be crucial in cushioning society from an employment crisis, but the unprecedented demands will strain kinship ties severely.

Comparing Africa's situation now with that of Europe on the eve of its nineteenth-century transition from very high levels of fertility, the differences point to grave social stress for African countries. Unlike the precipitate declines in mortality produced in Africa by imported health care packages, the fall in European death rates was slow, flowing from gradual improvements in the way people lived wrought by industrialization and development. European fertility rates were also much lower because people married late and often not at all. Where European populations doubled in about 90 years, African nations now reduplicate themselves in less than 30. This extraordinary growth also means that African populations have a much higher proportion of young people who will add to the momentum when they start having their own children.

Perhaps most importantly, Europeans were for the most part sharing an expanding pie. New jobs opening up in the cities provided outlets for most of those leaving the land; women, in particular, left farm work for cottage industries and factories in numbers and had fewer babies as a result. European societies also had another safety valve now virtually closed for Africa: international migration. In the nineteenth century the countries of Europe exported tens of millions of their citizens to various new worlds in the

Americas, Australia, and colonies elsewhere. With frontiers closed and hostility to immigration rising almost everywhere, flight abroad is not an option for most Africans.

Nor do they enjoy the ease of migration within their own continent that they had before colonialism, allowing them to pick up their belongings and move toward fertile soils and better rainfall, without borders to impede them. In African cities as well, guestworkers from neighboring countries nowadays may find themselves ejected, bag and baggage, when national politicians seek scapegoats for local economic discontents. Thus hundreds of thousands of Ghanaians were expelled from Nigeria by ship and truckload in 1981 and again in 1984.

The inordinate pressures that African countries face can work both for and against population limitation. If economic progress lags, so will positive incentives for change. It is when parents believe their offspring will have better lives than their own that they will begin to think about having fewer children in order to invest more time and resources in their future.

On the other hand, under the extreme stresses that lie in store, people's ideas about what is good and what they want from life may shift more quickly than we can predict. Here the tension—and seeming contradiction—between the tenacity of tradition and the inevitability of change is most striking. Though the strength of African traditions has been demonstrated, they are obviously under pressure, sometimes visibly and undoubtedly also invisibly. At the same time, the current sway of tradition over social order will make change all the more disruptive when it comes.

By its very nature, urbanization must now be making significant inroads: the sway of the ancestors grows increasingly remote the farther—and longer—you live away from their burial place. Among elites, notions about marriage, if not as often actual behavior, are shifting: the close-knit nuclear family and romantic intimacy between husband and wife are staple fare in the tabloid tales widely circulated in the cities. In the city many couples are now ignoring the bride price. When both partners are educated they are more likely to lean on each other for friendship and advice than in the village environment where each would turn more readily to family and age-group members. Illustrating the distance traversed and that still to be traveled, it is notable that many but by no means all urban wives now sit down to eat with their husband rather than waiting until he has finished—as their mothers did.

Changes in laws affecting women, marriage, and inheritance do not immediately equal changes in behavior, but in the long run they will broaden attitudes about what is socially approved. Issues of family law can be expected to cut to the quick in every African country, and the right of women to property within marriage is particularly sensitive in societies where wives were themselves regarded as the property of their husbands or their husband's family. Important reforms include recent laws in the Côte d'Ivoire, Ethiopia, and Kenya, giving women the right to inherit and own property. In the Côte d'Ivoire, the family code officially prohibits polygamy and dowry. More than in most African countries, Kenyan land is now owned by individuals rather than clan and family. Thus a law of inheritance passed in 1972 (but which was only beginning to be enforced five years later) has particular importance: widows and daughters as well as sons are to inherit the property. Similarly, four new laws on marriage and inheritance were enacted by the Ghanaian government in 1985. Superseding a prior ordinance that allowed a widow to be excluded from her late husband's home by his family, the legislation called for a careful differentiation of property belonging to the larger family and what has been "personally acquired," and stipulates that the spouse and children are entitled to all property within the household—and to the house.

In Zambia in 1986, the tax code was amended to give women 50 percent of a child allowance that had previously gone to men only. The hot debate that accompanied its publication showed how deeply the issues it raised are felt: despite the well-documented fact that women have customarily spent most of what money they had on their children, Zambian men complained that they would only waste the allowance on "perming their hair, buying make-up and expensive dresses," according to a male pundit quoted anonymously in the *Zambia Daily Mail*. In a number of countries, including Gambia, Kenya and Tanzania, governments have also established programs to broaden women's opportunities by giving them access to a wider variety of jobs, to credit, and to special training programs.

The pace of social change will also continue to be accelerated by Africa's permeability to imported cultural models and technologies. Where in nineteenth-century Europe the large family was normal and alternative examples hardly existed, in Africa today the current European norm of two or three children is well known and could help legitimize the small family. Then too, effective contraceptive techniques now exist, as they did not in Europe for the first century or so of its demographic transition, when people had to rely on abstinence and coitus interruptus. Fewer than 5 percent of couples use modern contraceptives in most sub-Saharan countries, and probably less than one-fifth of African couples now have convenient access to good family planning services, but evidence from places where family planning is available indicates that access may change attitudes faster than we might have predicted. Even in rural areas over one-fourth of couples choose such services when they can obtain them. Among single women in African cities, more than in Asia and Latin America, widespread premarital activity has created a market for contraceptives to prevent pregnancy out of wedlock.

Particularly in rural areas, attitudes of women and men toward contraception may be very different. For several reasons men are likely to be considerably less interested in family planning than women. As in other societies, contraception enhances women's independence on the most

109

basic level. African men's fear of wandering wives is often expressed in the common refrain that women who use birth control will "become prostitutes." As a Kenyan woman expressed it, "men fear that when a woman starts using family planning, she is in that way exposed to the world and can go with any other man, since she knows she won't get pregnant." Probably for this reason, in Zambian family planning clinics a woman is often required to show a letter of permission from her husband.

Further, one social wrinkle peculiar to Africa also inhibits men's concern about the burden of children: the major responsiblity women have assumed throughout the continent for feeding, clothing, and sometimes sheltering and educating the children. Because men monopolize the fruits of the wage economy, this is changing somewhat now, particularly in the cities. Yet men are used to thinking of children as a kind of free good: once they have secured a wife, the blessings should flow to them.

Women, on the other hand, must pay for their progeny, not only in hard labor but in bodily wear and tear. On average, African women have 18 to 20 years of childbearing, compared with about three to five years for women in developed countries. Aged before their time, African farm women's wrinkled faces and worn angular bodies often belie their young years.

Not surprisingly, Africa has a high rate of maternal mortality, fluctuating between two and six for each 1,000 births, some 100 to 500 times the Western European rates. Having many children and giving birth during adolescence or extending childbearing up to menopause, as many African women do, also intensifies the risks to women's bodies. In Senegal, for example, the risk of dying in childbirth is three times greater for a woman with eight or nine children than for one with only two. In Nigeria, a woman under 17 or over 30 is more than twice as likely to die in childbirth than a woman in her early 20s.

Complications stemming from frequent pregnancy undoubtedly drain the vitality of many African women.

Often malnourished themselves, mothers are further depleted by lengthy—frequently uninterrupted—breast-feeding. "I am always tired," sighed a Sudanese woman, the mother of seven, sitting in the sand outside a hut made of sticks and palm leaves, nursing a year-old baby. A common refrain from mothers throughout the continent, her plaint sums up the reason many African women appear receptive to family planning when it is available.

∽

A recent World Bank report on African population finds four reasons to conclude that the demand for family planning may be greater than expected: the unmet need, differences among age-groups about desired family size, growing numbers of abortions, and high use of contraceptives in some areas. The Bank estimates that about 10 percent of African women not now using family planning would do so if it were feasible: they want no more children but are not using contraceptives. Differences in desired numbers of children between older and younger women, urban and rural women, literate and illiterate women, also forecast change. In Ghana and Lesotho today, for example, women in their early twenties say they want around five children, while those in their forties see the ideal number as seven: if the younger women don't change their minds, average fertility will fall by one-fifth in those two countries. On abortions, while the data are scarce (most abortion in Africa is illegal), it seems clear from studies done in Zaïre, Ghana and Nigeria that the rate is significant (in Zaïre, for example, an estimated 50 to 200 for each thousand live births), especially among young women. Evidence from other countries where availability of contraception has increased greatly indicates that these women would be prime candidates for contraception, if they could obtain it. Finally, use of contraception is high in a few places in Africa where it is widely available. In Chogoria, Kenya, for example, where a pilot program serves a rural area of about 200,000 people, about 27 percent of couples use modern contraceptives, compared with about 8 percent in all of Kenya.

Until the present, efforts to meet the need have largely originated outside Africa. The African governments that have endorsed family planning with enthusiasm and started programs to deliver it can be counted on the fingers of one hand. Only Zimbabwe has pushed contraceptive delivery out from the cities to reach large numbers of rural women.

At this stage, most family planning programs still aim at helping women to space their children rather than limit their numbers. Moreover, almost everywhere rhetoric is way out in front of real commitment: population limitation is still largely an abstraction for people who grew up with dozens of brothers and sisters and had plentiful progeny of their own before any "population explosion" loomed on the horizon. In Nigeria, for example, the head of the fledgling population commission in the late 1970s had more than twenty children. In a few instances, governments may be significantly ahead of—if not at odds with—many of their people. In Kenya, the government tilted with the Catholic Church over artificial birth control at the time of Pope John Paul's 1985 visit. Popular suspicion of government designs started at least one riot there subsequently, when secondary school students jumped out classroom windows and ran into the bush to avoid drinking powdered milk rumored to be laced with contraceptives.

Nonetheless, much has changed since the Bucharest conference. Ten years later, at the 1984 conference at Mexico City, most African governments had come to support the goal of limiting fertility.* Nearly 40 African countries, meeting in Kilimanjaro before the Conference, adopted a Program of Action on Population calling for family planning services to be made available to all couples. Again at the U.N. special session on Africa's economic crisis in 1986,

---

* Only five countries—the Côte d'Ivoire, Guinea-Bissau, Chad, Gabon and Mauritania—still actively support population expansion or resist family planning.

population was a priority issue. Zimbabwe's program has led to the first recorded decline in fertility in Africa. Both Kenya and Botswana have declared a strong commitment and begun to organize, though they have not yet made contraceptives available beyond limited groups of women— mostly in the cities. In addition, Tanzania, Ghana, Nigeria, Malawi, Liberia and Rwanda have programs in initial stages.

Perhaps most importantly, Africa's most populous nation, Nigeria, has adopted a highly ambitious family planning program. Before their oil wealth began to fade, their country's burgeoning numbers were a source of pride to many Nigerians. Now, however, facing finite resources and seemingly infinite mouths to feed, the country is planning to spend $100 million over five years to make contraceptives available and to improve health care for mothers and children.

Is an end in view, then, to Africa's surging agglomeration of people? According to World Bank projections, by the middle of the next century Africa's population growth will have about ended. From the vantage point of the late 1980s the prospect of Africa's supporting nearly 2 billion more people by 2050 is hard to imagine. But how Africa will get to the point of stable growth is even more difficult to visualize.

The World Bank numbers assume steady though modest economic growth and development. For each country mortality and fertility are predicted to decline at varying rates. On fertility, the Bank bases calculations on predicted growth in education, infant survival, urbanization, and per capita income—as well as on the country's ability to supply family planning information and services. In six countries (Botswana, Congo, Ghana, Kenya, Swaziland, and Zimbabwe) projected growth in demand for and delivery of family planning services points toward falling fertility in the next several years. At the other end of the spectrum, it is assumed that most of the northern semidesert countries, and those like Angola, Mozambique, and Chad that are torn by civil war and foreign intervention, will probably start reducing fertility only between 1995 and 2000. Twenty-two countries in between—including Nigeria, Sudan, and Zaïre—are likely to see fertility fall between 1990 and 1995. The World Bank's end point, the world of population equilibrium, sounds decidedly idyllic from the perspective of the late 1980s: by 2050 both mortality and fertility will have dropped to low levels and average life expectancy risen from 50 to 70 years.

Clearly, the Bank's predicted future assumes a lot of government and private action and policy within Africa to strengthen the demand for smaller families and expand family planning services. The success of family planning will depend on the strength of health and education programs—particularly for women. Because African governments run or oversee virtually all modern institutions, they will have to play a major role—building infrastructure, training professionals, raising revenues. Because individuals ultimately make the decisions about procreation, however, reaching out to people through a number of different public and private approaches seems likely to work best. In Africa today, the private sector is often very much involved in purveying family planning services. In several countries commercial pharmacies and shops sell contraceptives at bargain prices subsidized by the government or nonprofit organizations. National family planning associations, partly supported by the International Planned Parenthood Federation, work in 25 countries, often in close tandem with the government.

Not surprisingly, many Africans who want to limit their fertility still prefer the more traditional magic or charms. In Kenya, for example, many women swear by "the curse of the aunt," wherein the husband's aunt (or sometimes a mother or grandmother) curses the woman by her grandfather's grave. When and if that fails they may then be ready to "go to the family planning."

When that moment comes, the record in Asia and Latin America shows how important family planning programs can be. Over time, access to reliable methods of birth control increases willingness to use them. The World Bank estimates that throughout the world 40 percent of the fertility decline between 1965 and 1975 can be traced to expansion of these programs. Thus direct government and donor intervention have changed demographic history.

Experience in Africa so far supports these findings. Looking at Africa's first effective national program, in Zimbabwe, the core of that operation is about 600 women on bicycles. Chosen by their own communities, they are trained for a month—after which they set out armed with contraceptive supplies and information for prospective users. Riding around a territory encompassing at least 5,000 and sometimes as many as 20,000 people, the women supply a dozen condoms or one-month's supply of pills to new clients, along with counsel on their use.* In the case of the pill they dispatch women for a checkup at the local clinic one month later and then offer a two-month resupply.

Together with the family planning services being offered by government hospitals and clinics, this program has made contraceptives readily available to most users, 75 percent of whom either receive their supplies at home or are within 30 minutes of a reliable source. But the personal visit of the population workers (every month or two) is undoubtedly the key to the acceptance of many clients. Both moral support and regular supplies bolster the resolve of women choosing to break with tradition and perhaps to defy their husbands as well. In the upshot, use of contraceptives in Zimbabwe has more than doubled in the last five years to around 27 percent—not high by international standards, but about seven or eight times that of most other African

* Among contraceptive methods, African women overwhelmingly prefer the pill. Both pills and condoms have the advantage, in African circumstances, that they can be delivered by nonphysicians, as IUDs, sterilization, and abortion cannot. More permanent forms of contraception, including the IUD, also run up against deep-seated fears about losing fertility.

countries. At the same time the country has recorded the first demonstrable fall in fertility in Africa: from very high to high—or about 7.5 to 6.5—according to a 1984 survey.

The importance of access to contraceptives comes through sharply in the account of a woman's group member, in Kenya's Rift Valley, of the obstacles to obtaining contraceptives once the social struggles have been resolved: "the nearest clinic is fifteen miles away and its service is spasmodic. The journey costs Kshs. 30 (= $1.50) and one is not certain of seeing anyone when one gets there. . . . I feel very strongly that if services were available within easy walking distance, the majority of our members would use the service."

In the long run, development gains—improvements in well-being and health—are essential to achieving lower birth rates. As we have seen, fears about survival still shape decisions about bearing children. Over the past several decades, Africans have made real strides in delivering health care, as shown in sharply declining rates of mortality and rises in life expectancy from under 40 three decades ago to nearly 50 today. Declining nutrition—with calorie levels now 13 percent below that of other low-income countries—and falling health expenditures are now threatening that progress.

Health in Africa is still wretched in comparison with that in Western countries and also worse on average than in most countries in other parts of the world. African death rates, for example, are still almost twice those of North America. To Western eyes, the loss of life and productive energy seems shockingly wasteful. Even if they survive their first year, one in four African children dies before the age of five. Moreover, malnutrition and infectious diseases in childhood permanently impair many African adults, with an estimated 40 percent carrying the effects of malnutrition into later life.

Compared with what most Westerners experience as "normal" health, many Africans feel permanently under par. Recurring bouts of malaria, internal parasites, and poor nutrition make fever, dizziness, fatigue, and pain so chronic in their lives as to pass almost unnoticed. Among farmers, the resulting physical apathy is reflected in lower crop yields. When illness confines them to their hut for some days, valuable cultivation time is lost. Once behind in the agricultural cycle, weakened individuals find it very difficult to catch up: they harvest less, eat less, and continue less resistant to disease.

With its mainly tropical climate, often meager diet, and scant medical facilities, Africa continues to harbor a lethal array of diseases and parasites—some indigenous to the continent and others that have been all but eradicated from the temperate regions where they once occurred. Probably the most pervasive is malaria; followed by parasitic invasions causing sleeping sickness and schistomosiasis (which subjects its victims to numbing, eventually fatal, paralysis and degeneration of the digestive system); as well as cholera and diarrhea-causing E. coli bacteria.

Research on these diseases has lagged because the problems did not seem immediate to the scientific communities in developed countries and the potential profits for Western drug companies appeared slim. Now, however, scientists are scoring the first real gains in some years on sleeping sickness and malaria, through a new drug developed by the Merell Dow Company of Cincinnati and a genetically engineered vaccine being tested by the Walter Reed Army Institute of Research in Washington, D.C. An 18-year program to curb the river blindness that has afflicted much of West Africa has brought the disease largely under control and reopened large tracts of arable land next to the rivers that used to be a spawning ground for host insects. Vaccines being developed through genetic engineering and new kinds of chemical synthesis also hold hope for major advances against cholera and other bacteria causing grave forms of diarrhea.

Looking at how health can affect fertility, one major imponderable must be the AIDS pandemic. Transmitted heterosexually in Africa, AIDS has spread with frightening speed throughout the central African countries of Zambia, Zaïre, Burundi, Rwanda, Uganda, and Tanzania (and somewhat more slowly in Kenya, Congo, Zimbabwe, and Malawi), infecting an estimated 1.5 million people by 1986. In its epicenter, an estimated 15 to 25 percent of adults are affected, and in Uganda, the worst-hit country, perhaps half of all adults may have AIDS by 2000. At least 50,000 people have died of the disease since it emerged in the late 1970s, and 1.5 million more may well perish in the next decade. Although only a few cases of AIDS have been reported in West Africa, epidemeologists point to several reasons why it could spread there rapidly as well: infection with other diseases widespread in much of Africa and the lesions due to untreated sexually transmitted diseases, also much more common in Africa than in the developed world, appear to increase susceptibility to AIDS; moreover, often rudimentary or nonexistent blood screening and unsanitary hypodermic needles heighten the risks in hospital care for other diseases.

Because AIDS strikes hardest in urban areas, and because most of the victims are young people of both sexes between the ages of 19 and 40, the effect on African economies—and fertility—may be devastating. Because so many mothers and children will die, a macabre "malthusian solution" will overshadow concerns about overpopulation where mortality is severe. Morover, the loss of so many productive people, a major share of those who have been educated and technically trained, could put all other aspects of survival on hold in a number of areas. In hard-hit countries an estimated 30 to 40 percent of military and civilian leaders are now infected. Zambia's President Kenneth Kaunda dramatized this threat when he announced to the American press during his fall 1987 visit to the United States that his son had died of AIDS a few months earlier.

118

Unlike many "tropical" diseases, however, the threatened plague has forged a link of fear between Africa and the West. Before the dreaded power of this twentieth-century scourge, people everywhere may be equally vulnerable. Therefore the push for a cure in countries like the United States and France is likely to have immediate benefits for Africa—as data on the African epidemic will play a major role in Western research on the disease. After refusing to acknowledge the problem, a number of African governments are now launching unprecedented public health campaigns to stop the disease's spread. In five to ten years, when those now infected have gone through the incubation period, we will know more about how bad it is likely to be—as we may also know more about possibilities for cure.

Apart from the apocalyptic possibilities presented by AIDS, all-out attacks on major diseases compare very favorably with other interventions aimed at helping Africa solve its problems. The drop in mortality rates and rise in life expectancy shows that this was so in the past, and the explosion of biological technologies now opens up enormous possibilities. Mass delivery of vaccines or drugs at periodic intervals can have highly demonstrable effects in ridding whole regions of a long-accepted scourge. Cultural barriers usually fall readily before the promise of "a medicine" against what is recognized as a dreaded affliction—whether its source be attributed to spiritual malfeasance or material microbes. And in organizing mass delivery campaigns, both governments and international agencies can tackle a fairly simple and appealingly finite task, with evident rewards.

Expanding basic health care also offers a relatively cheap way to improve the well-being of large numbers of people. Unfortunately national health departments have often forfeited the ounce of prevention in favor of the expensive cure. In most countries, the lion's share of health budgets still goes to staff and equip modern hospitals in the cities. Most doctors also cluster in the cities. Thus the investment in their training as well as the bulk of medical services

119

benefit only a few relatively affluent urbanites. Where rural health care is strong, however, life expectancy has risen measurably.

Improvements in health would certainly affect soaring population growth, at first probably swelling it still further. Yet evidence from Europe, Asia and Latin America strongly indicates that easing fears about survival also eases pressures for procreation. As more babies live beyond infancy and more children grow to adulthood, parents relax efforts to insure the future through lavish fertility.

Looking at the health of children themselves, although infant mortality has fallen sharply in many African countries during the past several decades, it is still way above that in any other region of the world. In West Africa in 1980, 145 out of each 1,000 infants died, while in the United States in that year the comparable figure was 12. African parents watch many children die. In a group of women interviewed in a village in Kenya, one said she had two living children, while three died in infancy; another had three alive and three dead; for another three had died while five survived; for another two lived while three had died; another's all had been stillborn; for another, one lived and one had died of measles. Except perhaps among the well-to-do in cities, uncertainty continues high.

The UNICEF campaign for child survival now gaining momentum in Africa and the rest of the Third World, in saving millions of children's lives, could also change the way people view their own future in relation to that of their sons and daughters. Joining expanded immunization with schooling in nutrition and the provision of simple remedies for the dehydration that accompanies diarrhea, UNICEF aims to reach all of Africa's infants by 1990. Begun in force several years ago, immunizations are beginning to pay off: in Somalia, for example, two-fifths of the country's children had been inoculated against the target diseases (measles, polio, diptheria, tetanus, and tuberculosis) in 1986, and in Ethiopia nearly 70 percent of the children in the capital, Addis Ababa, were immunized in 1986.

Starting later, the rehydration effort has gathered steam under the leadership of UNICEF Executive Director James Grant, who has succeeded in selling the strategy simultaneously to African governments, the U.S. Congress, and the World Bank. Because it works by teaching mothers, first, that babies with diarrhea need to have fluids restored—not witheld, as was often traditionally believed—and second, how to administer a solution of sugar and salt following attacks of diarrhea, the campaign requires instructions and packaging of the utmost directness. In 1985 UNICEF simplified the measuring and dilution process by including with every five packets of prepared salts a plastic bag to hold the correct amount of water, decorated with pictures and instructions in several languages. During the first six months of 1985, in Nigeria's initial demonstration unit, oral rehydration treatment led to a steep drop in deaths of infants treated there for diarrhea—from around 19 a month to a total of three for the entire period. All of Nigeria's 19 states have now set up similar units to counter a disease that formerly killed more than 500 of the country's children every day.

Family planning aimed at increasing spacing between children could also dramatically curb infant mortality: the World Bank estimates that if all birth intervals of less than two years were increased to two or more years, the number of infant deaths in Africa could be reduced by 12 to 20 percent. Limiting fertility would also decrease maternal deaths considerably: if family size fell from eight to six, maternal deaths could be reduced by 25 to 30 percent.

Apart from access to contraceptives, the most important single support for limits on fertility is women's education. Both family planning and health programs depend on the education of women (and indeed may be used as an opening wedge in teaching women basic literacy). The close correlation between a woman's education and her children's health is startling: in Kenya, for example, women's education appears to be responsible for more than 80 percent of the drop in infant mortality during the last two decades. Literacy does not of course work by itself but goes hand in hand with other positive influences on nurturing. UNICEF's 1984 report on the State of the World's Children described how this works very well:

> Usually it is the mother's level of education and access to information which will decide whether or not she will go for a tetanus shot; whether a trained person will be present at the birth; whether she knows about the advantage of breast-feeding; whether her child will be weaned at the right time; whether the best available foods will be cooked in the best possible way; whether water will be boiled and hands washed; whether bouts of diarrhea will be treated by administering food and fluids; whether a child will be weighed and vaccinated; and whether there will be an adequate interval between births.

In Africa today, women with ten or more years of education want 3.3 fewer children than women with no education. Learning what family planning is all about must be the first step. More important thereafter, women still bounded by subsistence will continue to see children as their main source of opportunity. On the other hand, once they find jobs and interests outside the home and farm, even those with domestic help may feel painfully stretched by the "normal" brood of seven or eight. Clearly, improvements in women's lives and livelihoods should profoundly affect attitudes toward fertility. When effective, women's organizations strengthen demand for family planning by enlarging skills and choices, but in some cases they also directly provide family planning services.

In Kenya's *Maendeleo ya Wanawake* (Development of Women), which fields 7,500 groups throughout the country, village women, trained for two weeks, lead discussions of health and family planning at regular meetings. Since

1986, the organization has sent out more than 1,000 volunteers to deliver information and contraceptive services. The payoff from *Maendeleo's* intensive form of communication has already been dramatic: over two-fifths of its members reported using contraception in 1986, compared with the Kenyan average of about 8 percent. In Somalia, the Somalian Women's Socialist Union (the main organ for women in the national political party) played a major role in establishing the national family planning association. In villages throughout the country the Union works both sides of the equation simultaneously, combining family planning services with training and credit opportunities that will increase women's income and scope.

Within the range of Africa's current urgent needs, family planning services come comparatively cheap. Estimates from Zimbabwe suggest an annual cost of about $20 per user. This would amount to about $.75 per capita out of the $3 to $15 per person that African governments allot to public health, seemingly affordable, given some private spending. According to the World Bank, total spending on family planning in Africa now totals under $100 million a year. Covering about a quarter of married women of reproductive age by 2000 would cost some $640 million.

With success, costs of course would rise: covering 70 percent of this group by 2030 would cost about $3.2 billion. In the short run at least, much of this would very likely have to come from donors. At present, around $50 million in aid goes to Africa for population programs. Although Africans represent one-sixth of the developing world, their governments' history of resistance to family planning has kept their share of population assistance to about one-tenth of the total. The United States, which contributes by far the largest share of aid to population programs worldwide, allots about one-fifth of its family planning budget, or $40 million, to Africa.

For the United States, during the 1970s population was a major cause. In Africa, American zeal may often have outstripped that of governments and people by some distance. American assistance to nongovernmental programs did, however, lay valuable groundwork—particularly through support for the United Nations Fund for Population Activities and for the International Planned Parenthood Federation, which worked carefully to build networks among private organizations where none had existed before.

Thus, at the Mexico City Conference in 1984 it came as a shock to Africans when the Reagan administration beat the drum loudly for what sounded like a pro-natalist stance—just as they themselves were moving toward concern about exploding populations. Although funding for U.S. population activities in Africa has remained constant, cutbacks in American support for the United Nations Fund and for International Planned Parenthood (because they work with countries that may supply abortion services) set back some existing programs. While early U.S. marketing of population control had seemed to many Africans fundamentally intrusive, the denial of funding to groups that offer abortion services projected yet another set of American values far from home. In classic fashion, a domestic American moral debate was carried to a conclusion for Africans.

∾

If Africans are to establish a livable balance between people and land, between traditional society and the evolution of institutions for modern life, they need help with funding and they need Western expertise in researching new forms of contraception and delivery of family planning. Nonetheless, the very moral and intellectual confusion manifest in the American turnabout of the early 1980s underlines the profound social force of the issue. If American society in the 1980s is riven by the question of family values, how much more so must the destruction of old

124

certainties torment the people of Africa. Demographers' talk of parents "replacing themselves" sounds rational and, indeed, to us and to many educated Africans, seems urgent for that continent. Yet the idea of neat nuclear families of mom, pop and two to three kids seems an unappealing and unlikely prospect for societies where so much seen as good flows from having children, and where comfort lies in manifold family relationships. If Americans have not yet succeeded in achieving a comfortable fit between new demographic realities and old social values, the pain for individuals and upheaval for societies of doing so in Africa would seem extreme indeed.

# 5

# Eden Eroding

*Why is the food of the people so scarce? . . . Where does the blame lie? . . . I have been unable to attain a proper balance between important and unimportant affairs. Let this matter be debated. . . . Let all exhaust their efforts and ponder deeply whether there is some way to aid the people.*

Edict of Emperor Wen on the Primacy
of Agriculture (163 B.C.)

For the foreseeable future, most of Africa will have to live off the land. Today the mass of its people still dwell in villages and earn their living cultivating family farms of five to 15 acres. Except in Kenya and Zimbabwe, most still hold the land communally, though often retaining private rights to its use that can be passed down to descendants. In a number of physical ways, work for many Africans seems hardly to have changed since before the arrival of the Europeans. The hoe is still their main tool for cultivating crops. To moisten the seeds, they wait for rain, and when the soil grows tired they burn the adjoining brush and begin to farm there. While the produce is ripening, they kneel or stoop long days to weed and spend a lot of time driving off cows and goats or rushing around the fields yelling loudly to scare away ravening birds. Unless they are lucky enough to live beside a stream, women trek daily for water, for longer and longer distances when the weather is dry. Before cooking over wood in a three-stone fireplace, they spend hours pounding the tubers or grain on which their families largely subsist. When their houses fall into disrepair, many farmers fashion a new dwelling the way their parents did, packing mud or mud bricks between a framework of poles and plaiting a thatched roof overhead.

126

Until you see the transistor radio hanging from a nail in a wooden doorjamb, or hear the motorbike put-putting down an unseen path nearby, time may seem to have stopped. To the early explorers, African villages and farms presented such a scene of unadorned rustic life. According to temperament and experience, European views of African existence ranged from savage to bucolic. In many accounts of farming, however, Europeans marveled at the abundance. A Portuguese sailor shipwrecked in 1633 on what is now the eastern coast of South Africa reported that the people he saw worked their fields:

> planting and tilling the earth with sticks to prepare it for their grain, which is millet as large or larger than linseed. They have maize also, and plant large melons which are very good, and beans and gourds of many kinds, also sugar canes. Cows are what they chiefly value: these are very fine . . . In the milk season they live chiefly on it, making curds and turning it sour.

In those days, before the Europeans, the forests, plains, and jungles of Africa usually provided most of what their people needed. There was plenty of land, and people asked only to subsist. Then as now, disease, drought, and tribal war periodically took their toll in lives and suffering, but then it was always possible to regroup elsewhere and recoup losses. Although in this Eden, people lived at the mercy of their environment, in their cultivating and herding they were usually able to sustain a workable balance between their own needs and the continent's often fragile soils and harsh weather.

Africa's croplands are not among the world's oldest, but few regions have a poorer natural endowment of productive soils. Glaciers that left fertile mineral paths across Europe and North America never reached Africa. In much of the region exceptionally heavy seasonal rains over thousands of years leached nutrients from the soil and left hard pans of iron oxide beneath the surface layer. When the Europeans arrived, most of the African landscape was over-lain by a perennial groundcover of forests or grasses and shrubs. Fallen leaves and dead grasses formed a protective mulch that shielded the soil base from direct exposure to the baking sun and assault by tropical rains while also build-ing up nutrients. Growth was sustained in parallel with decomposition.

African traditional methods of cultivation worked to maintain this balance. With few people and plenty of land, it was easy to practice shifting cultivation. When yields fell, farmers asked the chief for a new plot of land, and the one they had been tilling went back into the communal pool, sometimes lying fallow for as long as 20 years. After clearing trees and burning off the brush from their newly allotted acreage, they farmed it as long as it remained fertile. When land was less plentiful, farmers devised ways to protect soils by carefully mixing adjoining and successive crops, combin-ing those that took and returned different nutrients. Like the herders of the northern regions, however, cultivators almost everywhere depended on the ability to move about for survival.

Colonialism shattered this system. Three hundred years after the Portuguese survivor's report of plenty in southern Africa, a native commissioner in the same area pointed to serious privation, warning that:

> The menace of . . . [tuberculosis] looms very large and the general physique of the native is steadily deteriorating. The reduction in the milk supply and the lack of hygiene and nutritious food is predisposing the children to this and other diseases due to malnutrition.

Two things had happened in the interval. As we have seen, the enormous growth in human numbers in response to European medicine and public health measures funda-mentally altered the balance between people and land.

128

Growing numbers of people needed more to eat, and soils that could no longer be allowed to rest lost much of their fertility. As fallow periods grew shorter, yields fell sometimes dramatically. In several villages in eastern Nigeria, for example, cassava harvests fell from about four to less than one ton per acre as fallow time shrank from five to one and one-half years.

A secondary cause further increased pressure on the land. Beginning at the start of the century, the colonists introduced new crops that could be sold for money in the international marketplace. Without exception, the British, French, Portuguese, and Belgian administrators saw the sale of commodities like coffee, tea, cocoa, and tobacco as a way to support themselves and, in some cases, white settlers who came with them. In a number of colonies the administrators seized territory outright from "the natives," while in others they pushed African farmers to grow crops that colonial marketing boards could sell abroad for a handsome percentage of the take. Exploitative they certainly were, yet culpability is not the issue here. If the Europeans hadn't started mining Africa's soils for cash return, some enterprising Africans undoubtedly would have.

The consequences, however, have been far-reaching and are still not satisfactorily assimilated. In the first place, the introduction of export crops led to a direct assault on Africa's ecology. Not only did the requirements of cash crop production bring increasing acreage into constant use, but it also interjected what has been called the "temperate bias" of colonial administrators into African agriculture. The colonial administrators' experience of farming—if any— had been in temperate countries blessed with deep, fertile topsoil and year-round rains. Some of the crops they introduced, principally cotton and tobacco, make heavy demands on the soil, and, in Africa, require steady infusions of fertilizer and pesticides that have to be imported. Even seasoned "Africa hands" were prone to believe that Northern ways would work better and to view farming practices developed within Africa as a reflection of a prevailing back-wardness. So much of what Africans knew about their own physical environment and how to preserve it through combining and alternating crops as well as rotating acreages, got lost in the shuffle.

During a famine in Upper Volta in 1932, a French civil servant at Ouagadougou wrote home:

> One can only wonder how it happens that populations who always had on hand three harvests in reserve, and to whom it was unacceptable to eat grain that had spent less than three years in the granary, have suddenly become improvident. They managed to get through the terrible drought years 1912–1914 without hardship-... now these people, once accustomed to food abundance, are living from hand to mouth. I feel morally bound to point out that the policy of giving priority to industrial cash crops has coincided with an increase in the frequency of food scarcity.

For reasons stemming mostly from external commerce and internal politics, the colonial administration channeled the African resources at their disposal into one or two main export crops. Where there were no significant minerals, this left a number of countries at Independence dependent for foreign trade on highly fluctuating international markets in one or a few commodities. Nine African countries became reliant on just one crop for over 70 percent of their income. Coffee accounts for over 70 percent of Ethiopia's foreign exchange earnings, 70 percent of Rwanda's, and 90 percent of Burundi's, while peanuts provide 90 percent of Gambia's earnings, 60 percent of Guinea-Bissau's and almost 40 percent of Senegal's. Other nations depending on one crop for over 50 percent of their earnings include Uganda (coffee), Sudan (cotton), Ghana (cocoa), Kenya (coffee), and Mali (cotton).

In addition, customs about land ownership began to change: from an abundant free good it became in some places a scarce and contested resource. In Kenya and in what were then Northern and Southern Rhodesia (now Zambia and Zimbabwe), British emigres took the best land for themselves, creating huge plantations they cultivated with varying degrees of success, aided by whatever "native" labor they might require. The rest of the former inhabitants were crowded out onto marginal areas where the soils and rainfall yielded much leaner pickings.

In *Out of Africa,* Karen Blixen presides majestically over thousands of acres in Kenya's fertile highlands—and over the Kikuyu tribemembers who have always lived on "her" land. By the time we see them from her fascinated but elevated perspective, they seem a rather scraggly lot, though possessed of the innate dignity of people who have seen better days. When she left Kenya to return to her native Denmark, Blixen staged a one-woman revolution within the colony aimed at securing some of her choice land for the use of "her" Africans. By and large, however, the colonies settled by whites evolved a dualistic farming system—including both large and small farms, growing cash and subsistence food crops, respectively—where not only the best land but also virtually all government aid went to the whites. For the most part, Africans in these colonies were not allowed to compete with whites in growing export crops, but they were forced to work on European farms to pay new taxes levied against them.

In West Africa, neither the British nor the French viewed African lands acquisitively: the steamy bush of the "white man's graveyard" did not suggest stately manorial estates for transplanted gentry as did the rolling highlands across the continent. Instead, brandishing both carrot and stick, the colonial governors persuaded African small farmers to grow cocoa, coffee, palm oil, peanuts, and cotton. The carrot was the cash and the goods imported from the metropole it could buy. As in the white settler areas, the

stick was wielded through a variety of taxes and exactions—
sometimes, as in the Congo (Zaïre), taking the form of
outright labor impressment—that required Africans to
come up with some money (or its labor equivalent) some-
how. So African peasants took part of their land out of food
crops and grew what they could sell to government agents.
Thus were Africa's state trading corporations entrenched
many years before Independence.

The consequences of these European interventions
varied enormously, given different ecologies and historical
experiences throughout the continent. Yet everywhere the
advent of the money economy changed African societies
and their physical environments. The colonial governments
brought only the men into the cash economy. Except in the
white settler areas this meant that the new crops and farming methods were introduced to men only, while most of the
farmers—the women—were bypassed. In southern Africa,
many men were drawn out of the rural economy entirely to
work for wages in the copper, gold, and diamond mines.
Everywhere men began to leave farms to earn money in the
cities.

As a result, in most of Africa, clear divisions emerged
between modern and subsistence economies. Food production (largely a matter of subsistence) was neglected. Nutrition undoubtedly suffered as women found it harder and
harder to feed their families on the lesser (and often
poorer) acreage now allotted to them, particularly since
they still did much of the work on their husbands' cash
crops. With the growing attractions of school and the cities,
it was, in fact, becoming difficult to get the farm work done.

❧

With Independence in 1960, the advent of new African leaders bent on modernizing their countries as quickly
as possible only intensified agriculture's problems. Most of
the new elites had worked hard themselves to escape from

rural life and felt that farming was something that their countries had to put behind them. Kwame Nkrumah, for example, saw agriculture as servitude and deplored Ghana's dependence on the sale of cocoa in the international capitalist marketplace. The trouble was that cocoa supplied much of the country's wealth, and therefore casting off its shackles would be a highly risky exercise.

At Independence, Nkrumah reportedly made a bet with the Côte d'Ivoire's Houphouet-Boigny on the development of their respective countries. Noting the similarity of the resources they were starting with, Nkrumah wagered that his strategy of state-led industrialization (to be financed of course by cocoa as well as foreign aid and investment) would put Ghana far out front in ten years if the Ivoirean leader (himself a coffee planter) continued to support farming as the base of his country's economy. A decade later Nkrumah was in exile from his bankrupt country while Houphouet-Boigny and his countrymen prospered. (It is not known whether Houphouet-Boigny ever collected on the bet.)

With the exception of a few leaders like Houphouet-Boigny—Banda in Malawi and Ahidjo in Cameroon were others—the new governments continued the colonial policy of draining agriculture to finance everything else. Because they needed more money, however, to fulfill expectations and insure their own survival, they invested less, proportionately, than the colonial administrations, and extracted more. For example, government investment in Tanzania fell from over 20 percent at Independence to 10 percent at the end of the 70s, and about five percent in 1981. While an Asian country like Malaysia (a major competitor with African states in world palm oil markets) allocated around 25 percent of its budget to agriculture in the 1970s, the median for Africa from 1963 to 1973 was 7.6 percent. Zaïre has allocated two to five percent to agriculture since Independence. By the beginning of the 1970s, the bills were coming due. Africa's period of grace was over: the continent was selling fewer commodities, buying more food, fighting famine, and watching (mesmerized) the encroaching desert.

The spread of drought to eastern and southern Africa in the early 1980s, and its intensification in Ethiopia and the Sudan at the same time, riveted the world's attention on the prospect of African famine. Rainfall dropped in 1983 and 1984 to the lowest recorded in this century, following many years that were consistently below average. What made it worse was that almost a decade of above-average rain in the 1950s had encouraged extensive cultivation of fallow and marginal areas: the Sahel, Ethiopia, Somalia, Sudan, and Mozambique. These areas were, in most cases, hardest hit by famine, which drove people from their lands.

The current drought first struck the Sahel in 1968. Continuing until the present, though lessening somewhat after 1974–75, the drought fits into a pattern of sparse, highly variable, and unevenly distributed rainfall that has prevailed in the desert littoral for about 10,000 years. Early in this century, the severe drought of 1910 to 1914 reduced the annual discharge of the Nile by 35 percent and the depth of Lake Chad by about half. But the present drought may be different, for it follows 50 years of steady increase in the numbers of humans and animals using the area. Though the traveler might not see anyone in miles of sand dunes, the desert is crowded.

The Sahel (which means "the shore " of the desert) includes six French-speaking countries: Mauritania, Mali, Burkina Faso, Senegal, Niger, and Chad, plus Gambia and Cape Verde. Only about 8 percent of its land is considered arable. The very dry strip just to the south of the Sahara is mostly rangeland, which can support about 0.8 people in a square mile. Today it has about five inhabitants per square mile. Immediately to the south, where a little more rain falls (about 14 to 24 inches a year—slightly less than the 28 inches deemed necessary for crop cultivation), land that can support 37 people per square mile now accommodates around 50. The livestock population has increased at a similar rate.

People have been living in the Sahel for millennia. A thousand years ago, they were mostly nomads, subsisting by herding and hunting. The most powerful effects on the region's ecology came from brush fires that the nomads set to improve grazing or help flush out animal prey—and from the caravans plying their trade across the Sahara. To feed the several thousand animals in the trains and get wood for charcoal, the caravans sent out hundreds of advance teams that cut trees along the route. When Europeans arrived, pacification of warring local tribes brought the expansion of farming northward. At the same time camels were displaced as the mainstay of the nomadic economy by cattle, which need considerably more water and food per ounce of body weight than their desert-adapted predecessors.

As elsewhere, intensified human pressure reduced fallow periods—by 50 percent between 1961 and 1970 in Niger; eliminated much of the tree cover; cut mobility; and eroded cooperation between herdsmen and farmers, which had often permitted livestock to forage on harvested land, leaving their droppings for fertilizers. When the drought struck in 1972, there was no slack in the system: people competed for grasses and shrubs until they were gone; herds trampled the land hard as pavement for miles around waterholes and eventually began to die in great numbers; farmers ran out of seeds to sow in the parched ground and moved their families to refugee camps.

As people were leaving, the Sahara was moving south, sometimes reportedly by around 90 miles a year. In Mauritania, where herding is the main occupation, the capital, Nouakchott, has become less a city than an enormous refugee camp, as hundreds of thousands of people (half the country's nomads) pitched their tents around it. Their cattle had starved or been sold, and much of their land had been claimed by the Sahara. These people may hope their reassuring local proverb expresses the truth of their situation: "it is only the water that is spilt; the calabash is not broken!" But most of them will never be able to return to their homes.

In 1984 and 1985 around six million tons of food and $4.5 billion of emergency supplies poured into Africa to feed and shelter the millions crowded together, shriveled, dessicated, and almost immobile with hunger, in the camps. In 1985 more than 20 million Africans were at risk of starvation or actually died of starvation or disease. By 1986 the drought was officially over. Blessedly, the rains had come—to Ethiopia, the Sudan, parts of the Sahel, Zimbabwe, Kenya, Zambia—and refugees left the camps (though over half stayed). During 1987 the aid had trickled to around $500 million. Yet an estimated 150 million people—nearly a quarter of Africa's population—are still hungry or malnourished. In Mozambique in 1987 more than 4.5 million people (or about a third of the total population) were again threatened with famine, while in Zimbabwe excellent 1986 harvests diminished in dry weather the following year. As 1988 began, famine once again menaced southern Sudan and Ethiopia, as well as Mozambique and parts of Angola. Moreover, Africans in a number of other countries were still living so close to the margins of survival that the next drought would find them once again facing starvation. In 1987 over 2.7 million people were officially registered as refugees, but the real figure may be more than double that.

Significantly, the starving people are not in Africa's cities but in the rural areas where the food is grown; that is because famine, while often triggered by drought, is fundamentally a matter of poverty. In most famines, when shortages are threatened, food prices rise astronomically in local markets. Then farmers whose crops have failed begin to sell livestock, first sheep and goats, then oxen needed for cultivating fields. But as the market is flooded with farm animals, the selling price falls, and farmers have no money left for food or seed. Whole households move to the closest places where there is food—thereby increasing demand in nearby regions and again raising prices. In this way the famine moves outward, spreading like a rash or infection, until for many the only place left to go is to the edges of the cities—or, now, the refugee camps.

Grave in itself, African famine is the most dramatic representation of a much broader erosion that threatens the soils and forests that must sustain all the continent's people. Like the population explosion, which was largely ignored until it could be graphically rendered in swiftly rising curves, the threats to Africa's environment have tended to pass unnoticed until so much damage has been done that salvage becomes extraordinarily difficult. Except where disintegration has been dramatic, as in the enormous gulley erosions of Ethiopia's highlands, losses of soil and tree cover are often imperceptible. And when they are perceived, reversing the drain of resources may be as complicated as the African environment itself, entailing long years of investment just to retrieve what has slipped away. For Africa's environmental problems stem from the interaction of people, ground cover, climate, and policy—paralleling the reciprocal linkages among the basic physical elements of Africa's ecology: soils, forests, and rainfall.

Africa's environment is as diverse as that of any region on earth, though on the whole it is more difficult than most. Forty-four percent of the land is desert or semi-arid, 18 percent has low fertility, and 22 percent has shallow soils and excess water. Only 16 percent has no serious limitation for farming.

Although broad zones of population, climate, and vegetation can be traced across the continent, within them greatly varying soils and climate create numerous microclimates. Africa's patterns of soil, rainfall, and sunlight have been compared to an onion, with its center on the Equator in the humid tropical forests of Zaïre and the West African coast around the Gulf of Guinea. Though the forests are lush, tall, and green, rich in plant and animal life, their heavy rainfall and thick tree cover provide habitation for few people: even if cleared their metallic and lateritic soils do not yield much to domestic cultivation. North and south of the core, stretching through many West African states and the southern Sahel, as well as much of East and Southern Africa, are the grassy and wooded savanna regions, where most of Africa's people live. In the savannas, soils vary from fertile (in parts of West Africa and of the Sudan, Ethiopia, Kenya, and Zimbabwe) to sandy (in Botswana, Namibia, western Zambia, and Angola), and rainfall from moderate to low. Outside the forests, heavy rains are often concentrated in four or five months, and little falls during most of the year. In the few areas of exceptional fertility— southern Nigeria, around Lake Chad, the western Sudan, parts of the Ethiopian and Kenyan highlands, the volcanic highlands of Rwanda and Burundi—population densities are very high. Finally, the desert and semidesert areas bordering the Sahara in the north parallel those adjacent to the Kalahari and the Namib in the south, with sparse grasses, scattered thorn trees, and few inhabitants.

As in Africa now, environmental decline generally accelerates because the stages of deterioration reinforce each other: each speeds the onset of the next. The poverty of African farmers also increases the demands on their environment. Where they are too poor to buy fertilizers, overlapping uses of trees, soils, and wastes to provide both food and fuel hastens the exhaustion of all three.

The progression of environmental decline is triggered by the removal of trees. Ecologist Kenneth Newcombe has laid out its stages with particular precision: first, as forests retreat before the plow, trees no longer replenish soil nutrients and fertility begins to decline. Then, as populations grow, markets appear for wood, both for fuel and building. Farm families now sell wood cut from remnant forests and collect dung and crop residues to burn in their own households. Removing the layer of plant and animal wastes deprives the soil of renewed nutrients and leaves them more vulnerable to erosion. Once nearby trees are gone, dung and crop residues are traded in the market for fuel; with the steady export of nutrients and organic matter, fields and even pastures give back less and less. On sloping fields annual soil erosion of 20 to 40 tons per acre is common. Eventually, as harvests dwindle, cow dung becomes the main cash crop; people collect crop residues and feed them to their livestock, which can no longer survive on forage in their pastures. Massive loss of topsoil leads to total crop failure when rains fall off. Finally, agricultural productivity collapses completely. With the advent of a drought that formerly could have been tolerated, farmers leave the area en masse.

Overall, Africa's trees are being cut a good deal faster than they are being replaced. Since the turn of the century, Africa's forests and woodlands have been halved. In Mauritania, Rwanda, and Benin, forests have virtually disappeared. The Côte d'Ivoire, which once had 75 million acres of tropical rainforests, now has around 11 million acres. Much of Ethiopia, the communal lands of Zimbabwe, and the homelands of South Africa are now largely bare of trees. For the most part trees have fallen to make way for agriculture, though commercial logging has also taken a toll. In the Côte d'Ivoire, the biggest timber exporter in Africa, farming has taken 4.5 times as much forest as logging.

Felling forests to get at the land beneath, or mining them for valuable mahoganies and ebonies, usually wastes enormous quantities of wood, but while it is going on fuel is plentiful and often virtually free. The World Bank estimates that even if the demand for wood were decreased by 20 to 30 percent through conservation and substitution, current planting rates would have to increase 15 times to bring supply and demand into better balance by 2000. Although Africans use 200 times less energy than Americans, almost everyone depends on wood for cooking, heating, and often for light. In many poorer countries like Tanzania, Burundi, and Ethiopia, wood provides more than 90 percent of energy needs; even in oil-rich Nigeria wood supplies 80 percent of energy. Whereas rural people can gather what they need from fields and woods around them, city dwellers must buy it. In most places, woods have long since disappeared around the cities, which are often ringed by increasingly wide swathes of treeless plains.

Nonetheless, the price of wood is usually very low—far below the economic cost of producing it—because peasants or urban wood dealers pay little or nothing for cutting in official forest reserves or communal lands. In Niger, for example, the license to cut a cubic-yard stack is about 10 U.S. cents, less than 1 percent of the selling price. While this is the case, planting trees is obviously not a profitable enterprise. In Malawi, a cubic-yard of wood costs on average less than 2 cents in the rural area. Although growing that amount would cost about $16, it is probably impossible to raise the price very much or get farmers to grow wood to sell as long as they have access to free wood on customary lands.

In several countries, like densely settled Rwanda and semidesert Mauritania, firewood needs are as much as ten times what is regenerated each year; in Sudan, by comparison, they look almost manageable at about double the sustainable yields. Sudan's situation, however, illustrates how things can get out of hand before anyone realizes it. Annual demands for wood outdistanced supplies by around 1965. After that, cutting exceeded new growth, and as total stock diminished, so did the numbers of trees regenerated from existing stands. For some years the change was imperceptible: after 20 years, the forests had contracted by one-fifth. Given the country's population growth of 3.2 percent, however, the process is likely to accelerate wildly from here on out: in the next 20 years, only an extraordinary effort at tree planting and family planning can prevent the decimation of the remaining woodlands.

∽

As tree cover disappears all over the continent, scientists are beginning to ask how this may be affecting rainfall. Although the continent historically has experienced periodic droughts, since the beginning of this century the longest period of below-average rainfall lasted eight consecutive years and the others about four. From 1967 to 1984, however, Africa saw 17 straight years of below-average rain, and precipitation declined again in many places during 1987. Some meteorologists attribute this decline to a southward shift in atmospheric circulation of winds and ocean currents, which may be either temporary or permanent. Others argue that vast changes in African land use have altered the climate of Africa itself. Clearing woodlands and degrading farm and grasslands increases the reflectivity of the soil and decreases the retention of water by roots. Where forests have been cut, rain streams off into rivers very quickly, and what used to be held in the soils or recycled back into the rainclouds through evaporation from leaves instead flows back to the oceans.

Reducing evaporation may also weaken the atmospheric disturbances necessary for lifting and cooling the air to produce rain. The tropical forests of West Africa from Senegal to Zaïre "toss" moisture inland from the coast by converting rain into evaporation. Research on a watershed in Brazil's Amazon basin shows how much water is lost when the forest is cleared: on a healthy stand of tropical forest about a quarter of the rain runs off; after it is cut three-quarters runs off immediately, and only one-fourth evaporates to replenish rain clouds. If ecological changes are indeed reinforcing rainfall declines, for the first time in human history we may be witnessing what meteorologists are now calling "man-induced climate change."

Our understanding of these phenomena is highly inexact, and the jury will probably be out for a long time to come. A long period of good rains clearly would provide the most desirable answer to the debate. Policymakers, however, cannot wait to find out whether the dry spell is cyclic or reflects changes in the land. Regardless of what it may portend for long-term weather, this process has already left its mark on African farming. Ultimately, the erosion and degradation of soils underway now could lay waste to large chunks of arable land. The U.N.'s Food and Agriculture Organization (FAO) warns that without effective conservation more than 16 percent of Africa's rain-fed cropland could be lost by the year 2000.

Ethiopia presents an extreme example of erosion's progress. In that country's central highlands, which support about 80 percent of the nation's people and 70 percent of its cattle, more than a billion tons of topsoil erode each year, contributing to an astounding national erosion rate that is 137 times the world average. Denuded of trees, the land in many places is stripped down to bare subsoil and riven by gulleys. In the dry season soil from the barren surfaces of exhausted pastures and fields is carried off by whirlwinds; but when the rains come they often beat down in a deluge. On slopes of over 25 degrees, soil and boulders hurtle downward after the rains, carving ugly gashes in the hillside and spreading rubble in the valleys beneath. The cost of fertilizers to replace nutrients in soil eroded away in one year would be more than $1 billion.

As in other parts of the continent, overgrazing is a major cause of Ethiopia's soil problems. Although ninth in territorial size in Africa, the country has the largest number of livestock, which represent savings as well as a hedge against further drought (animals survive longer than crops when rains fail and can be driven to pastures not yet dessicated). Only about 8 percent are sold for meat each year (versus 11 percent for Africa as a whole and 44 percent for a major cattle exporter like Australia), and many live long beyond the point where their meat could be sold; as their numbers have grown in tandem with those of their human owners, competition for land between crops and livestock has sharpened.

142

The wholesale appropriation of fallow land all over Africa has brought parallel—though less visible—stresses elsewhere. Since 1920 about 175 million acres of land have been opened to cultivation in sub-Saharan Africa. In the 1960s, expansion was three times faster in Africa than in Asia, where the "Green Revolution" was raising incentives to enlarge cropland. Governments sometimes directly intervened to accelerate the process: in Senegal, the government decreed that any land lying unused for more than three years would be confiscated. Lacking new high-yielding seeds and substantial increases in fertilizers, growing numbers of African farmers were seizing their main option to raise yields. Now they have pushed about as far as they can. Even in a country like Zimbabwe, which enjoyed super-abundant harvests after the end of the drought in 1985, the country's Natural Resources Board has warned that over-farming threatens a quarter of the country's subsistence lands with severe erosion.

Centuries ago in Asia, an analogous process occurred. Farm populations pushed at the limits of available land and farmers responded by reducing fallow periods. But in Asia this transition from extensive to intensive farming took place under much more gradual population pressure. So farmers were able to concentrate on better soils; they invested more labor in destumping, irrigation, and terracing, used more manure, and switched from hand-held hoes to ox-drawn plows and then to tractors. In Africa now, farmers whom scarcity has already consigned to marginal land cannot afford new tools or fertilizers on the marginal output of those lands. And the good soils are also getting less nourishment now, as crop residues and dung that have traditionally served as mulch are increasingly being burned or sold by hard-up farmers.

A 1982 study of the potential carrying capacity of the developing world's farmlands by the FAO had alarming news for Africa. If the continent were a unit, and if all arable land were planted in food crops, at present levels of technology it could feed 1.6 times its projected population by the year 2000. Africa, however, is not a unit and much of its land is not planted with food. Looking at individual countries (even within which food distribution is highly fragmented), the FAO estimated that 14 countries accounting for 50 percent of Africa's population (including Nigeria, Kenya, and Ethiopia) could not support their current populations. In 2000, FAO estimated, seven more, including Zimbabwe and Ghana, would very likely no longer be able to do so without significantly increasing inputs. Forty-seven percent of the area FAO considered to be in critical shape worldwide was in Africa.

⌒

Given their main causes—poverty and population growth—there are no panaceas for Africa's current environmental problems. Technical solutions to many of Africa's environmental problems have been known and used by agriculturalists for a long time. Before the Europeans arrived, African farmers had evolved systems of cultivation that worked under local conditions. When the land was plenty and people few, shifting cultivation and fallowing made sense. Where more people crowded onto richer soils, methods of soil conservation including irrigation, manuring, and the stabling of livestock were developed in a number of places. At least 17 tribes and groups of tribes from Benin, Nigeria, and Cameroon on the west coast, and Tanzania, Uganda and Kenya in the east terraced their fields to prevent erosion. Though they seldom have seen the need to plant trees for fuel, most of Africa's farming communities already grow trees, which they value for many other uses. In the Sahel, the acacia tree has long been highly regarded for its shade as well as the fodder and mulch provided by its leaves, and it is planted by local farmers or left standing when land is cleared for agriculture.

"Conservation," however, was long resented as a colonial imposition on rural peoples and, indeed, had been used as a springboard for nationalist opposition in the Independence period. In the last decade, with the drought and bursting populations, government attitudes have changed markedly. Though action has seldom moved at the pace of rhetoric, East Africa in particular has enjoyed energetic leadership from Tanzania's former president Julius Nyerere, who began to warn his people about threats to forest and land resources as early as 1972; Kenya's president Daniel arap Moi, who has led a widely publicized personal campaign to build bench terraces and drains; and Rwanda's president Major General Juvinal Habyarimona, who has engaged vigorously in planting trees. (On a per capita basis, both Kenya and Tanzania spend six to eight times what the U.S. spends on nationwide parks and wildlife conservation.) The needs, however, are extraordinary.

Apart from overall progress in development and family planning, African governments will have to move on a variety of fronts to roll back destruction of trees and soils. Guarding and replenishing national forest reserves and building dams in watershed areas may seem the easiest answers technically and politically. The costs of both, however, are prohibitive. Supplying Africa's fuel through large-scale forestry or water through large dams would require enormous increases in expenditure from African governments and donors who are now cutting back. Ultimately, planting the trees, terracing the fields, and applying mulch to worn-out soils will have to be done by Africa's farmers—and they will make that effort only when they see a clear advantage in it for themselves.

It has often been noted that for poor farmers conservation is not an end in itself: you can't eat it and you can't sell it; most of its costs come now and the benefits much later. With their very pressing need for present income, poor farmers must see immediate as well as more distant rewards. Reversing processes of erosion, degradation, or deforestation usually takes a great deal of labor. Where returns are likely to be marginal farmers will rarely expend it.

145

Nor will peasants who are fully absorbed in a daily struggle for survival have much energy to spare for deferred gains.

Ultimately, poor farmers are unlikely to take much interest in planting trees unless these are clearly useful in themselves (other than as fuelwood) or increase the fertility and productivity of the land. In a World Bank tree-planting project dubbed "Johnny Appleseed," in Niger, farmers were given the opportunity to choose trees for planting from a central nursery, and they set to with gusto in the first year. When they had all the trees they needed for shade, fruit, and building poles, however, they stopped. They did not, as the donors had hoped, follow up by planting fuelwood trees outside their own property. In Kenya, farmers are planting increasing numbers of fast-growing leucana trees in alternate alleys with corn. These trees are burned as fuel, but they also fix nitrogen in the soil and provide both fodder and mulch.

Two contrasting tree-planting projects in Niger cited by ecologist Lloyd Timberlake show how demonstrated benefits make all the difference in securing peasant participation. In the early 1980s CARE painstakingly established a holding action against the desert in the small village of Yegalane in Niger. They carefully fortified and planted with grasses and shrubs a sand dune that was encroaching on the village's single stream and only patch of arable land. When CARE left, however, the villagers let their sheep and goats crop the vegetation, whereupon the dune blew onto their land: given the meager yields from farming that bleak landscape, they preferred to move elsewhere rather than work hard to hold back the desert. In the same valley, on the other hand, CARE gradually persuaded another group of farmers to plant 150 miles of trees as windbreaks to cut erosion and hold moisture in the soil on a flat, millet-growing plain. Villagers were convinced of the value of the trees by the 15 percent increase in yields on the protected fields. Because the villagers lived close to the main road, the trees could be profitably sold. About seven years later they faced the pleasant task of dividing the proceeds of around $80,000 from thinning the groves. The chances that the windbreak would endure for some years appeared good.

What this means is that there is no way to conserve Africa's environment on the cheap. Getting farmers to do the job takes less expenditure of cash than setting up government tree plantations or building big dams, but the money and effort will still go to waste unless schemes are implemented with intensive care as well as labor. Only if they pay heed at every stage to benefits for farmers are they likely to succeed.

Looking at how biological systems affect African agriculture, it is impossible to overlook the corollary—how rural poverty hastens the degradation of Africa's environment. Efforts to brake the deterioration seem unlikely to work unless the flow of resources out of farmers' pockets is reversed.

Stemming as it did from colonial stereotypes and the clear self-interest of African elites, the almost inevitable urban bias of African governments in the post-colonial era could be chalked up to learning experience had it not proved so destructive. Seeking all at once state control over national revenues; swift growth of industries; resources to expand education, health, and wage employment; and cheap food for city dwellers, African governments found a cluster of eminently serviceable policies ready at hand. Following a pattern commonly associated with import substituting industrialization, the governments erected a complex structure of tariffs and import licenses favoring the import of capital goods and components needed to build industries from scratch. They kept exchange rates for national currencies unrealistically high, facilitating imports and effectively discouraging exports. They centralized government control over all aspects of agriculture through maintaining colonial marketing boards and monopolizing the sale and transport of seeds and fertilizer as well as the harvested crops. Thus they could keep prices to farmers low and take a hefty cut out of overseas sales. Even in a state relatively supportive of agriculture like the Côte d'Ivoire, levies on commodities exports equaled a quarter to a half of public revenues at any given time.

Despite (or because of) this favored treatment, Africa's new industries languished. While the early entrants, serving basic consumer needs for beer, soap, cloth, and shoes, had some chance of profitability, most others had little prospect of achieving the size needed for efficiency while producing Africa's small domestic markets. Nor had they any hope of surmounting barriers to sales in neighboring countries, which all wanted *their own* steel mills, tractor plants, and glass factories. A good deal of capital was invested in enterprises that never got off the ground, ran swiftly into the red, or eventually collapsed for lack of spare parts or raw materials. In some cases foreign corporations engaged in joint ventures with African businessmen and in others foreign companies sold turnkey operations to African parastatals—but in virtually every instance most of the local money came from government coffers. Where a country's exchange rate was highly overvalued, as in Nigeria, local entrepreneurs largely busied themselves with securing foreign exchange for the initial investment and gave short shrift to setting up the enterprise. As in the United States during the late 1970s and 1980s, the profit was in acquiring the asset or in handling the money, not in making and selling a product.

One result of these patterns of investment was that balance sheets often were not taken very seriously by African partners or managers, either in terms of their financial accounting or their concern about oversight of operations. In addition, wage scales in the fledgling modern sector soared, both in relation to farm incomes and to amounts earned by workers in the rest of the Third World.

At the same time, the linked policies designed to favor industrialization progressively hobbled agriculture. First and foremost, low prices paid for crops—sometimes as low as 30 and most often around 50 percent of international prices—discouraged farm production. Further, while the overvalued exchange rates discouraged commodity exports by raising prices to foreign buyers, they also made it cheap to buy food abroad. While keeping city dwellers happy, imported wheat and rice cut into markets for domestically grown staples like millet and sorghum, further depressing farm prices. In Nigeria, people in 1981 were eating four times as much wheat as in 1960—in the form of government-subsidized loaves of bread. As more and more Africans move to cities, the new tastes for wheat and rice will be hard to break: the African staples, sorghum and millet, like the tubers, cassava and yam (and, though less so, corn), take hours of heavy pounding to prepare, grueling enough in the open spaces of the village but nearly impossible in cramped urban quarters.

In addition, the often slipshod performance of state corporations that were supposed to serve farmers also dampened productivity. With rain-fed agriculture, timing is all: unless seeds and fertilizers are delivered on time the entire planting cycle may be retarded. The meager proportion of government investment in rural areas also drained farmers' initiative. There is no point in producing a surplus if there are no roads to transport crops to market. Without schools, clinics, water supplies, and consumer goods comparable to those in the city, farm labor will flee the countryside.

In fact, the enormous gaps between urban and rural incomes have created a farm labor shortage in many places. Here African countries are faced with a painful paradox: although more and more people must be supported by the land, they don't want to work it. To some extent, the squeeze results from local growing conditions: compared with Asia and Latin America, African food crops need extremely heavy concentrated effort, as only one crop is generally grown each year, to coincide with the rainy season; in addition, labor productivity is much lower than in the other regions, partly because use of irrigation and fertilizer is much lower, and soils are poorer.

But the labor shortage also stems from the general poverty of Africa's farmers and particularly of food producers. Given urban wage scales and the flow of remittances back to rural areas, the cost of hiring workers even in farm villages exceeds the means of many farmers. The poverty of farmers also makes them less able to take risks in adopting new techniques or purchasing the fertilizers or tools needed to make them successful. In part because they can't afford pesticides or adequate storage, farmers lose 15 to 25 percent of their crop in the fields, and 15 to 20 percent after harvest—to rats, locusts, birds, beetles, moths, weevils, and countless microorganisms.

In most countries governments were able for some time to ignore happily the consequences of their policies for farmers while keeping food prices low in the cities. As a relief worker in the Sahel remarked, the equation is clear: "Starve the city dwellers and they riot; starve the peasants and they die. If you were a politician, which would you choose?" In the few instances where agriculture has become a target of investment for local elites, as in Kenya, Zimbabwe, and the Côte d'Ivoire, governments have given all farmers—small as well as large—a much better shake both on prices and investments in rural roads, bridges, waterworks. In most places, however, the small farmers who represent most of Africa's populace are politically mute. And none more so than Africa's women farmers, who grow perhaps 70 percent of the continent's food. As the Kikuyu proverb has it, "Let women spin and not preach."

෴

The position of women in African society appears to be a major contributing cause of Africa's food shortages. Traditionally, women were always subordinate to men. But women's control of their economic destinies has declined since the colonial era. While eroding traditional rights, Western mores also deprived women of membership in the new modern dispensation. In the pre-colonial era, men and women both worked within the subsistence economy. Women farmed and did household chores, while men focused on hunting and war and helped with clearing land and harvesting. Although accounts from the early twentieth century show that even then women usually did most of the cultivation, the men at least pitched in on the heavier chores when needed. Given plentiful land, women's rights to portions of family land for their own use were widely accepted.

As we have seen, however, with the introduction of cash crops by the colonial administrators, the division of labor shifted further against women and the division of spoils excluded them almost entirely. Regarding wives as homemakers and husbands as breadwinners, the Europeans either did not understand or refused to accept the fact that most African farming was done by women. The export crops grown by men benefited from research, extension advisers, marketing networks, and credit unavailable to the female cultivators of foodstuffs. In addition, women's responsibility for feeding the family cut back their ability to risk experimenting with the new methods.

Twenty-five years of Independence have done little to redress this balance. Because women are even poorer than their husbands and brothers, they are correspondingly less able to make the investments necessary to maintain or increase yields. Around the mid-1970s the food crisis and international women's movements caused donors to "discover" the woman farmer and to pressure African governments on her behalf. But inertia and social resistance have combined to insure that rationality and high-minded resolutions have not yet altered rural conditions markedly. An African woman farmer interviewed in 1984 expressed the anomalies of her position wryly, saying:

This one they call farmer; send in teachers to
teach him to farm (while I'm out growing the
food); lend him money for tractors and tillers
(while I'm out growing the food); promise him
fortunes if he'd only raise cotton (while I'm out
growing the food) . . . No, I daren't stop working . . . and I won't abandon that thing I was born
for—to make sure my children have food in their
bellies.

African farm women are almost certainly the most
overworked human beings in the world today, laboring 10
to 15 hours at a variety of jobs. A Zimbabwean woman
described her daily routine, beginning at 3 a.m. when she
awakens to pound grain into flour in a mortar: "At sunrise
one has to go to the river to fetch water" and then "to the
fields for weeding. If you have a baby, you breast-feed while
you work. And we must climb into the watchtower to chase
crop-raiders such as buffalo and elephants away." At sunset
the woman prepares supper, gathers more water and wood,
and "if she has energy, bathes herself and her children."

In addition to raising the family's food, she usually
helps her husband with cultivation of his cash crops. She
may also process the food she produces—threshing, drying, or grinding it—before carrying it on her head to sell in
the market. Drought and depletion of fuelwood has added
immeasurably to her load, as the miles she must go for water
and wood (sometimes twice a day) lengthen. In total, women work much longer hours than most men with consequent effects on their productivity as farmers. In the Côte
d'Ivoire, for example, the total workload of adult women is
twice that of men; in Burkina Faso, women spend 82 percent more time than men on agricultural tasks, in addition
to household chores. A Tanzanian man, describing women's burden from his own point of view, inadvertently
underlined this inequity, saying: "Water is a big problem for
women. We can sit here all day waiting for food because

152

there is no woman at home. Always they are going to fetch water."

The system, as embodied in law and policy as well as custom, hobbles Africa's main food producers in a number of ways. Most basically, women's rights to land are highly restricted. In Kenya and Zimbabwe, where land can be privately owned, a wealthy woman can in theory buy land as soon as a man, but for obvious reasons this opportunity can be enjoyed by very few. And despite Kenya's new laws protecting widows' shares in their husband's estates, land is commonly passed on to the eldest son.

Elsewhere, traditional land rights—as determined by village councils—still shape land allocations to a considerable extent. While the traditional right of women to hold land varies significantly from tribe to tribe, in practice women's access to land most often depends on having a living husband. For the most part women do not control the use of land. Even when their husbands work in the city and wives bear virtually the entire responsibility for cultivating family plots, often they are not allowed to decide what crops to plant. In Lesotho, for example, where the vast majority of men work as miners in South Africa, wives have to get their husband's agreement before starting a farming operation, employing a sharecropper, or getting a loan from the local credit union.

Almost everywhere women's tenuous rights to land make it extremely difficult for them to procure credit on their own—for most African farmers, land is the main collateral. In many instances, women are not permitted to participate in the cooperatives that often control credit as well as transport and marketing. Nor do wives have a right to the income from cash crops. When absent husbands retain most of their own wages—as in Kabwe, Kenya, for example, where husbands send home on average only 10 percent of what they earn—this leads to greater impoverishment of the farm sector.

Further, both government and donor programs have blocked women's chances to improve their farming skills.

Because the system is designed as if they do not do most of the work, they are bypassed by extension agents and agricultural information too rarely reaches them. Most extension workers are male, and social taboos may prohibit their spending time with women to whom they are not related. The few women extension workers are often trained in home economics rather than farming. In the World Bank-designed Training and Visit extension system, the farmers visited are almost invariably male.

The experience of rice farmers in a Gambian village shows what women are up against—and the benefits in redressing the balance. In the village of Jahally and Pacharr along the Gambia river, rice has traditionally been cultivated by women working with primitive tools in a swampland shaped like a saucer, with too much water in the bottom and too little on the sides. Although women are the majority of the tillers, they received only 16 percent of the government credits for land improvement; the rest went to men. And previously, each program for improvement and irrigation had led to a shift in control of land and its produce from women to men. Thus when the U.N.'s International Fund for Agricultural Development (IFAD) and a donor consortium proposed to set up a model $16-million project to increase rice production, the women resisted suspiciously. After IFAD drew up regulations protecting the women's rights, village men halted the process by demanding that women be ousted from the land allocation committee. Valuable planting time was being lost, so the women formed a committee and asked to launch the project on their own.

Eventually the unusual drive of the women and new savvy on the part of government and donors prevailed. After mediation, the men came around; 2,500 acres of swamp were drained and an irrigation system was installed. Like their male counterparts, the women received credit for seeds, fertilizers, threshers, and machines for land leveling and irrigation. Rice yields rose from a ton or less per acre to about 3 tons, reducing the area's rice imports significantly.

❧

Because farming will have to sustain most Africans for some time to come—and serve as the base for any viable industry—policies and pressures on the land need to change pretty quickly. The continent must achieve its own Green Revolution if it is to survive, and, eventually, diversify. With 72 percent of its people working in agriculture, small farms will have to remain the backbone of national economies for some time to come. With 40 percent of its export income flowing from farm products, Africa cannot afford further declines in either food or cash crops. All of Africa's major farm exports except for tea, sugar and tobacco fell by about 2 percent a year during the 1970s. Falling commodities revenues were paralleled by rising food costs, as commercial food imports rose about 9 percent a year. After exporting food in the early 1960s, by 1984 the continent was importing $7.5 billion worth of food (equivalent to a seventh of its total imports that year). Unable to sustain this sort of drain, most countries have increasingly depended on food aid, which rose by over 75 percent from 1978 to 1982 and is expected to reach $11 billion-worth by 1990.

The reliance of African countries on the sale of a few primary commodities already makes them highly vulnerable to the vagaries of international trends they cannot control. As their terms of trade have deteriorated, many African states can cover less than half of their import costs from export revenues. Foreign exchange has drained away; most countries now have foreign exchange reserves insufficient to cover even one month's imports. While they lack money for fertilizers, pesticides, machinery, roads, trucks, or gas, African countries will be hard put to farm better and grow more.

Paradoxically, Africa's decline is occurring in an era of worldwide biotechnological discovery analogous to that of

Columbus and Magellan: while the continent grows hungrier, most of the world is awash in farm surpluses. Despite the consequent abundance of donated food during the drought, the growing gaps in productivity will not make Africa's long-run prospects any easier. Food aid itself often worsens the very problems it is sent to assuage: it lowers farmers' revenues and frees African leaders from pressure to reform the policies holding down farm yields. While Africans have fiddled, Brazilians, Malaysians, and others have stolen a number of their customers for cocoa, peanuts, palm oil, bananas, rubber, sisal, and tobacco.

While Asia and some parts of Latin America have surged so far forward, why has the plant genetics revolution of the past several decades seemingly bypassed Africa? During the 1950s most of Asia (like Africa afterward) short-changed agriculture in favor of the spurious enticements of industrialization. When food shortages and famine followed in the late 1960s, the international donor community, led by the U.S. Ford and Rockefeller Foundations, rushed into the breach. The major push forward came from the broad dissemination of high-yielding wheat and rice seeds developed in international research centers in the Philippines and Mexico funded by Ford and Rockefeller. In the beginning of the 1980s, the Green Revolution had filled Asian granaries. In 1986 the chief basket case of the 1970s, Bangladesh, was feeding itself; India was enjoying surpluses; Indonesia, formerly the world's largest rice importer, was trying to staunch the flood of rice by encouraging farmers to shift rice lands to corn for feeding livestock.

During the two post-Independence decades in Africa, research efforts were conducted piecemeal. In the 1960s African states dismantled regional research institutes and converted them into national institutes. For donors, recognition of the depth of Africa's food crisis was a long time in dawning. When it did, many Western experts were convinced that "miracle" strains from Asia or Latin America would be just as prolific in Africa once farmers learned how to grow them. Unfortunately, it had become clear by the end of the 1970s that very few plant varieties could be directly transferred to Africa, and that agricultural miracles in the continent would be few and far between without decades of research focusing on Africa's unique problems.

Conditions for a breakthrough in Africa are very different from those in Asia. The Asian revolution was based on the broad dissemination of hybrid wheat and rice. Moreover, Asian soils and extensive potential for irrigation provided ideal conditions for a major push. What had to be done was relatively clear.

In Africa, however, the fragmentation that pervades research systems, staple crops, and climatic zones makes a sweeping effort much more difficult. For the most part, the many small, poorly supported national research systems are too isolated and impoverished to make good use of the trained professionals they may retain. Yet problems need to be coped with on a local level. African staple grains and tubers grow in a number of overlapping swathes: sorghum and millet, as well as chickpeas and cowpeas, stretch across the north from Mauritania to Somalia; the root crops (cassava and yams) run through humid equatorial areas from Guinea through Zaïre; and corn dominates in east and southern Africa from Kenya down to South Africa's Cape.

Compared with Asia's, neither African soils nor climate are widely adaptable to extensive wheat and rice cultivation. In most places Africa's old soils would need very heavy infusions of fertilizers, which farmers cannot now afford. (Africans now use about 1.5 percent of world fertilizers on about 10 percent of the world's arable land.) Moreover, very little land has been irrigated in Africa—about 2.7 percent (of which nearly half is in just one country, Sudan), versus around 30.8 percent in Asia. Where they have been tried, large-scale irrigation projects and big dams have proved highly costly and often of short-term usefulness. Kenya's Bura irrigation project has cost more than $12,000 per acre. In the Sahel, in the early 1980s where about

12,500 acres come under irrigation each year, the same amount of land goes out of production because of poorly managed irrigation systems.

Even in the American West, it took almost three decades to make irrigation work: a large-scale intervention of this sort demands the utmost care and understanding at every stage and every level—in planning, surveying, construction and maintenance. Officials, experts, and farmers all have to be committed, knowledgeable, and involved over the long haul. In Africa, unlike Asia, the knowledge and resources required are still in short supply. The continent's farmers will have to depend for moisture on rain and on small-scale irrigation for some time to come.

Thus the technology for an African Green Revolution is not, as it was in Asia, already on the shelf. Nor will the politics be as easy. When Asia's troubles mounted at the end of the 1950s, experts and governments agreed that intensive efforts should be poured into the most promising areas, which were quite easily identified. In Africa targeting is likely to be much more difficult. A lot of research must precede decisions about where success is most probable. After that national and ecological fragmentation will continue to limit choices.

⌒

Biology and politics have brought African agriculture to its present impasse; biology and politics will determine how—and whether—African leaders can stop the downhill slide. Until recently, African officials had every reason to view the costs of policies that bilked agriculture as negligible in relation to the enormous benefits. Not only did agricultural surpluses finance investments with a political payoff—in industry, education, and government salaries—but also pervasive state controls over inputs and marketing as well as foreign exchange and import licensing brought personal enrichment and enlarged patronage. Perversely, the greater the difficulties in obtaining or moving goods or money the greater the power wielded by those designated to allocate scarce commodities. Because liberating market forces would tie the hands of government officials who build compliance on patronage, economic and political rationality have often seemed directly at odds.

If the system had worked perfectly, Africa's food shortages would be even more severe: happily, food marketing boards have been able to control only about 10 to 30 percent of domestic trade in food; most food is sold for higher prices on the "parallel" unofficial markets. In Mali, for example, when the government set a price of 60 francs per kilo for rice that cost 83 francs for farmers to produce, most of the crop was privately spirited across the border into Senegal. Export crop producers have fewer choices, however; if they live near the border they may be able to smuggle it out, but often they must go through government channels to sell it abroad. What they earn then is the world market price for their produce minus the costs of the administering bureaucracy. The comparatively sharp decline in export crop production (in many places greater than in foodstuffs) during the 1970s corresponds to the rising costs levied by increasingly inefficient, sometimes corrupt, state corporations.

Now returns have diminished so far that political benefits are in jeopardy. Declining exports mean declining revenues—and patronage. Unless forestalled by food aid, food shortages lead to the high urban prices governments have sought anxiously to prevent. If the pie is not to disappear entirely, political and economic rationality will have to resemble each other much more closely.

Given the widespread excesses of state control in Africa, economic rationality right now does sound a lot like Adam Smith: cut back regulations and bureaucracies that stifle individual economic initiative and waste scarce resources—particularly inflated exchange rates, exploitive pricing of farm products, and licensing of imports and foreign exchange. Despite the cookie-cutter approach sometimes followed by the IMF, however, no one blueprint for "African policy reform" is appropriate for all. Different political, economic, and environmental circumstances in each country will dictate different priorities.

In addition, before they can expect policy reform to bring major leaps in agricultural output, African countries will have to build up their physical, technical, institutional, and human infrastructures greatly. Even more than prices, in Africa reliable delivery of inputs has been key to high yields. The cost of transporting food in Africa is extraordinarily high—typically double that in Asia. Getting fertilizers, seeds, and pesticides to the farmer at the right time demands working rural roads. More difficult, it requires middlemen and organizations—private or public—that serve the farmers' interests efficiently. Africa also lags far behind Asia and Latin America in trained scientific and managerial manpower. Building the technical base for agricultural takeoff will require 15 to 20 years. Western expertise and long-term donor commitment will be essential in carrying it through. As in Asia, enclaves of experts—many of them Westerners—will be needed for some time to come. But much more than in Asia, Africa's effort will have to involve local farmers at the earliest stages.

In great part, an African Green Revolution will have to be built from the ground up. For a number of reasons, small family farms are likely to continue to dominate African agriculture. Communal tenure will protect small farmers' land for some time to come. And for governments, the specter of increasing numbers of landless laborers reinforces support for traditional tenure systems. Fortunately, in this instance economic rationality is not at odds with social imperatives: small farms have proved more efficient than large combines under a variety of African circumstances—if they enjoy material support from government, or if they have effective private sales and distribution services.

Where research is concerned, because soils are fragile and because rainfall rather than large-scale irrigation will be the main source of moisture for some time to come, scientists should work now on farming practices that conserve soil and water, looking, as a priority, for inexpensive and easily maintained irrigation techniques. Improved seeds have to be sought for a variety of crops within widely differing climates. New tools and machines must be adapted both to seasonal labor shortages and hard-tilling tropical soils. Therefore, progress is likely to come at first from many small innovations, relying on detailed knowledge of the choices farmers make in extracting what they can from their fields under often difficult present conditions.

African farmers adopt changes readily when they see profit for themselves. A dry-seeded green bean developed at Uganda's Makere University in the 1960s (known as the "prostitute bean" because of its good looks) spread to southern Tanzania by the end of the 1970s without any government assistance—because it thrived and tasted good. Too often, however, farmers have been offered innovations that look good on paper or work somewhere else. When a World Bank adviser in a Kenyan village advocated a closer spacing of corn plants nearer to the surface, farmer Cleophas arap Moro planted an experimental plot with seeds close together at shallow depth. At night, however, field rats followed the rows and ate most of the shallow-planted seeds; later, heavy storms during Kenya's "long rains" period uprooted the rest. The bulk of his crop, nevertheless, which he had planted according to the older methods, came to fruition. Moro gave thanks that he had not followed the experts' advice over most of his acreage, graciously remarking: "They will eventually figure out how to increase our production, but more work has to be done." It is becoming clearer to all these experts that scientists will have to keep in close touch with individual farmers if their research is to bear fruit.

Some modest successes are occurring now. Building on traditional African systems, biologists at the International Institute for Tropical Agriculture in Ibadan, Nigeria, are working extensively on alleycropping as a means of arresting soil erosion. Crops such as corn, cowpeas, and yams are grown in four-yard-wide alleys separated by hedgerows of fast-growing trees or bushes, which can provide mulch, food for animals, stakes for climbing vines, and firewood. Another new anti-erosion measure, "no-till" cultivation, is being tried out in Nigeria and Ghana. Promoted as a labor-saving device, it encourages farmers to leave residues from the last crop on the fields, as they push seeds directly into the soil beneath with "jab planters."

More dramatic impacts on agricultural production may be expected only after several decades of research on high-yielding varieties. When improved seeds suitable for African environments become available, the sorts of leaps associated with the Asian Green Revolution may well be in the offing. And major technical innovations themselves can overcome obstacles within the broader system. After some 20 years of research, mostly in the colonial period, a high-yielding corn seed became available in Zimbabwe and Kenya in the early 1960s. With little effort at promotion or institutional development, people adopted it swiftly and widely, bringing new wealth and consequent major changes to the rural areas.

The only other innovation of this size was the improved oil palm also developed in the colonial period, in the Congo (Zaïre), and grown in Nigeria and Côte d'Ivoire as well. A bright possibility now, however, may be emerging with a new strain of hybrid sorghum in the Sudan. Developed by crossing seeds from Nigeria and Texas, the new variety has brought yields three times those of standard seeds on irrigated soils and almost five times those grown on dry land. In 1987 the sorghum harvest yielded an unprecedented surplus of a million tons over subsistence levels.

New government supports for farmers are also beginning to bear fruit. In Malawi, where the government formerly kept a large share of farm profits as an informal tax, higher prices and reduced taxes have caused cotton and corn production to soar. Kenyan corn production also rose by nearly 50 percent in 1985 when the government permitted artificially low prices to climb. Most strikingly in Zimbabwe, the government package of supports for small farmers has drawn a huge corn surplus from that nation's 8 million subsistence farmers for the first time since whites arrived and took most of the best land for themselves. In 1981, prices were raised, credit available to small farmers increased greatly, and depots for selling inputs and marketing grain were set up in the communal areas farmed by blacks. In the years since then, small farmers have increased their food production fifteen-fold (much faster than the white commercial farmers), raising their share of marketed corn from about 7 percent before Independence to around two-thirds in 1985. In one village in the country's fertile northeast, farmers brought 50,000 bags of corn to the depot in 1981, 270,000 in 1982, and in two drought years, 1983 and 1984, 390,000 and over half a million bags.

Even in sere Somalia, since 1982 higher prices and newly legal private marketing, as well as increased rainfall, have more than doubled sorghum and oil seed production. In addition the currency devaluations, combined with farm price increases, led to similar increases in corn and cotton production during the same period; corn output rose from 150,000 tons in 1982 to 350,000 in 1987 and fully supplied local needs for the first time in 10 years.

Zambia's experience, however, shows how hard it may be to sustain reforms that hit city dwellers in their most vulnerable area—their stomachs. Scarce foreign exchange cut imports of basic commodities: Zambians sometimes went for months without soap powder, cooking oil, or milk. After currency devaluations had cut urban incomes by around 50 percent, the removal of price controls on breakfast meal in late 1986 caused millers to concentrate on the production of that grain and to neglect roller meal, which is the staple food of most people. When, in the upshot, all cornmeal disappeared from store shelves, normally quiescent Zambian city dwellers were stirred to a violent protest in which 15 people were killed. The next day, President Kenneth Kaunda went on television and restored the controls, though declaring at the same time that the public was paying for them: the cost of subsidies would force cuts in some other part of the budget. In the aftermath, he nationalized the country's corn mills, and, in the spring of 1987 abruptly ended the far-reaching reform program undertaken over the preceding three years.

At the same time, harsh economic realities may in some cases, paradoxically, be giving hard-pressed governments assistance from an unexpected quarter—their own elites. In countries as diverse as West Africa's oil giant Nigeria and southern Africa's Zambia, some representatives of the rich and powerful are turning to agriculture as the surest source of wealth in a highly uncertain economic world. Since leaving power in 1979, Nigeria's former head of state General Olusegun Obasanjo has run an integrated group of four farms, raising chickens, feed, and a variety of other crops. At his main farm, between Lagos and his home area of Abeokuta, he roves about his acreage, fussing over incubators, holding impromptu seminars with workers, driving his Peugeot out to the corn stands, supervising the installation of a new separator at the feed mill. The general sold a bumper crop of chickens in 1986, and if Nigeria's structural adjustment program works, he expects his farms to grow and hopes move into export trade in the coming years.

On the other side of the continent, Zambia's Mark Chona, for many years President Kaunda's chief foreign policy adviser, has become an agribusinessman. From an office where Henry Kissinger and Peter Drucker share bookshelves with *Cattle World* and the *Elements of Accounts,*

Chona delegates most of the actual management of his 18,500-acre corn, vegetable, and cattle holdings to a trained agriculturalist and spends his time running marketing and freight companies. The political weight that each of these men—and others like them—can throw behind government reforms favoring farming is substantial.

More mundane are the strides being taken by ordinary farmers. In eastern Zimbabwe, about forty miles from Harare, extension worker Matthew Zende cycles back and forth across about 7 miles visiting hundreds of farm compounds; holding two-week in-service training courses on planting and cultivation of corn; organizing field days to demonstrate methods and rate produce. Expounding enthusiastically on the ideas he is trying to inculcate, he stresses energetic activity, saying "God, time, and money work together: if you want money, you must do it in time."

Sitting with a farm family in the sand before their conical cooking hut, Zende laments that the local ways discourage competition—rising higher than your neighbors creates envy. He tells, though, how he took a group of local farmers to visit the large irrigated land-holding of a young man who had risen above the rest. The rich young farmer, though only an elementary school graduate, had succeeded in amassing 80 acres of land, 550 pigs, 60 cows, a tennis court, a guest house, and "all the latest gadgets." The young man entertained the somewhat awed group all day and, as they were leaving offered to come visit them in return. Though all declined from shyness, afterward four of his visitors began to raise pigs and three others started to work on irrigation for their fields.

Speaking in English, which the farm family sitting around him could not understand, Zende also related proudly how the wife had passed the two-year master farmer course. Though her husband had for some time forbidden her to attend farmers' association meetings where Zende recruited for the course, eventually she came, joined, and excelled. Eighteen out of twenty of his master farmers, he recounted matter-of-factly, have been women.

In Mangaldié, in West Africa's Mali, a group of small farmers, through a process of trial and error, figured out how to make modern technology work for them. During the drought of the early 1980s, farmers in some dozen dusty villages on the treeless flood plain of the Niger delta banded together in order to build a dam. Using the mud, sticks, and stones they could find, they sought to catch the river's waters to use in irrigating their rice fields. When their dam burst they built another. When that was also washed away in 1984, they looked for outside help. In 1985, with $61,000 from the American private voluntary organization Oxfam and the technical assistance of a Malian engineer, they built two more dams—this time adding cement and iron reinforcing rods to the locally collected stone. In 1986 the villagers gathered the largest harvest in 30 years from their irrigated fields, and in 1987, when rains were less, the abundance was still attracting many new settlers to the area.

Clearly, the initiatives of all these Africans are limited by their national politics and local communities. But the relationship also works the other way. When the efforts of these peoples change their own lives, their societies will also change. In their learning process lies the best hope for Africa's future.

# 6

# A Learning Society

*The Dinka live in a world in which the dignity and survival of
the people depend largely on their effective participation in the
shaping and sharing of values as defined by global standards.*

Francis Mading Deng
*Tradition and Modernization*

*As long as you sleep on someone else's mat, you will never sleep
easy.*

Burkinabe Proverb

Where modern and traditional Africa intersect, every aspect of life seems to involve continuous tutelage. Mothers
bringing their babies for a checkup at a village clinic are
prepped about vitamins and protein, why sterile drinking
water will help keep their families healthy, how a dose of
water and salt can save the lives of babies with diarrhea.
Newspapers and radio offer daily lessons in how to dig a pit
latrine, accountancy for small businesses, running a meeting with Roberts' Rules of Order. Award ceremonies after a
race up and down Mt. Cameroon end with the planting of a
tree and a homily on the need for citizens to replenish
forests. Posters on the walls of a credit union office graphically illustrate the need for cooperation—as two goats on
one tether cannot reach the grass on either side because
they are pulling in opposite directions—and urge members
to "have a say in how your credit union runs!" Officers of a
women's self-help collective travel to the capital for a week-
long course in management techniques run by Church
World Services.

Scholars and would-be scholars are everywhere. In the
early morning, small boys and girls in patched white shorts

and dresses swarm down dirt roads and into long low structures of worn brick, cement, or thatch, where they open their throats wide to receive a lesson by yelling it back in unison. The smartest and luckiest of their older brothers and sisters crowd onto larger benches in somewhat sprucer structures often set in grassy "campuses," where they work and rework their way through worn texts and teachers' lecture notes.

Less visibly, almost everyone else who lacks the knowledge or credentials they need to move upward is trying to gain it through study. Thus education and the printing of texts or how-to manuals can be a good business. The casual academies that spring up in cities and towns frequently offer mainly hope to aspiring journalists, beauticians, accountants, or machinists, but nonetheless, at least initially they rarely lack for customers. A village school teacher, herself just out of elementary school, bicycles twenty miles every afternoon to and from a cram course for the teacher training exam. A farmer who cannot read her absent husband's letters enrolls in a basic literacy course given by a Peace Corps Volunteer. Other aspirants to upward mobility pore over self-help textbooks. When trade is slow, a sheet metal fabricator tries to master a primer on auto mechanics. Using a manual purchased in the local market, a Catholic catechist practices on the rectory's typewriter whenever he can, hoping for a clerk's job in a government office. A houseboy for a European family borrows their paperbacks to improve his English; he is also practicing algebra problems in preparation for another try at the secondary school certificate exam he failed five years before.

Since the white man first set out to administer Africa, education, with the riches and power it holds, has been the only passport to his world. From Independence onward, African nations have seen education as a main key to their own destinies. The revered teacher of Diallobe tradition in Kane's *Ambiguous Adventure* sadly counsels his people to enroll their children in the white men's school if they would save themselves, saying: "It is certain that their school is the better teacher of how to join wood to wood, and that men should learn how to construct dwelling houses that resist the weather." The father of the young hero agrees, reflecting: "It is certain that nothing pervades our lives with such clamour as the needs of which their school permits the satisfaction. We have nothing left—thanks to them—and it is thus that they hold us. He who wants to live, who wants to remain himself, must compromise."

Yet, the past several decades have shown that if Africans want to master the skills of the modern economy, setting up schools and universities is only the beginning. Besides learning the Western sciences that underlie economic life, Africans have to master the techniques of social organization that make them work—or devise their own ways of reaching the same end. For this they will need to meld their own culture with Western styles of work and production. Only if they can adapt imported institutions to their continent will Africans eventually be able to lift the psychological dependence which prevents escape from material dependence.

For better and for worse, Africa is firmly tied into the international communications network. Information and images flow at varying rates to African publics, depending on the receptivity and reach of their own (mostly government-controlled) radio, television, and newspapers. What happens in the West matters to African countries, and if the information is coming in Africans pay a lot more attention to news about and from Europe, America, and the socialist countries than the rest of the world does to them. On the day in early 1986 when the Philadephia police bombed a local neighborhood, cabdrivers in Nigeria expressed their amazement to American passengers. Again, in the summer of 1986, when the new Israeli ambassador to Cameroon went to a village deep in the interior rainforest, he met a man who heard him speak Hebrew and who realized he was from Israel. Greeting the ambassador, the villager asked him when Peres and Shamir would be changing jobs—and stated that he preferred Shamir because he was tougher on Qaddafi.

The dilemma of language exemplifies the painful cultural choices inherent in Africa's relationship with the West. Given some two thousand separate languages flourishing on the continent, the Tower of Babel might well have been sited there. Every African infant first learns one of these tribal languages. Only in ethnically homogeneous Somalia, Botswana, Lesotho, and Swaziland, however, does everyone start out with the same first language. Everywhere else, Africans have to learn at least one other language if they wish to communicate with most of their compatriots—much less with the outside world. In Tanzania and to a lesser extent in Kenya, the lingua franca is Swahili; in 21 countries it is French; in 14 English; in 5 Portuguese; in Ethiopia Amharic; in Sudan and the disputed territory of Sahara, Arabic; in Equatorial Guinea, Spanish. Only the Amharic people in Ethiopia had an alphabet and set down their words in writing before the missionaries arrived in the nineteenth century. Now all Africans have adopted either Roman or Arabic alphabet, with the Somalis holding out longest: unable to decide between the two, they approved an official orthography for Somali, using the Roman alphabet, only in 1970.

Not surprisingly, then, the spoken word was, and is, of primary importance throughout Africa's many ethnic cultures. Oratorical skills vary greatly, but Africans characteristically demonstrate a fascination and facility for using words and sounds that awe Western observers. History, cosmology, etiquette, scientific lore, and genealogy are passed down through eloquent speech and attentive memory. In his introduction to his transcription of an ancient Malian epic, Guinean novelist Camara Laye expanded upon the African "love of palaver and dialogue, the rhythm of talk, that love of speech that can keep the old men a whole month under the palaver tree settling some dispute." In many societies gifted speakers enjoyed special honor and authority. In Guinea and other areas of the upper Niger River, the "griot," historian and artist, was right hand to the king. Laye fervently renders homage to the ancient story-teller who was his source:

> We knew well that his wisdom and knowledge reached to the very boundaries of Malinke exis-tence; to the vast plain of the Malinke people, to its savanna, the most beautiful of all savannas, a savanna park; extended to its great river, to all that inhabits that plain's level distances, the all-powerful Djeliba River and the very sky itself; his wisdom extended to its animals and trees and plants, as his knowledge did to all its men, and to the ancestors as well; to the heavens, and to God also!

Because languages vary greatly in their ability to ex-press different meanings, choosing a European language over your African tongue means changing the way you think or even, perhaps, what you think about and feel. Students in a Nigerian secondary school said their lan-guages were more concrete than English: where an analyst might, for example, say in English that "U.S. policy is domi-nated by anti-Sovietism," a translation from Nigeria's Yoruba language might express the same idea by saying "the United States always has to cast its eye on what the Soviets are doing." On the other hand, they felt they had to switch to English—even in their minds—to formulate philo-sophical ideas. Senegal's first president, poet Leopold Senghor, executed an 180-degree volte face on the choice between European and indigenous languages, maintaining during the 1930s and 1940s that only African languages could capture the continent's soul, but arguing after Independence that French should be the national lan-guage, and that Africans could help make the Gallic tongue truly universal by developing it to its fullest range. A former

171

vice president of Zambia, Simon Kapwepwe, on the other hand, expressed the contrary conviction very vehemently in 1969:

> We should stop teaching children through English right from the start because it is the surest way of imparting inferiority complex in the children and the society. It is poisonous. It is the surest way of killing African personality and African culture.

Again, Jomo Kenyatta, in his first speech to parliament as Kenya's president in 1964 (given in English), ended with a few words in Swahili, saying: "Now that we have full independence we don't have to be slaves of foreign languages in our affairs. . . . " In fact, the use of Swahili (which is derived from Arabic and African tongues) gives rise to poetry in everyday discourse as neither English nor French are likely to: in Tanzania, people write letters to the editor of the Swahili newpaper in verse, which they would never dream of doing for the English-language *Nation* or *Standard*.

Tanzania chose Swahili as its official language in 1973, opting for a local language traditionally spoken all along the East African coast rather than the English or German of its colonial past. That meant switching from English to Swahili for most elementary school instruction and a good many secondary school subjects as well—and producing texts in the new lingua franca. All government business is conducted in Swahili, and Tanzania Radio has largely followed suit. There is some doubt about how widely the language is spoken inland, but none at all about the effect of the new regime on the use of English: now that literacy no longer implies command of the Western tongue, the general level of national competence in English has declined noticeably. Like other reforms he instituted, former President Nyerere considered the adoption of Swahili an investment in the future, in the long-term self-reliance of his people and possibly the unity of East Africa as well. One unintended effect, however, may be to create a class distinction that did not exist before, between English-speakers, who can do business with the world outside Tanzania, and the rest of their compatriots.

Only if the other East African countries followed Tanzania's lead might Nyerere's goals have a real chance of being achieved. In Kenya, where Swahili did not penetrate far inland from the coast before the arrival of the Europeans (as it had in Tanzania), embrace of the regional language has been merely half-hearted. One day in 1974, the language of parliamentary debate changed rather abruptly from English to Swahili, giving members of parliament from the coastal area an immediate oratorical advantage and silencing many others, at least temporarily. All official government papers are now published in both languages, but schools have gone on much as before, with most instruction in English and only occasional lessons in Swahili. Although perhaps 50 percent of Kenyans have some command of Swahili, it has traditionally had the low status of a tongue largely used for addressing servants. What is happening in effect is that English remains the language of power and privilege, while politicians declare Swahili's superior virtues.

For their part, Ugandans' level of competence in Swahili is even lower than that of Kenyans; moreover, their country has been too busy with internal military convulsions to pay much attention to linguistic revolutions. If all three members of the former East African community followed Tanzania's thorough-going approach, however, a block of some sixty million people would be linguistically united.

With its approximately hundred million people, Nigeria includes within its own borders all the language problems that afflict the whole continent. First of all, language cements the divisions among more than four hundred separate ethnic groups and particularly the three main tribes—the forty million Hausa in the north, twenty

173

million Yoruba in the Southwest, and ten million Ibos in the southeast. Spoken by millions of other people in countries adjacent to northern Nigeria, Hausa has been likened to Swahili as a possible lingua franca for West Africa; foremost among likely violent opponents of such a proposal, however, would be the Nigerian Hausa's southern countrymen.

For this reason no serious effort to depose English as Nigeria's national language is likely. Only a small elite use it for everyday communication—most ordinary transactions take place either in one of the three main languages or in pidgin-English (a saucy-sounding mix of English, Portuguese and various African vernaculars), while people speak their own ethnic tongues at home. Yet, after the first few weeks of school, English is the primary language of education. Thus children grapple with basic tools of alphabet and numbers for the first time while also trying to swim in a new and alien linguistic element. Their confusion is compounded by the poor English of many of their teachers—a good number of whom were recruited to elementary teaching after failing the West African School Certificate Exam, probably because they couldn't write understandably in English. The weaknesses continue to dog students as they climb the educational ladder: even the most talented who make it to one of the country's nineteen universities filter their training through the distorting lens of a language they only partially comprehend. A visiting examiner at one of Nigeria's top universities reported sadly, on marking student papers: "I often have to give credit not for what the student says, but for what I think he would have said if he knew how." When those who survive this experience are ensconced in the country's civil service, military or business—all run in English—their difficulty in understanding one another in that language slows things down considerably.

Problems in Nigeria's school system, most dramatically signaled by faltering mastery of English, seem inevitable given the approximately fourfold increase in elementary and secondary enrollment since 1970. In many ways, Africa's schools acutely reflect the continent's growing pains. The extraordinary expansion of education since Independence is the proudest achievement of many African governments. In delivering new schools, they have responded to the only insistent demand placed upon them by the mass of their people. Now, as everywhere else, they are having trouble paying the bills.

When the colonial governors decamped, only one-third of the relevant age-group were in elementary school, less than 3 percent in secondary school, and a minute fraction in the few colleges and universities that then existed on the continent. From that small base, total enrollments have increased fivefold, and they tripled between 1970 and 1983 (growing at twice the rate for Asia and three times that for Latin America). Elementary schooling is now virtually universal in many countries, and secondary schools have grown on average by about six or seven times, reaching about 20 percent of the relevant age-group today. Further, most African countries now have at least one national university, and the continent's total is up from 6 in 1960 to 80 today—with enrollment increasing by 14 percent annually. (Even with this growth only about 1 percent of the post-secondary age group reaches the university.)

African educators have also worked to transform school curricula imbued with European content and ethos into approaches appropriate to Africa. The glories of Britain and France throughout the ages have been subsumed into the sweep of world history: students who formerly would have struggled with the intricacies of Disraeli's diplomacy now consider the workings of European imperialism in Africa instead. At the same time, the expatriates who staffed and ran secondary education have given way almost entirely to Africans trained to take their places. As Africans themselves raised to revere classical education try to grapple with their nations' current needs, basic agricultural and technical know-how, adult education and literacy courses have gained increasing priority. In most countries, the enrollment of girls has risen from very low pre-Independence levels to half that of boys in elementary school and about 15 percent of secondary students.

In the past few years, however, these gains have been directly threatened. First of all, as Nigeria's situation shows, the pace of expansion has greatly strained available teaching and management skills. Second, in the grip of economic crisis, African economies can no longer sustain current systems—much less expand to accommodate the increasing numbers of children now reaching school age. From 1981 to 1983, elementary school enrollment in fact declined in twelve African countries. Spending also fell—except for teachers' salaries. Consequently, many of Africa's elementary, and some secondary, schools are being progressively hollowed out, as teachers without chalk, blackboards, maps, or charts face huge classes—often of one hundred students—without desks, chairs, paper, or books.

The question of resources is basic to the dilemmas of African education today. Beyond the support of schools themselves, however, African educators also face troubling questions about how well the existing education systems foster viable African economies. Looking at the workings of African bureaucracies, it is evident that schools in independent Africa have not dislodged the colonially implanted link between education and credentials for advancement. As in colonial days, education is still in most people's minds tightly linked to employment. Several decades ago, an elementary school certificate was considered a promise of a job. As more and more graduates emerged from secondary school, and then universities, lower school credentials lost their value. Nonetheless, schooling is still regarded chiefly as a ladder: you climb to one level so you can gain access to the next. Therefore, the purpose of elementary school is to prepare for the exams that open the way to secondary school.

In fact, only about half of African youth complete the seven years of elementary school, and less than 25 percent continue on to any kind of secondary training. Most of the rest of the elementary "school leavers" are left to earn their keep in agriculture or small-scale rural enterprises. How far their education has prepared them for productive lives as farmers is in some doubt. Secondary "school leavers," on the other hand, are in many cases alienated from rural life. Most of the time, they make their way to the city to seek a job, living in the meantime off the kindness of relatives.

Throughout the educational system, credentialism drives both purveyors and customers. Educators plan the curriculum around conditioning students to answer exam questions correctly. While the discipline of an exam can be used to inculcate basic skills, it can also lead to rote-teaching of canned material. A number of U.S. Peace Corps volunteers found to their chagrin that their African students resisted efforts to reason out answers together: students were used to their teachers' writing out sample problems—and solutions—on the blackboard for them to copy and memorize. With anything less concrete they felt short-changed.

Credentialism also shapes attitudes toward work. In effect, the value of the certificate is based on the level of access it affords rather than the training it requires. A typical water inspector, for example, probably has no intention of making his career amid the taps and pipes of the city, but hopes to move into a desk job in the ministry, and then perhaps to a more lucrative spot in, say, the light and power parastatal. Thus his interest in applying the skills and information he studied to grasp and to master the job itself may not be very keen.

The same interchangeability of parts often prevails at the top of the heap as well: a number of Africa's pre-Independence nationalist politicians were trained as medical doctors; again, after a cabinet shuffle finance ministers take over at public works, and foreign ministers move on to natural resources without missing a beat. Yet the effect on attitudes throughout the system is to shove most of the responsibility—and the work—up to the top officials. Senior bureaucrats in overstaffed ministries complain that there are no functioning middle-level personnel—"nobody between us and the drivers." Apart from the overriding concern with credentials, lack of supervision and supplies in overcrowded bureaus further weakens motivation among lower professional cadres as well as clerks. (If you can find a chair to sit in, your job is secure, no need to worry about a desk.) Problems in using European languages have also curtailed written output at this level and reinforced a trend toward oral decision-making flowing from the top. Thus provincial officials must spend a lot of time at headquarters, and ministry officials must travel in the field if anything is to get done.

Improving the training capability of African countries is a priority of Western donors. The question is how—and how much: what portion of African budgets should go to education, and how should resources be allocated among elementary, secondary and university levels? African governments often devote as much as 20 percent of annual budgets to education, and most experts would not have them spend less. Because the expansion of schools, with their still-implicit promise of employment, is so important to their publics, African governments are likely to resist overt tampering with the ideal of universal education. Nonetheless, everyone agrees that money is running out and quality is running down. Although donors are now beginning to contribute to annual running costs of schools, most Western analysts and many Africans see no economic alternative to parents and students paying a greater share.

In universities, costs per student are very high. At Independence, governments aimed to foster equity by granting free tuition as well as ample living allowances to those who made it to the university. Now, however, the cost per university student—around $3,000—is 8 times that in Asia and double that in Latin America. Probably because universities respond to the same employment pressures as government bureaucracies, the student-teacher ratio is 7 to 1, versus 12 or 15 to 1 in Europe and the United States. While continuing scholarships, governments may have no choice but to increase the share paid by students (many of whom are now children of the new middle class), and also to cut back the sizable subsidies on the secondary level. In addition, schools are now experimenting with productive activities, particularly farming, to improve diets and save on food costs. Most analysts agree that elementary schools need all the money that can be saved at the upper levels, and more. Double shifts (which would bring teachers' hours in line with other civil service jobs)—or "hotseating" as it is called in Zimbabwe—would help make places for more students without increasing already disproportionate salary costs.

Neither African nor Western analysts have found satisfying answers to the larger resource question—how to make education better serve the economic needs of African countries. Transferring more of the costs from the state to the individual will go part of the way toward bringing private calculations of the costs and benefits of education in line with its value to society. But credentialism—and the demand it creates—will persist as long as government pay differentials are tied to rigid qualifications. Given the personal interest of civil servants in the way it works now, credentialism would be very hard for political leaders to change once they decided to.

More support exists for a radical shift in elementary schools to stress the skills needed by the majority—who will leave and become self-employed—over preparation for the secondary school exam. Vocational education is not a new idea in Africa: it was also popular with colonial administrators. However, no one has come up with a very good notion of how to do it well: both at elementary and secondary levels it has proved so far comparatively costly and not very effective in teaching usable skills.

Should certificate exams themselves be scrapped? Despite the obvious logic of removing credentialism by eliminating the credential, African educators argue strongly that exams will be needed for some time to spur effort and maintain standards. They can be used, however, to teach skills that schools deem more relevant to most of their pupils' lives as well as to select the elite who will proceed farther up the ladder. They can also be used to diagnose weaknesses in students' mastery.

Apart from the resource crunch, Africa's educational dilemmas about the usefulness—and universality—of elementary and secondary education are pretty deeply rooted in local economic and bureaucratic culture. Thus, apart from possible emergency financial aid for running expenses, donors would probably be wisest to stay on the sidelines. On the university level, however, Western skills and commitment seem urgently needed. Compared with those of Europe or Japan (and less so the United States), Africa's universities were built in great haste. Tradition is coextensive with time: if the new academies are to acquire the tradition of high-level study and research needed to support self-reliant intellectual development, they will need technical, financial and moral support. Confronting dependency straightforwardly here, it seems clear that the transfer of knowledge largely derived from the West can benefit from immediate Western participation.

Thus, despite the poor record of direct interventions within African bureaucracies, African universities and research institutions will not be able to get along without donor-supported "enclaves" for some time to come. Clearly, donors' institutional improvisations will continue to work only as long as their creators are tending them carefully; Africans ultimately will have to come to grips with the institutional problems that plague research systems because these malfunctions are rooted in the local political and social order. But Western help in training the critical mass of Africans that will be able to change their country's intellectual and institutional climate is urgently needed in order to establish African centers of excellence—particularly in agriculture.

An initiative in agriculture is long overdue. During the 1960s, AID, the World Bank, and private foundations invested heavily in elementary, secondary, and university education. In higher education, both governments and donors aimed first and foremost at Africanization of the civil service. In accord with the traditions of the former colonial powers, arts and the law were the accepted training ground for the new African elites. The need was clear: at Independence the civil service even in a highly favored colony like Senegal was dominated by 1,500 Frenchmen. The University of Dakar was soon turning out first-class liberal arts graduates in droves. Not until 1979, however, (nineteen years after Independence), did Senegal set up a university-level school of agriculture.

The donors were no swifter on the uptake. Around 1970, as we have seen, marching to the new drumbeat of Basic Human Needs and designs for Integrated Rural Development, most of them withdrew from the business of formal education almost entirely. Since then, U.S. AID and the World Bank have allotted only a minuscule portion of their worldwide assistance for education to Africa. Most of agriculture's share in that has supported postgraduate study in America and Europe.

Now that Africa's agrarian crisis has been the focus of people's minds, technical—and particularly agricultural—training has come to the fore. After nearly three decades of Independence, Africa lags far behind the rest of the Third World by every measure of human resources: literacy, portion of population in secondary school or university, percentage of scientific, managerial and academic positions held by expatriates. Much of the continent's technical capa-

181

bility is still in expatriate hands. In the Côte d'Ivoire, there is 1 Frenchman for every 160 Ivoirians; Kenya, twenty-two years after Independence, still depends on a large team of foreign economic advisers, a number of them provided by Harvard University's Institute of International Development. In 1984, 26 percent of all professionals in agricultural research, extension, and university education in the nine member countries of the Southern Africa Development Coordination Conference (SADCC) were expatriates.

Overseas training often gives students excellent skills and exposure to mainstream research in their fields. It may not prepare them to work on their own continent, however. Unless they carry out their main thesis research in Africa on local agronomy, horticulture, or range management—as few African agricultural students in Europe or America have chosen to do—what they learn in the temperate, high-tech climes of Michigan State or Reading may not prepare them very well for the rain-fed small farms of their native lands. Moreover, only when research on Africa is rooted in the continent will Africans experience the home-grown symbiosis between ideas and institutions that must sustain self-reliant development.

A good deal of donor effort over the next several decades will undoubtedly go into strengthening African university training of scientists and managers. In 1986 AID set in motion a 10-to 20-year plan to strengthen agricultural research services and university departments of agriculture in Africa. Within that effort, Africa's pressing need is for doctoral-level training, with all dissertation research carried out in Africa. Viable institutions with strong local roots seem most likely to emerge where there are local scholars and researchers who will benefit from them.

৵

Formal education is of course only part of the learning process needed to support growing productivity. Exposure of Africans to Western public administration or business curricula, for example, though a valuable stimulus to thought, will not solve African management problems. Sharpening African technical skills is an absolutely essential first step, and familiarity with how organizations work in other societies undoubtedly provides a starting point. Yet, in the long run, the success of African officials or entrepreneurs in running their bureaus or industries will also depend on their ability to rise above the immediate demands of their economic culture. To make organizations productive they will have to challenge and adapt the rules underlying their entire society.

These rules, stemming from ethnic ties, shape the economic behavior of most Africans today. Apart from their effect on government they also determine how individuals invest and how work is organized. The link between wealth and kinship was cemented in colonial times: with the state's largesse as a kind of El Dorado, ethnic groups closed ranks to secure their share. The effect of this magnetic attraction for individual and group initiative was to strengthen styles of leadership and cooperation that already existed within ethnic groups. Within this system, patronage rather than productivity ruled economic decision-making.

A careful study by economist Sara S. Berry of Yoruba cocoa farmers, teachers, and mechanics in two towns in southern Nigeria shows how these styles have shaped their choice of investments and the way they run the businesses they do invest in. Because their lien on wealthier kin provides their main opportunities—particularly for access to state resources—they sink much of their surplus income into strengthening kinship ties. They are thereby diversifying their investment portfolios.

Education is the ticket to a state job, and consequently, through your support of children and relatives, the main chance to tap into the mother lode. Beyond that, the dues to be paid expand with your means: the system of exactions is as complicated as your extended relationships with family and friends. Celebrating nuptials, mourning the departed, taking a chiefly title, honoring a friend's chieftiancy, helping build a new palace for the Oba, building your own palatial home in the village, subscribing to your village union's welfare fund, paying respects to your cousin who is a public works official—are both obligations and investments. For people (like most Africans) whose income is always uncertain, patronage offers a way of diversifying risks and increasing opportunities. What you've put in should come flowing back to you in the form of jobs, scholarships, emergency aid, or shelter when needed by you or your children.

Not much is left, however, for upgrading your coffee trees or expanding your repair shop. Nor, on a national scale, do Nigerians or other Africans with surplus income invest very much of what they earn or take off the top in local profit-making enterprises. Those with big money spend some on real estate, put a good deal into consolidating their access and influence, and send the rest out of the country. In terms of economic rationality it makes sense: for the most part, investing in Africa is not a very good risk— for Africans any more than for foreign private companies.

Previously, African states depended on foreign capital for around 50 to 60 percent of investments—and the least developed countries for as much as 80 to 100 percent. As we have seen, African debt and the international downturn cut back investment flows. Now that African economies will have to depend much more than before on domestic sources of investment, the heavy risks arising from both policy and economic behavior can no longer be sidestepped. Since Independence, government policies reinforcing the distortions wrought by patronage have made profit-making enterprises very chancy in many countries. But in addition, the influence of patronage on the organization of work has also made it difficult to run businesses efficiently.

The operating style of a Yoruba mechanic in southern Nigeria depicted by Berry gives one example of how this can work. When the mechanic succeeds in building up his clientele and needs to take on help, he will rarely hire another trained mechanic: wages are too high; his own receipts are likely to be irregular; and the demands on whatever surplus he may have put by are already great. Instead, he will procure the services of relatively untrained workers through reciprocal obligations, which in West Africa takes the form of apprenticeship. Thus, he will bring in one or more apprentices, who will contract to stay with him for two to five years, learning his craft in exchange for their labor and a modest fee.

Under the terms of this relationship, as under traditional patronage obligations, the apprentice owes his master loyalty and obedience—but not efficiency. For most of his tenure, the apprentice is not skilled enough to take responsibility for customers' property, and the mechanic is unable to delegate authority to him. When the boss is away, the apprentices may well be found buying peanuts from a passing vendor, cooking lunch, swapping tales with fellow apprentices or the blacksmiths next door, washing clothes, or merely waiting for someone in authority to take charge. Though to Western eyes this looks like laziness or malingering, both apprentices and master accept the fact that very little work will get done unless the latter himself is present.

Expanding the firm, on the other hand, depends on the proprietor's spending a lot of time away from the shop. Like everything else within this system, success flows from personally cultivating good relations with customers, suppliers, creditors and bureaucrats. While the owner is bringing in more business, current repairs are grinding to a halt. So the demands of efficiency and expansion run directly counter to each other.

In bigger enterprises, the organizational problems are obviously somewhat different, but attitudes of both workers and bosses about work, incentives, and responsibility flow from the same sources. Where personal relations rather than output are widely accepted as the main determinant of success, both the quality and efficiency of production will depend on close supervision. For the chain of command to operate effectively, however, it has to be driven by a concern for profits or quality. Again, that will usually require constant oversight by the owner himself.

∽

Can expatriates intervene positively in what is essentially an African cultural dilemma? Proponents of capitalism have often touted foreign private investment as a valuable leavening force within African economies, inoculating Africans with technological know-how and the virus of free enterprise, while turning a smart profit for them at the same time. Alas, it has too seldom worked out that way. International contractors oversold export opportunities and delivered shoddy and obsolete machinery; African officials took exorbitant cuts and changed the rules in midstream. For investors the uncertainty of the legal environment, where regulations seemed to proliferate around them, has probably been the greatest disincentive. To compensate for the risks they demanded special concessions to ensure high short-term profits.

Along the way, what flourished most luxuriantly was not the enterprises in question but rather the opportunism of their principals—both Western and African. The interaction helped nourish the climate of "buccaneer capitalism" in which many Africans learned the ground rules for modern business. While production and sales often languished, those alert to opportunities learned much from their Western counterparts about working the system and cutting into lucrative deals.

Not surprisingly, eventual balance sheets recorded a high quotient of disillusionment on both sides. In the 1970s, governments aiming at "Africanizing" their economies bought out foreign corporations when they could afford to and enacted laws to curb their activities when they could not. Between 1970 and 1980 foreign private investment grew half again as fast in all developing countries as in Africa. By the beginning of the 1980s, growth in foreign investment had trickled to a virtual halt—except in mining and oil—throughout most of the continent.

Since Africans will have to learn how enterprises work from the rest of the world, this seems unfortunate. As American employees of Japanese corporations realize, well-run foreign private firms are the best schools for teaching managers about other economic cultures and technology. A Nigerian pharmacist at the Lagos branch of Pfizer International, for example, is taught how to gauge the potential sales for a new pain remedy that his department will produce and distribute, but more importantly, he absorbs the idea that market research is basic to planning for new products. A Kenyan senior accountant at the Nairobi office of Barclays Bank goes to the Great Britain for a special course in programming bank ledgers so he can help install a new computerized system for recording deposits and withdrawals; in London he spends more than a month looking over the shoulder of a branch manager, watching her close supervision of the clerks and tellers manning the new system. A Zambian economist working in the Lusaka office of the Equator merchant bank of Hartford joins two American colleagues in marathon twelve-hour days devoted to developing a plan for restructuring Zambia's largest parastatal—and through extraordinarily painstaking effort snagging the contract from much larger rivals.

Like the West African apprentice, these professionals get a big head start in understanding what they have read in university texts about productivity in modern enterprise: the combination of zeal for profits; for getting there first with the most; and of systems for enlisting workers to fulfill these goals. Whether or not Africans eventually organize their enterprises along these lines, they need to see at first-hand the peculiar cultures capitalists have evolved to make their businesses grow and profit. If the multinational

branch affiliate is itself efficiently run, African professionals can experience the impersonal goad of the bottom line
and the more personal rewards for the quality of their
contribution.

In the last decade, as foreign equity participation in
African economies has fallen off, other kinds of contractual
arrangements involving expatriates in African economies
have been on the increase, including leasing, licensing,
management service, and production-sharing contracts. As
parastatals have failed, some African governments have
also brought in expatriates to whip them back into shape.
Not only their skills but also their insulation from local
politics gives these hired guns an edge over many of their
African counterparts.

In Zambia, for example, a Scottish plant manager was
brought in several years ago to run a heavily indebted
government oil extraction plant. After six months on the
job, he was happily reporting, in a nearly impenetrable
burr, that the operation had broken out of a long spiral of
deterioration by fabricating its own parts to end bottlenecks
in oil and margarine assembly lines, and had already turned
a profit. As the pale oil funneled into clear bottles and the
whipped gold margarine poured into plastic bags, his Zambian workers labored with seeming enthusiasm. Proud of
their energy and skill, the Scotsman bustled among his
"lads" with the euphoria of a green expatriate but also the
practical know-how of his twenty years experience in
Glasgow and Liverpool.

For African states, the return of expatriate managers
represents both an assertion of government control over the
country's economic fate and a retreat from self-reliance.
While staunching the flow of red ink that threatened to
bankrupt parastatal coffers, the appointment of the Scotsman inevitably reinforced the notion that had bolstered the
authority of the colonial administrators and never quite
disppeared even though most of them did: only Europeans
can run things. Yet in the case of that oil extraction enter-

prise, the Zambian government was realistically drawing on its twenty years of experience since Independence to seize whatever opportunities it could. Today the expatriate is no longer the master but rather the hired hand—all the decisions about how to invest the proceeds of his labor rest with his African bosses. Whether or not the Scotsman's personal enthusiasm carried far enough to institutionalize the systems that worked for him, the best training for future Zambian executives can be found within an efficiently run operation, whether it be headed by a Scot, Zambian, East German, Indian, or Ghanaian.

As Africans gradually gain experience, will entrepreneurship just emerge like spontaneous combustion? Within their various diverse cultures, Africans as people are not slow to seize economic opportunities. Particularly in West Africa, trading enterprises—often operating over long distances, from the coast across the Sahara—have been thriving since before the time of Mohammed. Today much of West Africa's trade in foodstuffs, cloth, and a wide range of consumer goods is controlled by a formidable group of women traders. Wrapped in yards of colorful and stylishly tailored cloth, they preside majestically over the sprawling markets of the seacoast and river cities, selling almost anything you might dream of from rude thatch or concrete stalls. (Rumor has it that in the enormous Aba market in eastern Nigeria the traders do have their limits—if you want a 747 you have to order ahead.)

Apart from family obligations, Africa's merchants reinvest often sizable wealth in enlarging their stock and extending their reach. In real estate as well, Africans use their money to make money. Almost everywhere, apartments and houses in the cities command high rents from the diplomatic and foreign business communities: most officials, businessmen, or large-scale traders are also landlords. Industry, however, except on a very small scale, has been financed almost entirely by governments or foreign patrons. This is undoubtedly one main key to its widespread failure.

The most likely incubators for industrial entrepreneurship seem, in fact, the businesses employing fifty or fewer people, set up with modest cash stakes to offer services and fabricate light consumer goods in cities and farm areas throughout the continent. These enterprises supply most of the clothing worn in a country like Nigeria, as well as furniture, metal goods, prepared foods, and beer. They also repair almost anything—keeping cars, bicycles, and shoes on the road, and electrical appliances wired together. Most are diminutive—almost half consist of one individual, and 95 percent employ fewer than five people. Nonetheless, they provide two-thirds of the industrial employment in Africa, consistently generating more jobs in relation to capital invested than larger firms.

These small, privately owned businesses also operate significantly more efficiently than their larger counterparts. Seemingly, this is true for several reasons: they are highly labor-intensive in an environment where labor is abundant; at small scale, management is much less complicated; and, perhaps most importantly, less than 5 percent of the capital in these firms comes from government or bank loans: where personal funds are at stake, proprietors appear to keep close tabs on the books. For whatever reason, these businesses get higher rates of return on the money invested than those on a larger scale; they also succeed where major enterprises in Africa often fail—in adding to the value of the materials used in manufacturing processes. Something of how this works can be glimpsed in several enterprises created by small-scale African entrepreneurs.

Ruben Angwafor, a tailor in Bamenda in western Cameroon, has been working out of one tiny room in a poor residential neighborhood for the past 15 years. Side by side with a printer, a photographer, and a store selling softdrinks, cigarettes, and canned goods, his shop opens wide to the street on one side. The tailor sits at his sewing machine where the front wall would be, looking up to greet customers as they scramble across the gutter on wooden

190

planks and up his front stoop. Inside, a young girl, a boy, and an older woman crouch before battered old Singers, stitching up a consignment of pale muslin slipcovers for a local furniture factory. Angwafor himself stops work to look at the blouse and wrapper-style skirt his customer has brought as a pattern for the outfit she wants him to make out of a bolt of orange cloth stamped with green and yellow swans. Similar blouses in crisp prints, eyelet, heavy pale cottons, with wrappers folded underneath, hang with school uniforms, men's shorts, laces, ribbons, and silken braid from pegs on the walls.

Angwafor is well known and business is brisk. Counting the cash in his Cadbury's cookie tin before closing at 7 p.m., he totals $40 for the day. Over the years he has expanded his equipment from one to five machines (one for back-up when others break down) and hired an experienced seamstress as well as two apprentices to help with the growing volume. Regular customers include the furniture factory and two of the town's hotels. Working ten hours a day except on Sundays, he has recouped his original investment many times and saved enough to buy the building he works and lives in, after sending most of his seven children to secondary school and two sons to university.

After more than twenty years drying and selling fish caught by her husband and other men in their seacoast village in Senegal, Martha Diop went into business when her last child was weaned six years ago. Her original stake of $50, borrowed from her husband and brother, went to purchase her first stock of fish and a cylindrical drying oven. Her early profits, after selling the dried fish to a trader from Dakar, were meager, barely enough to feed and clothe her family. Eventually, however, (after three years) she was able to repay the original loan, and then, at intervals of several years, to buy four more ovens, which she rented to other women. When she decided to set up her own processing enterprise, she built a pole and thatch shed near the shore where the fishermen unloaded their catch from dugout canoes, and enlisted help from other women in return for use of her spare ovens. Except when the guardian spirit of the seas withholds the men's catch, her current profits often reach $125 a month. Her contributions to the schooling of her kin have made Diop influential in her family, and now she is planning to hire her sister to manage the ovens so she can travel in a lorry to sell the fish in the market at Dakar.

Kabiru Kamau recently moved his metalworking shop from the outskirts of Kenya's capital, Nairobi, to the industrial park near the center of the city. Now he has space to expand his repair and metal pressing enterprises into the manufacture of gray metal cabinets and typewriter tables. Borrowing cash from his brother in the postal service and from a moneylender, he has purchased two secondhand presses and a metal lathe. He has also hired away a former employee of the Asian tool and dye works company that has dominated the fabrication of this sort of furniture locally for the last twenty years. Kamau and his six employees rattle around a bit in the front of a shed that could accommodate triple their number. Shaping, welding, and painting the cabinets to a uniform standard still involves a lot of trial and error, and Kamau cannot afford many mistakes. For a while all his receipts will go into expenses. If his new foreman can keep production humming while he is out lining up orders from the postal service and other government bureaus, however, he should be solidly established in another year.

Looking at these small businesses, we see much that is familiar: hard work, thrift, ambition. Horatio Alger would have felt right at home. The question now is what it would take to make this ingenuity and drive effective in larger enterprises. Might Ruben's or Ngugi's son or daughter expand their parents' shops into a shirt or furniture factory? It seems likely they will not choose to do so as long as jobs in the government or with international companies offer more money and greater security, and while investment in real estate, importing, deal-making, or foreign opportunities is more profitable.

つ

Governments committed to the hard choices underlying growth could go a long way toward making entrepreneurship happen by altering the opportunity structure to
make it a viable alternative. This would mean, first of all,
adopting policies that encourage savings, investment, and
exports. To a great extent these are the same measures that
seem most likely to stimulate agriculture as well—bringing
exchange rates in line with international values, eliminating
complicated licensing and other regulations. Productive industrial investments, however, will also require raising interest rates considerably. The effect of cheap credit policies
followed by most governments has been to discourage savings and dry up wellsprings of capital while at the same time
leading to a profligate use of cheap money. Extending women's access to credit also seems likely to pay off significantly. Apart from the kinds of discrimination already described, the entrepreneurial women who dominate much of
Africa's domestic commerce face direct competition from
the various state trading companies and retail outlets that
monopolize most available resources while operating at a
loss.

Looking at the investment climate more broadly, it
seems very clear, at least to Western observers, that governments desperate for capital to invest need to create an
environment of stability for both foreign and domestic investment. In some African countries today, following the
abrupt changes in rules and procedures for carrying on
business and trade requires a local guide with the skill and
stamina of a Nepalese Ghurka: in a country like Nigeria,
savvy professionals make their living doing it full time.
Where shifting rules of the game may change rates of
return in midstream, few investors will be willing to take the
risk. If private money and energy is to help spur growth,
governments and private individuals will have to evolve a

commonly shared set of business practices that will provide a basis for mutual trust. This climate of trust between individuals not linked by blood or feudal ties but rather by common economic interests was basic in the emergence of the unfettered Western growth accompanying the ripening of capitalism. Unless they opt for pervasive state control—and find the means to make it work—Africans now have to do in a relatively short time what Europeans took several centuries gradually to accomplish: develop business codes that reinforce legal codes of behavior. Only in a climate of trust based on the viability of contracts between economic partners will the primacy of patronage over productivity be broken.

Policy changes that release private economic initiative and reduce state interventions may also, in the long run, mitigate some negative effects inherent in weak government accountability. First of all, separating economic institutions from the state could reduce occasions for corruption as state controls over allocation of economic opportunities diminish. Second, as the profit motive sharpens, proprietors may begin to give concern for efficiency a greater edge over patronage in decisions about the management of their enterprises. Achieving this sort of cultural change in time to matter (that is, soon) would seem to require the chicken and egg to emerge at the same time: with the rewards for productivity rising as the acceptability of corruption falls. Currently contented fat cats may be expected to resist this sort of change with great energy and resourcefulness for some time to come. What remains to be seen is how strong countervailing pressures already evident in many places may become.

Aspiring industrial entrepreneurs in Africa today are to some extent playing the role of missionaries. Chief Michael Ibru is an early example of what may be a new breed. The son of a Nigerian civil servant in the colonial administration, he grew up in relative privilege. After taking a university degree in Great Britain, he returned home infused with the idea of starting an enterprise that would add something to the economy of his country—and also make money. Looking at the cost of protein in the Nigerian diet—about a day's wage of the average worker for a pound of beef or chicken—he decided to go into the fish business. After setting up huge cold stores in the port cities of Lagos, Port Harcourt, and Warri, he installed three hundred selling points with walk-in refrigerators all over the country. First fishing locally, with small boats, he handled about 4 or 5 tons a day—not nearly enough to supply the market; next he began to buy from Russian and Japanese ships; finally, he acquired the fleet of state-of-the-art factory ships that supplies his network today.

Fishing off Angola to the south and northward off Mauritania and Senegal (where most of the fish are), he was in 1986 able to supply Nigerians with protein for about 10 cents a pound. To get the fish to the people at that price, his company enlisted a sales force of market women—"the men were too greedy, they wanted a large margin on very small volumes"—who understood his idea of charging less and selling more. In the process of building a clientele, he had to overcome local prejudices about frozen produce: for some time people thought something was very wrong with food that steamed when the carton was opened but in fact felt frigid to the touch. Sooner or later, however, they began to buy—the price was irresistible.

More recently, the Ibru combine has diversified widely. Their cold storage capacity led directly to another major interest in poultry, when the Americans who had leased refrigerator space for the produce of their local chicken farms decided to sell out and return to the United States. Ibru complained that previous government policies penalizing agriculture and supporting cheap food imports had made poultry-raising unprofitable: only because they turned their small size into a virtue, emphasizing the superior freshness of home-grown birds, did they survive.

In his choice of investments, Chief Ibru was following what is probably the most promising path for industrial enterprise at this stage of development in most African countries—farm-based business. Both for export and for home consumption, agribusiness enjoys advantages that many African industries do not: a local market and often, immediately available raw materials. At the same time, links between local industry and farming enrich farmers and create jobs in the rural areas—all of which increase consumption of local manufactures.

In Zambia, businessman Fred Mwananshiku exhibited the instincts needed to make modern enterprise thrive when interviewed in early 1986. After investing income he had earned managing several different government corporations in the purchase and stocking of a twenty-acre pig-farm, he then branched out into fruits and vegetables. With the profits he amassed over a few years, Mwananshiku bought up several small factories, including a meat-packing plant where he turned his pigs into pork and ham to supply much of the Lusaka market. He was aiming to build an "integrated" economic empire, where his businesses would supply parts and raw materials for one another. Thus he also acquired a spinning factory and a knitting mill. His future goals include a vegetable cannery.

Despite his enthusiasm and acumen, Mwananshiku almost certainly is having great difficulty staying afloat in Zambia today. Nor could Ibru tell his story with the same elan in 1988, with Nigeria struggling to maintain its grip on the hard contours of austerity-induced reform. Inside and outside Africa today, the institutions shaping the efforts of people like Ibru and Mwananshiku have come under increasing pressure. Whether and how they can evolve remains an urgent open question.

# 7

# "Seeing Is Different from Being Told"*

*The vision of a new society in Africa will need to be developed in Africa, born out of the African historical experience and the sense of continuity of African history. The African is not yet master of his own fate, but neither is he completely at the mercy of fate.*

Jacob Ajayi

Because productive economic institutions will not emerge without extensive reform, the most important learning experience in Africa today is that taking place in state houses and cabinet ministries across the continent. The enormity of the crisis they face has by all signs struck African leaders forcibly. Senegal's current president and former head of the Organization of African Unity, Abdou Diouf, expressed it dramatically at the organization's summit in 1985, declaring: "At stake is our credibility before our people, before the entire world, indeed before history." What is more important, African leaders appear to be confronting the more painful realities of their Independence in a new way: no one else can solve their present problems; they have to do it themselves. The president of Botswana, Quett Masire, said it explicitly in 1986: "We have graduated from the stage of blaming our condition on colonialists to taking positive initiatives on our own behalf."

From our faraway Western vantage point, a trend toward policy reform and looser state controls is the wave of

*Kenyan Proverb.

197

the future. Whether Africans themselves intend—or would be able—to steer their economies by the Western road map for the longer term is much less clear.

First of all, African governments have a hard time saying an outright no to Western advice. They are too vulnerable both economically and intellectually. Popularly known as "conditionality," the new policy usually sounds a lot more like Adam Smith than anything most African economic officials ever expected to encounter at close range. But African governments want Western aid, and right now many of their major creditors and benefactors are insisting on reform as a quid pro quo for debt relief or new money.

Second, African leaders also have a difficult time defending past policies on the basis of results. It seemed easy enough for former Senegalese president Leopold Sédor Senghor to say in 1961 that "the market economy will have to be abolished and replaced by a rationally planned economy. Hence, an inventory is being made of resources, deficiencies and potentialities. Already the guidelines of local and national planning are becoming clear." Now the confident socialists of the 1960s have to face the eloquent polemics of adverse balance sheets.

It is, in a way, mortifying. Since Independence the benefit of the doubt has shrunken away along with monetary reserves. In *A Bend in the River,* V.S. Naipaul describes the glorified image of the new African fondly held by his would-be patrons in the early days; he was "the new man whom everybody was busy making, a man about to inherit." For donors the romance of African development is over, and the possibilities shimmering out there have dwindled and dulled. Confidence is a major casualty of the crisis. African governments by and large may be too hard-pressed to afford a luxury like an economic strategy of their own design.

Because of their extremity, African policymakers are looking for new ideas, as the U.S. Treasury reported to

Congress in 1986. For a number of them, a little magic of the marketplace may now look like a palatable antidote to the current malaise. Whether or not the dose will be strong enough to make a difference, however, remains to be seen.

Where it endures, Africans' dawning realization that they must themselves cope represents a major change for the continent. While most nations resort to scapegoating in times of trial—Americans, for example, often appear to view Japanese malfeasance as the root of their own diminishing competitiveness—Africans have been encouraged since Independence to believe that the sources of both their problems and their salvation lay outside themselves. The primacy of external capital in early donor formulas for "takeoff" by the underdeveloped, the growing contribution of aid to capital investment in Africa, and the continuing intellectual dependency of African states on Western patrons all reinforced attitudes from colonial times. Further, Africans' image of government as a fount of resources "out there" at some remove from their loyalties and real lives has often paralleled international relationships. A key cabinet official of a southern African country described the attitudes of his people toward government with some exasperation, saying that "if you ask people in the towns why they are here, they will in turn ask why can't the government give them jobs." He hoped people would say instead " 'I have waited a long time and suffered long enough; now let me get involved.' "

Both internally and internationally, hopes for rescue by a deus ex machina have been roughly buffeted by continuing economic blows. In a number of countries, governments have recently signaled the change by abdicating their role as employers of last resort, with heads of state and chief ministers explicitly abrogating the unwritten law that every university graduate would be guaranteed a job. Governments' expectations about aid as the answer have been shrinking as the Western economies settle into prolonged period of sluggish growth—or worse. Always a favorite slogan in African politics, "self-reliance" now has acquired considerably sharper emotional reality. Were it not for the very narrow margin it leaves African states to apply their painful lesson, the current crisis could be considered a blessing in disguise.

⌒

African discourse about their economic situation has shifted markedly since the beginning of the 1980s. After the second oil shock of 1979, African heads of state met in Lagos, Nigeria to agree on a continent-wide response. The resulting Lagos Plan of Action of 1980 placed most of the onus for Africa's straits on the hostile international environment, citing "the political constraints on the development of [the] continent caused by colonial and racist domination and exploitation." Though the plan stressed the need for food self-sufficiency, the overall strategy put industrialization first. On tactics, the plan leaned heavily on the idea of inter-African cooperation: in the best of all possible Africas, national self-sufficiency was to be fostered through African regional links. But increased aid levels were, still, the bottom line, as the African states declared they were "owed a massive and appropriate contribution by the developed countries to the development of Africa."

Resistance to the idea of agriculture as the engine of production died hard. At a meeting in Harare, Zimbabwe, in 1982, for example, education ministers identified science and technology as the "priority of priorities" because they would provide the basis for *industrialization*. By the OAU summit of 1985, however, the winds of change were blowing stronger. The summit was the first in 22 years that focused on economic issues. The atmosphere was serious, as the countries of the region acknowledged that most of them were near "economic collapse." While placing most of the blame on "an unjust and inequitable economic system," Africa's leaders also declared "that the development of our continent is the primary responsibility of our governments and people." While reaffirming most of the goals of the Lagos Plan, they made agriculture their chief priority, suggesting that 20 to 25 percent of each country's budget should go to agriculture.

By 1986, African delegates to the May U.N. special session on Africa's economic crisis were beginning to sound a lot like officials at the World Bank. In a session characterized by a paucity of political rhetoric and striking economy of public discourse, the Africans relegated everything else but agriculture to supporting roles: they considered industry only as "agro-related." While calling on the international community to enter a "new era of cooperation based on a spirit of genuine and equal partnership," they acknowledged their own mistakes and stated flatly that "Africa has taken the main responsibility for its own development." Echoing donor prescriptions, they cited the need for exchange rate adjustment, wage and salary reductions, and a public employment freeze. Regimes that had until very recently been assiduously expanding government's economic role affirmed (as though it were in some doubt) that "the public sector will continue to play an important role in development," but went on to say that "the positive role of the private sector is also to be encouraged."

Looking at the session realistically, a fair amount of lip service was undoubtedly involved in an exercise aimed primarily at translating international momentum for relief into support for development. One West African official described with mordant candor the reason for his country's conversion to Western notions like "privatization," saying:

> We need two legs to walk—a strong state and a strong private sector; we are like a cripple I saw recently with no legs, pushing himself around on a crude board with wheels, surviving only by begging and trying to look sympathetic to the potential alms giver. Talking about privatization is one way to try and look sympathetic.

Two months after the May U.N. session, in fact, at their July 1986 OAU summit, African heads of state accused one another of wholesale capitulation to Western pressures in the session's final program. The leaders' debate vented very real feelings they had largely suppressed in New York—dominated by anger at the lack of concrete response from donors to the session. Again, strong disaffection surfaced at the February 1987 meeting of the French West African Monetary Union. There, Côte d'Ivoire, Senegal, Mali, Burkina Faso, Benin, Niger and Togo launched a collective attack on the International Monetary Fund's structural adjustment reforms. Echoing the revolt of the major Latin American debtors, they argued that the IMF programs and debt service together were strangling their economies.

African hostility to painful, frequently hastily conceived, and often externally imposed, programs should come as no shock. Because they are the weakest, African countries are more vulnerable to international pressures than any other set of debtors. More than the Latin Americans or Asians, Africans probably have felt those pressures as the strongest goad for reform.

But, it is also clear that for a number of African countries the new directions represented not just a rhetorical shift but an attempt to create a new reality. Beyond the undoubted importance of IMF pressures, the reform packages also sprang from the desperate quest of finance ministers for anything that would get their economies going again. For it had become obvious to many that the state controls they had elaborated just did not work. "Privatization" means very different things to different people, but clearly it was an idea whose time had come. In their search for new answers, many governments were turning their polities into laboratories for the new Western development theories.

Africa's main financial institution, the African Development Bank, led the way, pushing structural adjustment energetically from the early 1980s. The triple-A-rated bank, which expanded its lending by 42 percent in 1986 and tripled its capital in 1987, recently has put a large chunk of its money into agriculture (doubling the farm sector's share of bank lending to 40 percent in 1985) and has set aside 60 percent of its resources for Africa's poorest states. In addition to farming, the ADB President, Babacar N'diaye recently laid out as priorities "policy reforms and policy dialogue; inter-African trade; the promotion of the private sector; the insertion of women into economic development; and the problem of the environment."

∽

Looked at cumulatively, the reforms undertaken by African governments from 1982 onward are impressive. "Privatization" itself—or the sale of government enterprises to private bidders—did not find many takers, and those who did emerge may be exactly the sort of "buccaneer capitalists" the continent does not need. But, the record as of 1986 showed, Africa was moving to the beat of reform. To sum up briefly, ten countries[1] decontrolled agricultural prices and nine[2] decontrolled consumer prices, particularly of food. A number of countries decreased the share of production controlled by the state: eight[3] greatly reduced their fiscal deficits; twenty[4] froze public sector hiring or actually reduced public sector employment; thirteen[5] permitted private competition in the marketing of farm products or eliminated government marketing boards entirely;

---

[1]Burundi, Ghana, Madagascar, Mali, Mozambique, Niger, Nigeria, Senegal, Somalia, and Zambia
[2]Ghana, Guinea, Madagascar, Malawi, Sierra Leone, Somalia, Tanzania, Zäire and Zambia
[3]Ghana, Kenya, Madagascar, Niger, Senegal, Swaziland, Togo, and Zäire
[4]Burundi, Ghana, Guinea, Guinea-Bisseau, Lesotho, Madagascar, Malawi, Mali, Niger, Rwanda, Senegal, Sierra Leone, Somalia, Swaziland, Tanzania, Togo, Uganda, Zäire, Zambia, and Zimbabwe
[5]Gambia, Ghana, Guinea, Kenya, Madagascar, Mali, Niger, Nigeria, Senegal, Somalia, Tanzania, Togo, and Zambia

six[6] turned over imports of agricultural inputs to private concerns; nine[7] transferred some state corporations into private hands; eight[8] shut down some state corporations completely; nine[9] reduced subsidies to state corporations or improved the efficiency of their management; and fourteen[10] eliminated or cut subsidies on raw materials used by state corporations.

A great many countries also moved to reduce the urban bias: twenty-one[11] raised prices to farmers substantially; eight[12] cut back or ended subsidies on food; and sixteen[13] cut or ended subsidies on petroleum. And a number quite directly benefited farm exports by reducing supports for import-substituting industrialization: sixteen[14] aligned their exchange rates much more closely with the real cost of foreign exchange; and nine[15] phased out or lowered taxes on exports. By the end of 1987, except in Zambia and Somalia (which had each fallen off stringent structural adjustment programs), most of these reforms, reportedly, were still in place.

When we look more closely at this mass of data, several details stand out. First of all, everyone's favorite policy disaster, Tanzania, swallowed a healthy dose of the Western

---

[6]Gambia, Ghana, Nigeria, Senegal, Zäire, and Zambia

[7]Ghana, Guinea-Bisseau, Malawi, Mali, Senegal, Sierra Leone, Somalia, Tanzania, and Zambia

[8]Burundi, Guinea, Madagascar, Mali, Niger, Senegal, Tanzania, and Togo

[9]Ghana, Guinea-Bisseau, Malawi, Mali, Senegal, Sierra Leone, Somalia, Tanzania, and Zambia

[10]Chad, Gambia, Ghana, Ivory Coast, Kenya, Madagascar, Malawi, Mali, Niger, Nigeria, Senegal, Somalia, Tanzania, and Zambia

[11]Burundi, Cameroon, Chad, Gambia, Ghana, Guinea, Ivory Coast, Kenya, Madagascar, Malawi, Mali, Mozambique, Nigeria, Rwanda, Senegal, Sierra Leone, Tanzania, Togo, Zäire, Zambia, and Zimbabwe

[12]Guinea, Guinea-Bisseau, Madagascar, Senegal, Sierra Leone, Tanzania, Zambia, and Zimbabwe

[13]Cape Verde, Ghana, Guinea, Madagascar, Malawi, Mali, Niger, Senegal, Sierra Leone, Somalia, Swaziland, Tanzania, Uganda, Zäire, Zambia, and Zimbabwe

[14]Burundi, Ghana, Guinea, Guinea-Bisseau, Kenya, Madagascar, Malawi, Mauritius, Nigeria, Rwanda, Sierra Leone, Somalia, Tanzania, Uganda, Zambia, and Zäire

[15]Burundi, Chad, Gambia, Ghana, Malawi, Mauritius, Senegal, Tanzania, and Uganda

medicine. In addition to launching major cuts in public sector bureaucracies with the lay-off of 25,000 government employees in 1985 and a freeze in 1986, it moved on several fronts to support the long-abused private sector. It released a major share of food marketing from the clutches of the National Marketing Corporation; began to divest the major state corporation for agricultural exporting; closed down state corporations for cold storage, transport, automotive and tractor assembly, domestic appliances and bicycles, livestock development and marketing, timber marketing; and ended subsidies to unprofitable state corporations. While raising the prices to farmers of both food and export crops, it also ended subsidies to consumers on corn and most other staples.

Second, several countries with strong records—such as Côte d'Ivoire and Cameroon—did not figure prominently in this listing because they had for a number of years been implementing many of the policies that others were undertaking. Nor does this run-down take account of Nigeria's reform program, largely adopted in the latter part of 1986. With the largest economy in sub-Saharan Africa, Nigeria could become a catalyst for the whole region if it recovered from its oil-induced binge of the 1970s and early 1980s. At the time of its 1983 military takeover, the country's debt was soaring and its reserves hardly covered essential imports. Although the crisis was well known to the Nigerian public, who read about the follies of their leaders in Africa's freest press, Nigerians vociferously resisted any cession of their sovereignty to the IMF. In late 1985, the country's new leader, General Ibrahim Babangida, summoned the entire citizenry to engage in a national debate on economic policy. Over several months, carpenters on construction sites, cab drivers, and women traders in the market could be heard sounding off about "IMF," imperialism, corrupt politicians, and the general evils of borrowing. Nigerians wanted no part of the IMF or any of its works. Having gotten that out of their system, however, the following year they settled into

205

an extremely far-reaching reform program embodying virtually everything the IMF had asked for.

While ostentatiously refusing an actual IMF loan,
Nigeria did come to an agreement with the Fund that paved
the way for successful talks with its commercial bank and
foreign government creditors to reschedule its $20 billion-
debt. Nigeria's own blueprint was radical indeed: almost all
price controls were lifted; rice and wheat imports were
banned to encourage local production; private traders took
over inefficient agricultural marketing; around 100 state-
owned companies were to be sold or run on a commercially
profitable basis. Most importantly, the nation's currency,
the naira, was devalued 75 percent and the most important
source of corruption was curtailed when a weekly currency
auction eliminated the old import licensing system by issu-
ing licenses to successful bidders for scarce foreign exchange. With a World Bank loan of $4.8 billion assured over
the next three years, inflation down from 40 percent in
1984 to 15 percent in 1986, and the budget deficit reduced
from more than 11 percent of gross domestic product in
1983 to less than 1 percent in 1986, the Nigerians had taken
decisive steps.

But some very tough times would lie ahead. Until the
end of the 1980s, the country would have to borrow $3 to 4
billion a year to keep up with its debt service obligations and
maintain a level of imports permitting modest growth.
Without major investments in rural areas, the plan's goal of
greatly increased farm exports would remain just that.
Moreover, the shakeout in industry—most of which relies
on imports for 50 to 60 percent of raw materials—would
cause major shock waves. In the first quarter of 1987, for
example, Volkswagen Nigeria manufactured only 777
models of a car that had previously been purchased by
hundreds of thousands of Nigerians—and sold only 147.
The most difficult part for Nigeria would lie in weathering
the long haul. Over the next few years it would not be at all
clear to most people that things were getting better.

West Africa's star reformer, Ghana, has already taken a good deal of fallout from its ambitious—and in many ways successful—structural adjustment program. In the preceding review, Ghana stands out as the most zealous, with reforms in almost every category. At the beginning of the 1980s, few would have believed it possible.

The career of Ghana's charismatic leader, Flight Lieutenant Jerry Rawlings, embodies Africa's current learning process almost visibly. After two decades of economic and political turmoil in Ghana, characterized by accelerating corruption and declining farm output, Rawlings and a group of colonels seized power in June 1979. Carrying the banner of the urban workers, they vehemently denounced a proposed devaluation that would greatly raise the prices in the cities. Soldiers enforcing draconian price controls physically assaulted venal officials and traders known for gouging, threw consumer goods on the open market at greatly slashed prices, and bulldozed down the largest market in Accra. Retreating from the scene to allow the country a brief fling with an elected civilian government in 1979 and 1980, Rawlings returned in 1981 with rhetoric undimmed. During 1982 he put his populism into action, cutting salary differentials and replacing professionals with workers and citizens' committees.

At the beginning of 1983, however, a devastating drought cast the country's bankruptcy into stark relief. In its wake, Rawlings' government executed a 180-degree shift. Declaring that "small is beautiful, at least for us," he pushed through a series of reforms bearing a striking similarity to the stabilization programs of the IMF—reducing state controls and supporting rural development. He also enacted a harsh austerity program that squeezed the already hard-pressed urban workers as well as the middle classes. By 1985 he had devalued the national currency, the cedi, by over 1000 percent, tightened tax collection, cut government payrolls, doubled prices to cocoa farmers, spurred rural banking and shunted consumer goods into rural areas. By 1987, inflation had dropped to 5 percent, the corn crop had doubled, and cocoa yields had jumped by 25 percent. Once-scarce goods and foodstuffs filled the shelves of city stores—though at prices most workers could not afford.

But while urban austerity apparently persuaded at least some city dwellers to look for a better life back on the farm, it also alienated many of Rawlings' most loyal supporters. Urban workers reacted violently in the spring of 1986 when the government tried to rescind large salary increases proffered in compensation for sharp drops in urban incomes, and a general strike was narrowly averted.

Rawlings' initial popularity and the Ghanaians' history of constantly declining expectations probably gave him more room for maneuver than many other African leaders enjoy. But as he learned painfully in 1986, people can't eat policy reforms, and the table may look pretty bare before anyone can see the fruits of austerity. Holding onto power while elite privileges are vanishing and the masses grow hungry offers challenges most African politicians would undoubtedly prefer to avoid. If they are serious about reform, African governments would do well to look for alternative economic payoffs that do not obstruct productivity as subsidies and patronage have done. Road building and other public works projects can, for example, be delivered as tangible rewards both to construction workers and local people—without the permanent drain on revenues that comes when government bureaucracies are expanded to serve as employers of last resort.

Switching from patronage to pork barrel, however, would require more than ingenuity from hard-pressed leaders. What Ghana's experience—like Zambia's—shows is that the flexibility of African governments will disappear entirely if food is not available and affordable and if they cannot maintain imports to keep systems going. Where it is used to induce policy reforms, food aid can be useful in giving governments leeway. Yet, for a country like Ghana, where 35 percent of export earnings go for debt service, the government will not be able to deliver incentives to farmers and forestall violent upheaval in the city without substantial debt relief and some balance of payments support.

෴

For their part, the donors have not remained entirely immune from the lessons of the past few decades either. Over twenty years, aid practitioners heard enough horror stories about white elephants foundering in the sands of cultural and environmental ignorance to have humbled the most complacent of do-gooders. For Americans, admittedly, acting on this awareness meant rising above their native impatience and culturally ingrained can-do instincts. But reportedly they were doing so.

The most acute Western myopia about how things worked was in the failure to recognize that African women produce most of Africa's food. By the mid-1970s, U.S. AID planners routinely began to scrutinize women's participation in farm programs. And study of traditional African farm methods came into its own. At the Rockefeller Foundation's International Institute for Tropical Agriculture in Ibadan, Nigeria, scientists studied the way Nigerian women cultivate 50 or more different kinds of plants to provide proteins and vitamins year round. In research stations throughout the continent, scientists looked at current applications of the traditional African practice of intercropping.

For all the donors, shrinking budgets have spurred stock-taking on their own records as well as those of the Africans. Now they are honing an essential tool that they largely lacked until a few years ago—evaluation of their projects. Assessment of aid efforts has always lagged behind design. For U.S. AID, reporting to Congress has meant documenting whether the money has been spent according to plan—often an extremely expensive process in itself. Only recently have AID, the World Bank, and other donors tried to gauge what difference projects actually made. At last they are creating an institutional memory. The process promises to check the zeal of aid officers who want just to get something going and to disburse the money. It will also enable them to learn from their mistakes.

One of the lessons staring them in the face is the appalling waste in competing and duplicative programs. But though "donor coordination" now has the status of motherhood and apple pie, it is a very hard rule to live by. There are 82 bilateral and multilateral donors, including Western and Eastern bloc countries, the World Bank, the IMF, U.N. agencies, the regional development banks, and special funds like the Commonwealth Development Corporation and the Arab Fund for African Development. In addition, another group of private and voluntary organizations funded by churches and private philanthropy comes to some 1700 organizations worldwide. With each of them looking to make a mark of some sort, the problems of coordination resemble those of the great Crusades.

Recently, however, consultative groups of the main official donors have been established by the World Bank in the African countries undergoing IMF structural adjustment. Obviously, much of the impetus behind these collaborations right now flows from the debt crisis. Yet, their very existence sharpens the donors efforts to make scarce resources go further.

For the moment, donors and Africans appear firmly agreed on one way to do that: available aid money should be spent keeping up existing infrastructure, institutions, or enterprises rather than creating new ones. Thus donor money earmarked for elementary schools will go to directly support a government's education budget—rather than, say, to build a hundred new schools. Close monitoring of how the money is used will replace the direct control over each stage—location, design, procurement, and construction—that would often have characterized the donor's drive to get those schools up and operating. Although straitened

210

circumstances led us to it, the leaner approach has distinct advantages: it is simpler and less intrusive.

By now the virtue of simplicity should be close to a first principle for donors. Except where donors are personally active in scientific training or research, sorry experience leads to wariness about complicated projects. Using grants for education, agriculture, health, and population to encourage reform gives Africans ultimate control of the process. This does not mean that benefactors should just "throw money at" recipients. Quite the contrary, if they are serious about policy reform, donors will pursue it more attentively than ever before—maintaining strict financial accountability—with African governments that are equally serious.

Many African governments are, regrettably, still forced to rely on foreigners for help with long-term planning and even for basic information about their own economies. Much of the data about how things work—even within local farming systems—is processed in the West and then returned to Africa. It is no secret that the outlines of the reform programs now underway in some 22 African countries originated in the World Bank, the IMF, and the headquarters of various donors.

Yet, the nature of the conversation between donors and recipients has changed a lot since the early aid programs in Africa. At Independence most countries were looking quite indiscriminately for just about any sort of technical assistance. Now African governments have built up much more local expertise, and they have become a good deal more focused in their planning. In the old days aid officials went out to set up ministries, and African governments invited Western scholars to delineate national problems. Now Western experts are more typically asked for help with specific management problems or feasibility studies.

Over the past few years, the imperfections of government-to-government efforts have increased the appeal of work at the grass roots by private voluntary organizations (known as PVOs). Reaching out to village people directly, these organizations often gain an understanding of what's happening on a local level that official donors, spending much more money much more widely, can seldom match. Their modest grants are often administered through African organizations. In 1986 one such private group, Oxfam, funded over 2,000 separate grants, mostly to local organizations, out of a $4.5 million budget. Even more striking is the Trickle Up program, which is run by a New York City couple out of their apartment. They have provided grants of $100 apiece to more than 3,000 small groups and businesses throughout the Third World.

Because Africa's population and environmental problems have to be coped with on the level where people live, the skills of private voluntary groups can be essential. Their workers, often motivated by humanitarian or religious concerns, live close to the people they are trying to help and spend time learning how these people see their own needs. At their best, they offer people new ways to meet these needs. For example, Catholic Charities in Zambia ran a farm where they taught 12 Zambian families how to use new agricultural techniques—instructing them when and how to cultivate first 5 and then 12 acres using oxen, plows, fertilizers, and new types of seeds. After two years the farmers not only had absorbed the new methods but also saved enough capital to buy oxen and plows to take back to their villages. There it was expected they would serve as models for others, exemplifying the value both of the new technologies and of thrift.

For these achievements, PVOs are now being touted in some quarters as the new answer to Africa's development dilemmas. Their primary virtue, however, makes it hazardous to try replicating them on a much larger scale—size would be likely to blunt their sensitivity. Nor would increasing numbers of foreign voluntary workers be a healthy addition to the local African scene. It is a truism, but one

Westerners often forget, that African institutions have to evolve from the interaction of African leaders and people. Once back in their villages, the Zambian farmers will probably find their new accomplishments and possessions threatened both by extended family claims and by kinks in their country's marketing system. When they succeed, PVOs can help to shift the process of change toward the interests of the people. But more well-meaning foreigners with open purses moving through African villages will only delay and distort the accommodations that Africans themselves must make.

In this situation, the growing activism of *African* private voluntary organizations is encouraging. Though again not "the answer" to Africa's problems (as philanthropic fashion will at some point undoubtedly decree), these new African groups obviously bring to the grass roots an innate understanding of the villagers they work with. They will make their own mistakes, but they will not be able to retreat from them, to another country. They will of course still depend largely on aid from Western governments and PVOs.

Inevitably any form of aid raises the risk of dependency. The outstanding question now is to what extent African policy shifts result from pressure from donors, and to what extent they result from the desperate search of Africans for new answers. How deeply African commitments go will be determined over ensuing years. In this worst and best of times, falling levels of aid, by default, provide a partial answer: more than most had acknowledged before, African leaders *are* clearly responsible for the fates of their nations. Though external trends will shape their opportunities, how they use their own capital will determine their future.

So donors have to walk a fine line, foreswearing direct interventions into African economies but holding up government records to frank and open scrutiny. Paradoxically, increased African vulnerability can give donors an opportunity to press African governments to take more responsibility.

⌒

At the same time, the present desperately low starting point of most African states will make it almost impossible to increase their economic self-reliance without substantial external assistance now. Falling Western aid and rising debt service deprive African governments of crucial flexibility in selling unpalatable austerity. Reforms are unlikely to be sustained in very many places unless declines in aid are halted during the coming decade.

As the 1980s were drawing to a close, debt relief clearly would be the crucial factor. During 1987 several African countries, including Liberia, Sudan, Zambia, and Sierra Leone, had reportedly, without fanfare, stopped making their required payments to the International Monetary Fund. While care was taken to avoid talk of "default," the trend posed ominous portents for international credit mechanisms. By the end of that year, the IMF was working energetically to obtain longer-term relief for Africa. The Fund's Director, Michel Camdessus, had obtained agreement from the donors that the Fund's Structural Adjustment Facility should be expanded sharply—from about $3 to 11 billion—to subsidize interest rates and stretch out periods of repayment. And pledges of that amount appeared to be on the table. Citing its trade deficit, the U.S. administration continued to balk at conceding new money, but supported the expansion in principle. How far the new measures would go toward meeting Africa's need remained in question.

In 1987, amid market crashes and deficit cuts, U.S. development assistance for Africa held at about two-thirds of the 1985 figure. In the next few years the most important new investments in Africa seemed likely to come from the World Bank. With the money they do spend on bilateral aid, the United States and other donor countries should try to accomplish a goal that is the obverse of that embodied in debt relief: that is, they should reward success. What that is will always lie in the eye of the beholder. If donors are flexible, their definition of "success" will change with circumstances. But apart from food aid and disaster relief, the countries judged to use the money or technology most effectively should have first shot at it.

Is this a proposal for some form of triage? From its earlier use to denote the sorting of battle casualties, "triage" has come to mean, more dramatically, jettisoning the weakest to save the strongest—pushing the feeble off a crowded life raft so the most vigorous will get a larger share of common rations. When it comes to Africa, the lifeboat image has very limited relevance. From the donors' standpoint, aid to Africa has never been a matter of equitable sharing of rations; it has been apportioned according to strategic and political priorities, occasionally for more purely developmental ends, and, particularly in emergencies, from fairly immediate humanitarian impulses.

No matter what choices we make in the future about allocating aid, emergency relief must and should flow where famine threatens. Fortunately, the citizens of the developed world have demanded that, and very likely will continue to do so. Apart from relief, however, the limited resources available should go to the states with the best prospects of success. This means the countries whose leaders are both committed and capable of using them to increase their people's productivity. Often those will be countries that lead us rather than follow along, those who organize the donors rather than letting their economies be shaped by a cacophony of foreign notions. Successful African leaders do not have to be—cannot be—replicas of George Washington or Abe Lincoln. Shrewd and ruthless as well as strong, they will need to have a vision of their society that can sustain them and their people. Turkey's Kemal Attaturk is probably the best model, but Jomo Kenyatta will do.

In the future, the consensus that chiefs formerly arrived at through palaver in palace courtyards or town meetings will have to be writ much larger through modern communications and transportation. In a country like Ghana, Jerry Rawlings' early charisma was vulnerable to ongoing economic reverses. In order to carry through programs of economic reform and austerity African leaders like Rawlings will often have to stump their countries on a continuing basis, as in the traditional run-up to an American election, and to mount media campaigns as well.

For our own part, effective choice does not mean rewarding those leaders who slavishly follow our advice. It does mean reinforcing links between aid and results. As logical as this principle sounds, the primacy of politics in our own aid program has made acting on it anything but easy. Not entirely coincidentally, the recipients of the largest American grants for security assistance in Africa—Liberia, Zaire, and Sudan—are among the continent's basket cases. Buying the loyalty of local elites, we are at the same time buying their continued purchase upon power. The terms of exchange are clear to both sides and just as clearly corrupting.

An excellent obverse example here was the U.S. effort, launched in the spring of 1987, to rescue Liberia's deteriorating economy—in effect colonizing the main economic institutions of the country by sending in cadres of American "advisers" to run them. Pouring bad money after bad, and then jumping in to protect our investment, we increased Liberians' sense that they could not solve their own problems, and that in the long run they did not really have to. If we can, instead, channel more of our aid to the states that are increasing productivity and laying the groundwork for future progress, rewarding merit rather than allegiance, we will be strengthening the values that underlie efficient performance in modern economies. Countries like Ghana, Cameroon, and Zimbabwe—all of which have constructively confronted a variety of economic dilemmas—are good candidates for assistance on that basis.

If, over time, Africa's better off states become more prosperous while the worse off get poorer, this is an inevitable result of any sort of progress. (The most potent leveler of all is likely to be pervasive failure.) In the long run the growing inequities among nations may well be beneficial. For they may spur forms of hegemony that break down regional economic barriers. And they will throw up home-grown models for other African states to emulate. In the long run, African countries will learn most from what is working for them and for others on their own continent.

# 8

# A Future in Shadow

*That is why the Black Continent is groping in the dark. It is a continent in quest of a vanishing spirituality, a continent pursued by a too-immediate reality, a continent in search of itself.*

Camara Laye
*The Guardian of the Word*

For all the tenacity of tradition, Africa is changing, and changing fast. As more and more people pour into the cities, extended family ties sit more loosely on the shoulders of second and third generation urban dwellers. To Westerners looking on, evidence of basic change must seem highly circumstantial compared with the weight of tradition, but it is equally as foolish to doubt the importance of what is taking place as to overstate it. Westerners, viewing kinship bonds mainly as an obstruction to modern political and economic progress, see chiefly their enormous power. Africans, on the other hand, viewing kinship as the main structure of society and source of security see these bonds grow brittle as the old order falls apart.

Both concerns are well warranted: both tradition and change hold grave pitfalls for Africa. This truth captures much of the pain Africans are now experiencing and what lies ahead. "Progess" brings upheaval—to some extent economic development must be based on wrenching social change. Thus, in the coming years, the transition of Africans will take the form of a struggle, or layering of struggles. Falling backward—retreating into further fragmentation— Africans risk submersion in a rising tide of material problems. Therefore rationality dictates that they must try to go

218

"forward." But where "forward" lies exactly is less than clear to many Africans as well as to most knowledgable outside observers. A good deal of energy, commitment and awareness within the continent is focused on exactly this question.

In *Ake: The Years of Childhood,* Nobel prizewinner Wole Soyinka compares his hometown in his early youth with its present-day Westernized veneer, which for him represents a vulgar colonization of his townsmen's spirits:

> The hawker's lyrics of leaf-wrapped *moin-moin* still resound in parts of Ake and the rest of the town but, along Dayisi's Walk is also a shop which sells *moin-moin* from a glass case, lit by sea-green neon lamps. It lies side by side with McDonald's hamburgers, Kentucky Fried Chicken, hotdogs and dehydrated sausage-rolls. It has been cooked in empty milk tins and similar containers, scooped out and sliced in neat geometric shapes like cakes of soap. And the newly rich homes stuff it full of eggs, tinned sardines from Portugal and canned beef from the Argentine. . . . Today's jaws on Dayisi's Walk . . . champ endlessly—on chewing gum. Among the fantasy stores lit by neon and batteries of coloured bulbs a machine also dispenses popcorn, uniformly fluffed. Urchins thrust the new commodity, clean wrapped, in plastic bags, in faces of passengers whose vehicles pause even one moment along the route. The blare of motor horns compete with the high decibel outpouring of rock and funk and punk and other thunk-thunk from lands of instant culture heroes. Eyes glazed, jaws in constant, automated motion, the new habitues mouth the confusion of lyrics belted out from every store, their arms flapping up and down like wounded bush fowl.

So much is borrowed; so much is jerry-built. Where is Africa?

Fortunately, people are rarely able to see themselves in a historical continuum. Rather, rooted in the seeming solidity of everyday life, they feel themselves subject only to the foreseeable demands of that limited place and time. If Africans compared their own situation today with Europe's leisurely meander over five centuries toward nationhood and prosperity, the prospect would look even more daunting than it does already.

First of all, compared with Europe's gradual evolution from feudalism to industrialization, social change is coming to Africa with extraordinary velocity. In the face of modern education and of urbanization, the hierarchies of traditional society—largely based on seniority—are unlikely to remain in place. Africa has the youngest population of any continent (nearly half of its people are under sixteen); for those who live in cities traditional attitudes cannot escape the invasion of modern images. As sons go to school and begin to accumulate wealth, they gradually displace their fathers within the family. As children of the shantytowns scramble for a bare existence, the settled order of the village recedes, even as a touchstone. Because change means adapting or giving up much that is good in the old ways, in order to get new things that are also good, it can happen only with a struggle.

Sometimes, it becomes a battle. Recently a Kikuyu widow in Kenya engaged in a well-publicized tug-of-war with the Luo kinsmen of her husband over the burial of her deceased spouse. Revolting against tribal tradition, this unusually strong-minded mixed couple brought up their children to speak neither of their tribal languages but only English and Swahili, and schooled them as well to despise tribal customs. The father was a prominent attorney, and when he died, his widow successfully resisted the seizure of all his possessions that is customary among Luos. But she still was forced into court by her in-laws, and eventually she lost jurisdiction to them over the location of her husband's grave. Despite the deceased's explicit repudiation in life of his family's customs, the court accepted the argument made by his brother that unless the late lawyer was buried on his ancestral farm, the dead man's spirit would roam angrily abroad, making life miserable for his relatives.

In this struggle, most Kenyans—and probably most Africans—would probably come out somewhere in the middle, with the older people of the villages at one extreme, and the educated young people in the cities on the other. If possible, many thoughtful Africans very likely would choose to hold onto the awe, altruism, and security that they value in tradition, while also taking on the initiative, technological mastery, organizational skills, and broader identity needed for entry into the modern world. Traditional rules and customs represented the conscience of the whole people or tribe. But tradition will evolve as the collective will of Africans shatters and regroups.

Then too, the actual physical pressures generated by economic change in Africa are intensifying more swiftly than those experienced by the Europeans at similar stages of development (or, for the most part, those felt elsewhere in the Third World). As populations double and redouble, their rate of increase becomes almost visible. And the deterioration of the land has in many places been evident for some time.

In addition, history, geography, and culture have all conspired to fragment Africa and erect barriers impeding growth. Africa's many tribal groups divide its people both politically and economically, even within their own countries, into separate enclaves of trust and responsibility. Further, nature has so varied Africa's climate and soils that a map of adjoining crop and farming systems often resembles an intricate mosaic. And colonial boundaries emphatically didn't help: they halted the evolution of African political forms, leaving African fragments in structures of European design—with international legitimacy but without political or economic viability. Too small to provide strong domestic markets for home-grown industries, the states still resist any inroads on that one precious commodity that modern times have surely placed within their grasp—sovereignty (and the elite privilege it underpins). Thus they forgo the larger benefits of economic community with their neighbors.

What will look like a heightening of the disorder on a continental scale may sometimes accompany attempts to create larger wholes. Some countries may eventually break apart, and others absorb parts of their neighbors. Over time, differences among African countries in strength and in performance are likely to become more pronounced. Both Nigeria and South Africa (after apartheid) are obvious candidates to become regional catalysts, creating—perhaps partly by coercion—the larger markets and resource bases necessary to support industry.

One of Africa's wisest statesmen, Nigeria's former head of state General Olusegun Obasanjo advocates a visionary scheme for creating six African confederations in the twenty-first century, arguing that otherwise there is "no viable future for many African states, and perhaps for all of them politically." Kenyan Central Bank Governor Philip Ndegwa similarly calls for a revivified "pan Africanism," which he defines as "nationalism" not of "an individual country but of the entire continent." In his view, without continental unity many African countries will find it "impossible to achieve the required progress in both agriculture and industry."

Finally, beyond drawing the borders, the Europeans substituted alien authority for African, enshrining their dominance in African psyches with gunpowder, machinery, the alphabet, and afternoon tea. Western material superiority has preyed insistently on the sense of values of Africans, as it has changed their world, ever since. In Ghanaian Kojo Laing's novel *Search Sweet Country,* Professor Sackey ruefully declares: "We really must learn that ideas do not exist merely in relation to the past or to exams, to books, articles or to other countries." Africans cannot now afford

Western life-styles and may not want Western individualism, but, if they are to grow, neither can they afford to reject Western technologies and styles of organization. At the same time, Africans rely on the countries of the West only at their own peril. Like that of the Wizard of Oz, Western magic can take its devotees very little farther than they are ready to go themselves.

Thus even with the real progress we can see in specific instances, the broad picture of Africa will look fairly bleak for some time to come. Falling incomes lead to rising struggles over shares of the pie. As traditional authority is altered, and national authority struggles to assert itself, as cities explode in hasty, grimcrack swathes, and new forms of social organization are tacked together swiftly, the cracks in public order will in many places appear wider than ever. The simultaneous erosion of authority and material well-being has spurred a rise in crime, ranging from the theft of vegetables from neighbors' gardens in Zambia to the invasion of fortified city mansions by heavily armed bands in Nigeria.

∾

And that may be the optimistic scenario. All our predictions about patterns of change may be overshadowed, at least temporarily, by apocalyptic outbreaks of famine and plague analogous to those that afflicted Europe in the fourteenth century. Whether the current drought is an aberration or part of a new climatic pattern, the damage already done in an number of areas may periodically intensify the chronic poverty and hunger. Beyond the human suffering involved in each famine, the recurrence of these crises could exact a heavy toll on available energies, draining away support for progress, even where genuine promise does exist.

The prospect of the AIDS epidemic is harder to envision. Although it would not, as in Camus' parable of the plague, come as a surprise, a calamity of such potentially major dimensions is probably impossible to prepare for. The *Economist's* June 1987 supplement on East Africa said it succinctly: "if the worst forebodings prove true, nothing written [in this survey] will make sense ten years from now. . . . " Where it strikes in force, AIDS would bring development to a virtual halt while almost all human energies would be focused on caring for the sick and burying the dead. In those areas, current estimates on population growth would, of course, be irrelevant, and the sorts of societies that might emerge afterward could hardly be predicted. For this reason, and because the intensity of its onslaught will vary a good deal from region to region, for the time being we cannot allow a preoccupation with AIDS to threaten efforts at improving the odds in other ways. Apart from public education campaigns, and until real palliatives are found, thinking the thinkable is likely to be more useful.

What we have been thinking about in this book, that is, economic reforms and an infusion of skills and technology to move Africa forward, ought to prove useful if these initiatives can be sustained. For all the reasons elaborated, that is a very big if. As the African transition continues, what happens within individual countries will depend mainly on the evolution of their elites and of the relationship of these leaders with the people. For their part, African citizens, though often passive and detached from the affairs of government, by and large have no tradition of slavish obedience to authority. In most places Africans were governed by a king, groups of elders or titled men who were responsive in varying degrees to public consensus. (Nigeria's IMF debate is an example, though unusual, of how this has worked at national scale.) For Africans today, fears about social and economic security dominate shared concerns. Despite very real aspirations for democracy, present just about everywhere on the continent, Africans seem most to want a stable framework within which they can survive and thrive.

With the deaths of Kenya's Jomo Kenyatta and Guinea's Sékou Touré, and the resignation of Tanzania's Julius Nyerere and Senegal's Leopold Senghor, the first generation of charismatic African leaders has come to an end. (Of the original group, only Houphouet-Boigny in Côte d'Ivoire, Kenneth Kaunda in Zambia, and Hastings Banda in Malawi remain at the helm.) More than ever, though, Africa cannot do without strong leaders. For the next generation will need to wean its people from the negative pulls of tribalism at the same time that the appeal of kinship—as the major solace from austerity—may be growing.

Since Independence, Africa-watchers have been waiting for class differences to erode tribal alliances. As inequalities and urban-rural gaps persist, class differences will increase. Already, the new middle class is perpetuating its own advantages through the education of its children. Even now Africa's extraordinary social equity, which allows rich government officials to move about in their home villages at little social distance from their illiterate brothers and sisters, is probably fleeting. Technocrats are emerging in numbers from universities throughout most of Africa. Urbanized and educated, they are a different breed from their parents. Given their growing numbers, these new trained professionals will affect the way systems work if they can see concrete benefits for themselves—that is, if their societies begin to hold out real rewards for merit and achievement.

Yet while gaps have been widening, class alliances have proved fairly weak when faced with ethnic solidarity. Rather than diminishing with the growth of class links, ethnic ties are likely to percolate in new ways through altered social structures. So African leaders pursuing national cohesion will have to fortify the positive associations of citizenship. This means, in the first place, selling their people the idea of a common good that supercedes that of each individual group, and then convincing their people that both adversity and progress are being shared in some way that serves the common good.

Admittedly, the various mandates to African leaders are often contradictory. How many people could fulfill this job description? All at the same time African officials need to: cut back government involvement, employment, and patronage while demand grows; build infrastructure while cutting back government expenditures; persuade their people to curb their expectations of the modern economy while also persuading them to curb their traditional zeal for fertility; persuade farmers to conserve land resources while also urging expanded production. Most difficult, leaders will have to intervene actively to break the links between accumulation and patronage.

How far is the choice of economic liberalism—or socialism—likely to affect the ability of African leaders to fulfill these mandates? Apart from the effect of African indebtedness in bringing on the constant and unloved ministrations of the International Monetary Fund, since the end of the 1970s the handwriting on the wall has looked pretty clear from within the continent: if you have any hope of economic development, you had better look to the West. In this calculation, hopes for greater shares of aid certainly spurred a number of governments to engage in "policy dialogue" with the donors. The expectation of positive results from reform was also real: since free enterprise was demonstrably more productive than any other economic system—even the Chinese thought so—something more like it might help turn things around in Africa.

As time goes on, economic rationality will in many places be hard-pressed by events. Clearly, the results of current reforms in Africa will be imperfect and at times politically disastrous. Where pain comes quickly and rewards arrive only at length, backsliding and backlash are inevitable. In the African states where economic reforms appear to have few discernible payoffs (except perhaps for the central banks and the IMF), governments are likely to react against what can be labeled a Western plan for their economic management. Recognizing that the rules of the game that Africans must play by have been set virtually in their entirety by the former colonial powers and their allies, many African intellectuals have reflexively resisted the idea of capitalism as a Western creation and will continue to do so at some level.

$\sim$

Facing the facts squarely, for some time to come fewer countries are likely to succeed in maintaining health and growth than will fail. Looking at the historical continuum, the present reform era can be seen as the second phase for Africa in its post-colonial pursuit of economic growth. The first phase, following Independence, involved Africans and outsiders in exuberant expansion through proliferating state bureaucracies. Now that the exuberance is gone and the bureaucracies don't work, the need to contract is evident. As we have seen, however, prescribing the medicine is a lot easier than administering it. Because it will probably work in some cases but not in others, yet a third phase lies ahead. What we may expect after the results of reform are clearer is much greater differentiation among states, arising from their different ways—and powers—of coping.

What may come next for states where reforms fail will be harder for us to face than either the neat blueprints for "takeoff" of the first phase, or the remedial reforms of the second. In reaction to failed hopes, ideology may be the surest political balm, and a recourse to religious fundamentalism and millenarian traditionalism the most likely social refuge.

Wherever privation increases—even where political leaders are strong enough to maintain economic reforms—the seeming failure of the modern economy is likely to loosen the hold of the West. Twenty-five years ago, the decline of tradition in the face of modernity seemed not only inevitable but, in more ways than not, also desirable: many were enjoying the rewards and all might hope to have their share. Now that Western-style economic plenty appears far beyond reach for most African states, the attractions of the whole Western package, of values and ·social organizations, may well weaken.

But few of the discontented are likely to choose a retreat to rural life when growing populations constrain access to land. Nor does African tradition provide a doctrinal system that could become a magnetic alternative to the Western ethos. What does seem likely is that where Western culture loses some of its potency, African languages and popular arts will gain much greater sway over elite as well as mass self-expression. Like the flourishing of the informal economy within the tumble-down structures of the formal, African popular music, drama, and fiction may provide the cultural foundation previously lacking for a genuinely African synthesis of the traditional and modern.

The decline of old certitudes, both traditional and Western, may also lead to a greater role for both the Christian churches and Islamic movements, as well as to a resurgence of fundamentalist churches offering a blend of Christianity with local religious practices. Both Christianity and Islam offer a kind of refuge from a world of unattractive options, whose appeal has been demonstrated both in parts of the Middle East and in the United States. The evangelist Bishop Budu in Laing's *Search Sweet Country* was beloved by his congregation because he carried "their worries to God on [his] broad bright back."

Heightened religious fervor could have a number of effects. Fundamentalist religious churches often preach a deeply conservative message, upholding order and authority, but they also provide an alternative to constituted authority. Then too, as has been found in Latin America, the Middle East, and the United States, religious denominations can mobilize their followers' zeal for defined social goals. Thus greater popular activism by the Christian churches and by Islam in Africa could spur greater participation in African politics by Christians and Muslims. In states like Nigeria where Christian-Islamic cleavages already exist, this could add sectarian divisions to societies already seriously rent by tribal splits. Both Islam and Christianity, could, however, provide a moral basis—transcending ethnic loyalties—for concerted efforts to advance the general welfare.

During the 1980s, ideology has been shunted to a back burner in much of the continent. The appeal of the Soviet Union, and socialism, for African intellectuals has been chiefly in their opposition to the West and to capitalism. That appeal has waned as the persistence of Soviet economic backwardness has become clear over the past several decades. Nor—aside from its largely military involvement in Angola and Ethiopia, and its aid to South Africa's liberation movements—has the Soviet Union taken much interest in the continent since Rhodesia became Zimbabwe in 1980.

However, where reforms prove too difficult or unrewarding, and where political reactions dim possibilities of economic growth, socialist ideology—or left-wing populism—may well enjoy a resurgence, supplying a rationale and sometimes an organizing pattern for tightening authoritarian control. In several African countries, populist military leaders like Jerry Rawlings have been able to use socialist ideology to deflect blame for failure and support promises of better times. Before his overthrow in October 1987, Burkina Faso's Captain Thomas Sankara had became a role model for many young Africans—that of an egalitarian leader whose personal incorruptibility gave credibility to his stern demands on his people. In both impoverished Benin and oil rich Congo, military regimes have smoothed over sharp divisions and shored up authoritarian order with the soothing nostrums of socialism. For, apart from anything the Soviet Union does or does not, socialism continues to connote egalitarianism, redistribution, and rejection of colonialism. It can be seized both by those who seek those ends and those who use them to consolidate control. A reaction against reform is likely to generate more left-wing populism of both varieties.

229

But in Africa's current circumstances only a fairly draconian system of control can make such a system work politically—and economically the chances are much slimmer. Because most African states are dependent in so many ways on the West—and because the Soviet Union is unlikely to fill the gaps—a full-fledged ideological turnabout would have the effect of isolating a Marxist regime from most potential sources of material assistance. Thus, a pendulum swing from the current reforms to resurgent state control would in many cases probably result in more of the same but worse for the economy.

For some time to come, our own involvement with African development will be subject to the strong undertow of the continuing crisis. Periodic major efforts to cope with African famine threaten to turn our development assistance policy into pure and simple relief. Clearly, our enthusiasm for involvement in Africa will also be affected by the results of current reforms.

For the Western donors, the question of ideology has mattered in varying degrees. For the United States in particular, in the age of Reaganomics, the economic systems chosen by Third World countries became a matter of wins and losses: of being right. The argument of this book has itself supported the Western-backed reforms as "best" for Africa—as a corrective to the stagnation induced by all-embracing state control and the ethnic patronage systems feeding on it. To the extent they can be administered, these reforms will be "good" for African economies. However, any chance of their succeeding depends on a high degree of realism on our part as well as Africans.

Because the kind of far-reaching adjustments needed represent vast changes for many African societies, the prescription has to be varied according to the constitution of the patient. How much importance should be placed on economic planning, how many state enterprises should survive, how far African policy should rely on exports and how far it should be used to encourage production for domestic consumption—all of these much-debated issues may be decided in a number of different ways within African economic strategies. But the indicated remedy is not one of laissez-faire. If the result of reform is merely to privatize patronage or transform ethnic levies into an out and out license for exploitation of the poor by the rich, things could well be worse than before. Thus weak government is not the answer no matter what the strategy. Where privation is increasing, the best hope of many Africans would be for leaders who would combine strong economic control with "clean" fiscal management and concern for their people. Equally, if moves toward more "liberal" economic structures are to have the desired effect, African nations will need strong regimes that can build infrastructure and enforce ground rules leading to productivity and equity.

Realism should also extend to our own role. Structural adjustment is highly unlikely to have a widely beneficial effect unless African nations get more aid over the next decade than seems likely to be forthcoming. After the Western countries began encouraging and recognizing African "pragmatism" in economic reform, U.S. aid to Africa fell by nearly 50 percent. While the promises of socialism, may, like religion, inflate people's spirits, those of capitalism probably will not work unless they fill people's stomachs. While Western education and know-how can help Africans over the longer run, direct and swift infusions of debt relief are needed to sustain reform now.

In the drive for reform, as in all else, Africa cannot live with the West and it can't live without it. To the extent that the structural adjustment/austerity plans are externally derived, they are less likely to work. Where they fail, however, they may, paradoxically, spur reforms that will work better, not because of their technical superiority but because of the commitment of those who implement them. Thus, where reforms come pouring in, as where they succeed, what happens next depends greatly on the imponderable of leadership.

If we hadn't all—Africans and Westerners alike—thought it would be easy, the tortuous twists and turns of this path would surprise no one. It will take a lot of time. Obviously, Africans have to be in it for the long haul. The question for us, if we now realize how difficult, messy, and protracted this process is likely to be, is whether we have the patience to stay the course—offering counsel, encouragement and specifically targeted aid—alongside the Africans. Concerning ourselves with the welfare of Africans, as with that of most others of our species, requires overcoming our own tribalism. The reasons for doing so are compelling: only if we can, may our world—like that of the Africans—be an agreeable place in which to live.

# Notes on Sources

In telling the story of Africa's current struggle, I have been fortunate in the extent and kind of attention that Africa's crisis has received over the past few years. Thus, I have been able to draw on excellent studies by experts in a number of fields who, perhaps spurred by the enormity of the crisis, have been able to see the roots of problems more clearly as surface veneers erode. An account of my debts, and of some excellent work that has been done on Africa's economic situation, is found in the notes on individual chapters which follow. I have tried to acknowledge debts at both micro and macro levels, ranging from anecdotes found in newspaper articles to seminal books that have influenced my thinking. I hope these sources may be as instructive to readers who wish to push further as they have been to me.

## INTRODUCTION

On page 2, paragraph 2. David Lamb's *The Africans* (New York: Random House, 1982) attracted an unprecedentedly large audience for a book on this subject (even including President Ronald Reagan, who said in the *The New York Times* Christmas book review section that it was one of the three books he read in 1983). The former African correspondent for the *Los Angeles Times* is an extraordinarily well-informed and sympathetic observer, but the total effect of his vivid assemblage of anecdotes and facts was, finally—how strange Africa seemed! Xan Smiley probably reached even more people with his article on Africa in the September 1982 *The Atlantic Monthly;* in that piece, the former *Africa Confidential* editor found the cause of the highly complicated mess he described pretty obvious: that is, the well-nigh universal corruption of Africa's elites.

On page 6, paragraph 2, re variation in statistics, see the *World Bank Research News* (vol. 7, no. 1, Summer 1986); also Carl K. Eicher and Fidelis Mangiwiro, "A Critical Assessment of FAO Report on SADCC Agriculture," in *Food Security for Southern Africa,* by Mandivamba Rukuni and Carl K. Eicher et al, for University of Zimbabwe/Michigan State University Food Security Project, February 1987.

On page 8, paragraph 2, re the end of apartheid: with the end of apartheid, these problems would not go away. In fact, a majority rule government in South Africa would in certain ways would have a harder time because it would no longer be able to sweep them under the rug. Depending on what the struggle for majority rule involves, the country may or may not continue to enjoy the advantages of the industrial infrastructure that has been built up. The leaders will have to integrate into its economy large numbers of blacks who have been excluded from the system and, unlike the case in other African countries, unemployed workers will not have subsistence farming to fall back on: for many, if not most, agricultural roots have dried up long since, both in the cities and to some extent the homelands as well.

# 1: PRE-MODERN STATES IN A POST-MODERN WORLD

For a good overview of Africa that emphasizes political development, see Sanford J. Unger, *Africa* (New York: Simon and Schuster, 1985); also Richard Sandbrook, *The Politics of Africa's Economic Stagnation* (Cambridge: Cambridge University Press, 1985).

For a full explanation of the external and internal causes of Africa's decline, see Robert J. Berg and Jennifer Seymour Whitaker, eds. *Strategies for African Development* (Berkeley: University of California Press, 1986). See also John Ravenhill et al, *Africa in Economic Crisis* (New York: Columbia University Press, 1986), which succeeds very well in laying out the political and economic pitfalls that lie in wait for most reform strategies; Toré Rose et al, *Crisis and Recovery in Sub-Saharan Africa* (Paris: OECD Development Centre, 1985), which surveys remedies in a broad range of sectors, with some skepticism about conventional wisdom. An early analysis by Carol Lancaster, "Africa's Economic Crisis," *Foreign Policy* (Fall 1983), laid out the main trends. On Africa's trade problems and their causes, see Stephen R. Lewis, Jr., "Africa's Trade and the World Economy," in *Strategies for African Development*. See also Michael F. Lofchie, "Africa's Agrarian Malaise," in Gwendolen M. Carter and Patrick O'Meara, eds., *African Independence*, (Bloomington: Indiana University Press, 1985) pp. 168ff. See also: Kevin Danaher, "Can the Free Market Solve Africa's Food Crisis?" *TransAfrica Forum*, (Summer, 1987), for an argument emphasizing the relative helplessness of Africa's small farmers due to their dependence on the world economy; and G. K. Helleiner, "Outward Orientation, Import Stability and African Economic Growth: An Empirical Investigation": paper prepared for the Paul Streeten Festschrift, April 1984, which makes a good case for the primacy of import volume stability in African economic growth.

The epigraph by Arthur M. Schlesinger, Jr., is quoted from an article in *The New York Times Magazine* (July 27, 1986), which was adapted from Schlesinger's *The Cycles of American History* (New York: Houghton-Mifflin, 1986).

On page 13, paragraph 1, "Even the vultures have fled," is quoted from the *Christian Science Monitor* (April 9, 1984).

On page 15, paragraph 2, for a balanced appraisal of Africa's integration with the West, see I. William Zartman, "The Future of Africa and Europe" in Timothy W. Shaw et al, *Alternative Futures for Africa* (Boulder, Colo.: Westview Press, 1982).

On page 15, paragraph 3, studies on the evolution of Western European states and economies that profoundly influenced the argument of this chapter and this book include: William H. McNeill, *The Rise of the West: A History of the Human Community* (Chicago: University of Chicago Press, 1970); Nathan Rosenburg and L. E. Birdzell, Jr., *How the West Grew Rich: The Economic Transformation of the Industrialized World* (New York: Basic Books, 1986); Charles Tilly, *The Formation of National States in Western Europe* (Princeton: Princeton University Press, 1975); and Grace Goodell, "The Importance of Political Participation for Sustained Capital Development," ARCH, *Europ Sociol:* (XXVI, 1985) pp. 93–127. In this regard, see also Thomas R. Callaghy, *The State-Society Struggle: Zaïre in Comparative Perspective* (New York: Columbia University Press, 1984), an impressive survey of Zaïre's progress toward patriarchal absolutism through a comparison with the seventeenth- and eighteenth-century French Monarchy as well as through a close scrutiny of local bureaucratic pulling and hauling in the mid-1970s.

On page 15, paragraph 4, Chinua Achebe, *Things Fall Apart*, (New York: Ballantine Books, 1984), p. 155.

On page 23, paragraph 3, on ethnicity and economic organization in Africa, see Goran Hyden, *No Shortcuts to Progress: African Development Management in Perspective* (Berkeley: University of California Press, 1983), for a pathbreaking study of the difficulties of achieving economic growth in a society where family and clan interests still largely supercede the profit motive. Another groundbreaking study on this subject is Sara S. Berry, *Fathers Work for Their Sons* (Berkeley: University of California, 1985), cited extensively in Chapter 6.

On page 26, paragraph 1, James Ngugi, *A Grain of Wheat*, (Heinemann, London, 1966), p. 136.

## 2: WHAT WENT WRONG

On the economic effects of African social organization, I am particularly indebted to Hyden, *No Short Cuts to Progress*, Berry, *Fathers Work for Their Sons;* Gwendolen M. Carter and Patrick O'Meara, *African Independence: The First Twenty-Five Years* (Bloomington: Indiana University Press, 1985); and to an excellent overview by Christopher Clapham, *Third World Politics: An Introduction* (Madison: University of Wisconsin Press, 1985), which traces these social patterns throughout the Third World.

On page 32, paragraph 3, while most Western analysts agree that Africa's crisis stems from both external and internal factors, the balance between the two has been the object of some debate. The World Bank's analysis, *Accelerated Development in Sub-Saharan Africa: An Agenda for Action* (Washington, DC: The World Bank, 1981), emphasizing policy failures, provoked a spate of reactions (see below). For an analysis stressing problems with policy, see Stephen R. Lewis, Jr., "Africa's Trade and the World Economy" and also Ravi Gulhati and Gautam Datta, "Capital Accumulation in Eastern and Southern Africa: A Decade of Setbacks," *World Bank*

*Staff Working Papers*, no. 562, (Washington, DC: The World Bank, 1983), which analyzes the impact of government policy on productivity in capital investment. David Wheeler, on the other hand, argues in "Sources of Stagnation in Sub-Saharan Africa," *World Development*, (vol. 12, no. 1, 1984), pp. 1–23, that the environmental variables have had the most impact. See also Caroline Allison and Reginald Green, eds., *IDS (Sussex) Bulletin* (no. 1, 1983), for a highly critical examination of the World Bank's diagnosis of Africa's ills; and Ravi Gulhati and Satya Yalamanchili, "Contemporary Policy Responses to Economic Decline in Africa," paper presented at the conference on *The Crisis and Challenge of African Development*, September 26–28, 1985, Sugarloaf Conference Center, Temple University.

On the formation of African states, I am particularly indebted to the work of Robert H. Jackson and Carl G. Rosberg, including *Personal Rule in Black Africa: Prince, Autocrat, Prophet, Tyrant* (Berkeley: University of California Press, 1982), a fascinating study of African governance since Independence, which focuses on individual leadership styles; "Democracy in Tropical Africa: Democracy versus Autocracy in African Politics," *Journal of International Affairs* (Winter 1985); and "Popular Legitimacy in African Multi-Ethnic States," *The Journal of Modern African Studies* (22, 2, 1984), pp. 177–198. See also Thomas M. Callaghy, "The State and Development of Capitalism in Africa: Some Theoretical and Historical Reflections", to be published in *Balancing State-Society Relations in Africa*, Naomi Chazan and Donald Rothchild, eds. See also Aristide W. Zolberg, "The Formation of Weak States in Tropical Africa," in Aristide W. Zolberg, Astri Suhrke, and Sergio Aguayo, *Escape from Violence* (New York: Oxford University Press, 1988).

An excellent study of the workings of ethnicity, emphasizing the psychological motivation in mass movements and the value of the prestige of the entire group, is Donald L. Horowitz, *Ethnic Groups in Conflict* (Berkeley: University of California Press, 1985).

On page 32, paragraph 3, for an excellent discussion of some reasons why investors soured on Africa, see Pauline H. Baker, "Obstacles to Private Sector Activities in Africa," prepared for the Bureau of Intelligence and Research, Department of State, January 1983.

On page 32, paragraph 4, on the lack of flexibility of small poor economies see G. K. Helleiner, "The IMF and Africa in the 1980s," *Essays in International Finance*, No. 152, July 1983 (Princeton, N.J.: International Finance Section, Department of Economics, Princeton University).

On page 35, paragraph 1, see Bill Freund, *The Making of Contemporary Africa: The Development of African Society since 1800* (Bloomington: Indiana University Press, 1984), which scrutinizes the institutional legacy of the colonial period and also shows clearly the persistence of pre-capitalist economic and social patterns throughout the colonial period and into the present; another valuable account of the impact of colonialism in Africa is Crawford Young, "Africa's Colonial Legacy" in Berg and Whitaker, *Strategies for African Development*. See also David B. Abernethy, "European Colonialism and Post-Colonial Crises in Africa," prepared for the conference on "The Crisis and Challenge of African Development," Temple University Conference Center, Philadelphia, September 26–28, 1985; Thomas M. Callaghy, "The Political Economy of African Debt: The Case of Zaïre" in Ravenhill, *Africa in Economic Crisis.*

On page 36, paragraph 2, the assertion about the settlers' civilizing mission was made by M.F. Hill in "The White Settler's Role in Kenya," *Foreign Affairs* (July 1960), p. 659.

On page 37, paragraph 2, see Young, "Africa's Colonial Legacy."

On page 38, paragraph 2, *Ibid.*

On page 40, paragraph 2, General Olusegun Obasanjo, *Africa in Perspective* (New York: Council on Foreign Relations, 1987), p. 5.

On page 42, paragraph 2, Stanford J. Ungar, "The Military Money Drain", *Bulletin of the Atomic Scientists* (September 1985).

On page 43, paragraph 2, for general discussion of the military in African politics, see Henry Bienen, *Armies and Parties in Africa* (New York: Africana Publishing Co., 1978).

On page 47, paragraph 2, for an illuminating case study of the interplay between venality, bad policy, and the international marketplace, see Sayre P. Schatz, "Pirate Capitalism and the Inert Economy of Nigeria," *The Journal of Modern African Studies* (22, 1, 1984), pp. 45–57.

On page 49, paragraph 2, Chinua Achebe, *No Longer at Ease* (New York, Ballantine Books, 1984) p. 81.

On page 51, paragraph 2, Pale Walde is quoted from *The Wall Street Journal,* July 15, 1985.

On page 52, paragraph 1, the story about the gold pin stripe suit comes from *Ibid.*

On pages 52ff, three papers by David B. Abernethy provide the best sources on relationships between bureaucracy and productivity in Africa. These include: "Bureaucratic Growth and Economic Decline in Sub-Saharan Africa," paper written for presentation at the 26th Annual Meeting of the African Studies Association, Boston, MA, December 1983, pp. 12–13; "European Colonialism and Post-Colonial Crises in Africa;" paper prepared for the Conference on "The Crisis and Challenge of African Development," Temple University Conference Center, Philadelphia, September 26–28, 1985; and "Bureaucratic Growth and Economic Stagnation in Sub-Saharan Africa," unpublished paper.

On page 53, paragraph 4, Abernethy, "Bureaucratic Growth and Economic Decline," p. 9. See also Paul Bennell, "The Colonial Legacy of Salary Structures in Anglophone Africa," *The Journal of Modern African Studies* (20, 1, 1982), pp. 127–154.

On page 54, paragraph 2, see Abernethy, "European Colonialism and Post-colonial Crises," p. 19.

On page 54, paragraph 3, Abernethy, "Bureaucratic Growth and Economic Decline," p. 14.

On page 55, paragraph 2, Abernethy, "Bureaucratic Growth and Economic Stagnation," p. 19.

On page 55, paragraph 4, Abernethy, "Bureaucratic Growth and Economic Decline," p. 21.

## 3: THE WAGES OF ALTRUISM

Surprisingly little has been published on the subject of U.S. aid to Africa. Therefore this account relies to a great extent on interviews with practitioners. The thoughts of Frank Ballance and his unpublished paper, "Aid and Congress," were a major resource. Bob Berg, Bill Diebold, Haven North, Mark Edelman, Raymond Love, Philip Birnbaum, Alex Shakow, Roy Stacey, and Carol Lancaster were all extremely helpful. For the historical material, I owe a major debt to Gerald N. Meier and Dudley Seers, eds., *Pioneers in Development* (Washington, DC: the World Bank, New York: Oxford University Press, 1984). For a helpful summary of the main trends in U.S. aid to Africa, see Carol Lancaster, "U.S. Aid to Africa: Who Gets What, When and How," *CSIS Africa Notes* (no. 25, March 31, 1984).

On page 59, paragraph 2, the quote from Lord Keynes is from Gerald N. Meier, "The Formative Period," in *Pioneers in Development*, p. 9.

On page 59, paragraph 3, see *Ibid*, p. 14.

In the same paragraph, Harold Laswell is quoted from "The Policy Signs of Development," *World Politics* (no. 17, 286, 1965), p. 337.

On page 60, paragraph 3, Bill Diebold has pointed out the salient arguments made at the time for concentrating on industry. On this point, see also Meier, "The Formative Period," pp. 11–13.

On page 61, paragraph 4, on Africa's aid dependence, see Robert J. Berg, "Foreign Aid in Africa: Here's the Answer—Is it Relevant to the Question?" in Berg and Whitaker, *Strategies for African Development*, p. 506.

On page 63, regarding the direction of World Bank lending, it should be recognized that the Bank has been, in fact, for most of its existence a significantly more conservative organization than the U.S. Agency for International Development. As its name indicates, it is primarily a lending institution. About a third of its loans take the form of long-term credits to the poorest countries (through the International Development Association). Most of the bank's capital is not granted but lent (at the lower end of prevailing interest rates, fifteen to twenty years for repayment) and it must be repaid. Therefore, the Bank has less flexibility than the United States or other national donors. By and large, its projects are expected to have a good rate of return, and basic components of development—like roads, water and power systems, schools and universities—have dominated its portfolio. Now the crisis is changing the Bank's profile within the continent as nearly interest-free grants disbursed from the Bank's soft-loan window become the norm.

On page 64, paragraph 2, on the proportion of U.S. aid to Africa that takes the form of U.S. military assistance, see "U.S. Military Assistance to Africa," by William H. Lewis, *CSIS Africa Notes* (no. 75, August 6, 1987).

On page 65, paragraph 3, Sir Abubakar Tafawa Balewa, "Nigeria Looks Ahead", *Foreign Affairs* (October 1962), p. 134.

On page 66, paragraph 2, Meier, "The Formative Period," p. 18.

On page 67, paragraph 2, re aid in Vietnam, see Ballance, "Aid and Congress."

On page 68, paragraph 1, Zablocki quote, *Ibid,* p. 12.

On page 69, paragraph 2, for a full account of the Bank and its policy shift, see Robert L. Ayres, *Banking on the Poor: The World Bank and World Poverty* (Cambridge, The MIT Press, 1983).

On page 71, paragraph 1, see "Can More Be Done To Assist Sahelean Governments to Plan and Manage Their Economic Development?" Study by the Staff of the U.S. General Accounting Office (Washington, DC: U.S. GAO, September 6, 1985).

On page 71, paragraph 3, Ballance, "Aid and Congress," p. 36.

On page 74, paragraph 1, on failed efforts in the Sudan, *The Washington Post* (March 12, 1983).

On page 74, paragraph 2, on the story of the Turkana, *The Washington Post* (April 30, 1986), and *The Christian Science Monitor* (August 5, 1985).

On page 75, paragraph 3, on the failed eucalyptus forest in Senegal, *The Wall Street Journal* (July 29, 1985).

On pages 75 and 76, regarding overall aid to Tanzania, *The Christian Science Monitor* (February 4, 1986).

On page 76, paragraph 2, on Tanzania's cashew industry, *The Washington Post* (November 19, 1984); on the pulp and paper mill, *Christian Science Monitor* (August 5, 1985).

On page 76, paragraph 3, re the proliferation of donor projects, see Elliott R. Morss, "Institutional Destruction Resulting from Donor and Project Proliferation in Sub-Saharan African Countries," *World Development* (vol. 12, no. 4, 1984), pp. 465–470.

On page 76, paragraph 4, on the "tying" of aid, see "Monitoring for Aid to Developing Countries," *World Development* (vol. 12, no. 9, 1984), pp. 879–900.

On page 77, paragraph 2, on adverse views of aid, critiques include William and Elizabeth Paddock, *An Independent Audit of What They Call Success in Foreign Aid* (Ames, Iowa: Iowa State University Press, 1973); Francis Moore Lappé, Joseph Collins, David Kinley, *Aid as Obstacle* (San Francisco: Institute for Food and Development Policy, 1980); P. T. Bauer, *Equality, the Third World, and Economic Delusion* (Cambridge, Mass: Harvard University Press, 1981); Nick Eberstadt, "Famine, Development & Foreign Aid", *Commentary* (March 1985) pp. 25–31; Jack Shepherd, "When Foreign Aid Fails," *The Atlantic Monthly* (April 1985) pp. 41–46.

On page 78, paragraph 2, *The Washington Post* (April 14, 1981).

On pages 79–83, on the policy discussion, the debate about "liberalization," the priority of agriculture, and what difference policy itself makes in relation to other factors such as government delivery of services, the weather, and international economic trends was initiated by the World Bank report cited above, *Accelerated Development in Sub-Saharan Africa: An Agenda for Action,* commonly known as "the Berg report." Reactions to Berg include David F. Gordon and Joan C. Parker, "The World Bank and Its Critics: The Case of Sub-Saharan Africa" (Ann Arbor, MI: Center for Research on Economic Development, Discussion Paper no. 108, March 1984); *Rural Africana,* special issue on the Berg report (nos. 19–20, 1984) and the *IDS Bulletin,* (no. 1, 1983). Studies debating or describing the policy issues include Berg and Whitaker, *Strategies for African Development;* Toré Rose, ed., *Crisis and Recovery in Sub-Saharan Africa* (Paris: OECD, 1985); *Africa: Crisis and Beyond*, special issues of the *International Journal,* Canadian Institute of International Affairs (vol. XLI, no. 4, Autumn 1986); Reginald Herbold Green, "Africa in the 1980s: What are the Key Questions? What is to be Done?"; paper presented at the Society for International Development, Kenya Chapter Conference, "Development Options for Africa in the 1980s and Beyond," Nairobi, March 1983; Manfred Beinefield, "The Lessons of Africa's Industrial 'Failure'," *IDS Bulletin* (16, 3, 1985) Sussex: Institute of Development Studies, pp. 69–87; and Christopher Colclough, "Competing Paradigms in the Debate about Agricultural Pricing Policy," *Ibid*, pp. 39–46; Kevin M. Cleaver, "The Impact of Price and Exchange Rate Policies on Agriculture in Sub-Saharan Africa" *World Bank Staff Working Papers* (no. 728, Washington, DC: The World Bank, 1985). Later World Bank perspectives on issues raised by the Berg report are *Towards Sustained Development in Sub-Saharan Africa: A Joint Program of Action* (Washington, DC: The World Bank, 1984); and *Financing Adjustment with Growth in Sub-Saharan Africa, 1986–90* (Washington, DC: The World Bank, 1986).

On pages 83–86, for good general discussions of Africa's debt crisis see Carol Lancaster, John Williamson et al, *African Debt and Financing* (Washington, DC: Institute for International Economics, special reports no. 5, May 1986); and Chandra S. Hardy, "Africa's Debt: Structural Adjustment with Stability," in Berg and Whitaker, *Strategies for African Development*. An important perspective on the IMF's role is John Loxley, "The IMF and the Poorest Countries: Performance of the Least Developed Countries Under IMF Standby Arrangements," (Ottawa, Canada: the North-South Institute, 1984).

## 4: THE BLESSINGS OF CHILDREN

In this chapter, I am greatly indebted to several studies by demographer John Charles Caldwell, including his paper, "Cultural Forces Tending to Sustain High Fertility in Tropical Africa" and his book, *The Persistence of High Fertility: Population Prospects in the Third World*, (no. 1 in "The Family and Fertility Change: Changing African Family Companion Series," Department of Demography, Australia National University, Canberra, 1977). Of particular value within *Persistence* is Helen Ware, "Economic Strategy and the Number of Children," an impressive overview of relationships between culture and economy. Together the studies go far to explain why Africa's demographic pattern looks so different from that of other world regions. Also of real value on spurs to fertility arising from African tradition are Jack Goody, *The Character of Kinship* (Cambridge: Cambridge University Press, 1973); Margaret J. Field, *Search for Security: An Ethnopsychiatric Study of Rural Ghana* (London: Faber and Faber, 1960); and Lucy Mair, *African Marriage and Social Change* (London: Frank Cass and Co., Ltd., 1969). Valuable references on marriage and social relationships include Margaret Jean Hay and Sharon Stichter et al, *African Women South of the Sahara* (London: Longman, 1984); Denise Paulme et al, *Women of Tropical Africa* (Berkeley: University of California Press, 1963); Nancy J. Haskin and Edna G. Bay et al, *Women in Africa: Studies in Social and Economic Change* (Stanford, California: Stanford University Press, 1976); *Population Growth and Policies in Sub-Saharan Africa* (Washington, DC: The World Bank, 1986), a World Bank Policy Study, was equally important in documenting changes now occurring, though as yet hardly discernible to the naked eye.

On page 88, paragraph 1, Chinua Achebe, *Things Fall Apart*, p. 163.

On page 88, paragraph 2, re the European demographic transition, see Michael Teitelbaum, "Relevance of Demographic Transition Theory for Developing Countries," *Science*, May 2, 1975, pp. 420–425, and John Knodel and Etienne van den Walle, "Lessons from the Past: Policy Implications of Historical Fertility Studies," *Population and Development Review*, (2, June 1979), pp. 217–245.

On page 88, paragraph 3, comparative figures for Kenya come from David Lamb, *The Africans*, p. 7.

On page 90, paragraph 1, Caldwell, *The Persistence of High Fertility*.

On page 90, paragraph 2, Cheikh Hamidou Kane, *Ambiguous Adventure*, (New York: Collier Books, 1972), p. 130.

On page 91, paragraph 1, on the Bera of Tanzania, see Marc J. Swartz, "Some Cultural Influences on Family Size in Three East African Societies," *Anthropological Quarterly* (42, 2, 1969), p. 82.

On page 91, paragraph 2, on the Yoruba of Nigeria, see the useful essay by I. O. Orubuloye, "High Fertility and the Rural Economy: A Study of Yoruba Society in Western Nigeria," in Caldwell, *Persistence*. On the links between children and ancestors, see Caldwell, "Cultural Forces," *Persistence;* and Goody, *The Character of Kinship*.

On page 92, paragraph 2, Orubuloye, "High Fertility," p. 363.

On page 92, paragraph 4, Thayer Scudder, *Gathering among African Woodland Cultivators: A Case Study—The Gwembe Tonga* (Manchester: Manchester University Press, 1971), pp. 61ff.

On page 93, paragraph 1, on the Sisala of Northern Ghana, E. L. Mendonsa, "The Explanation of High Fertility among the Sisala of Northern Ghana," in Caldwell, *Persistence*, p. 237. On the Nuer of Southern Sudan, see Mohamed El Awad, "The Economic Value of Children in Rural Sudan," in Caldwell, *Persistence*, pp. 624–625.

On page 93, paragraph 3, on the Gonja of Northern Ghana, Orubuloye, "High Fertility," p. 363.

On page 94, paragraph 1, on the power of the father, see Helen Ware, "Economic Strategy," p. 488.

On page 94, paragraph 2, on the Mossi of Burkina Faso, *Ibid*, p. 496.

On page 94, paragraph 3, on Nigeria's Igbo people, *Ibid*, p. 490. In the same paragraph, regarding unemployed school teachers, see M. J. Field, *Search for Security*, p. 31.

On page 95, paragraph 3, on the effect of urban life on fertility, see Helen Ware, "Economic Strategy," pp. 512–529.

On page 97, paragraph 2, on the army officer in Congo, see Lucy Mair, *African Marriage and Social Change,* p. 551.

On page 97, paragraph 3, on the Banyankore of Western Uganda, see Tarsis Kabwegyere, "Determinates of Fertility: A Discussion of Change in the Family Among the Ahamba of Kenya," in Caldwell, *Persistence,* p. 191.

On page 98, paragraph 2, on the Coniagui in Guinea, see Paulme, *Women of Tropical Africa,* p. 24.

On page 98, paragraph 3, on male-female relationships in marriage see Lucy Mair, *African Marriage and Social Change.*

On page 99, paragraph 4, regarding woman-woman marriage, see Hay and Stichter, *African Women,* pp. 57–62.

On page 100, paragraph 3, Camara Laye, quoted in Hay and Stichter, *African Women,* p. 112.

On page 100, paragraph 4, Buchi Emecheta, *The Joys of Motherhood,* (New York: George Braziller), p. 32.

On page 101, paragraphs 2 and 3, see Caldwell, "Cultural Forces," pp. 10–16.

On page 102, paragraph 1, see Field, *Search for Security.*

On pp. 103–123, the data on population, urbanization, employment, and health, as well as information on family planning throughout this section come from The World Bank study, "Population Growth and Policy in Sub-Saharan Africa." See also Fred T. Sai, "Population and Health: Africa's Most Basic Resource and Development Problem", in Berg and Whitaker, *Strategies.* General sources include Frank L. Mott and Susan H. Mott, "The African Paradox of Growth and Development," *Bulletin of the Atomic Scientist* (April 1986), pp. 26–29; and Rashid Faruqee and Ravi Gulhati, "Rapid Population Growth in Sub-Saharan Africa: Issues and Policies," World Bank Staff Working Papers, Number 555, (Washington, DC: The World Bank, 1983). See also Edwin Green, "U.S. Population Policies: Development and the Rural Poor" in *The Journal of Modern African Studies* (20, 1, 1982), pp. 45–67, which illustrates the need for policies aimed at achieving economic equity in coping with Africa's population surge.

On page 104, paragraph 3, on African labor and land, see Food and Agriculture Organization of the United Nations, "Potential Population Supporting Capacities of Land in the Developing World," (Rome: United Nations, 1982).

On pages 106 and 107, on the differences between Africa's situation and that of Europe, see Teitelbaum, "Relevance of Demographic Transition Theory."

On page 107 and ff, see Caldwell, *Persistence,* pp. 5, 19, 36, 41, and 42; Christine Oppong et al, *Female and Male in West Africa,* (London: George Allen and Unwin, 1983); Lucy Mair, *African Marriage and Social Change,* pp. 49ff; Mary Steimel Deru, "Continuity in the Midst of Change: Underlying Themes in Igbo Culture," *Anthropological Quarterly* (56, 1, 1983), p. 5.

On page 108, paragraph 2, on laws affecting women, see Dina Sheikh el Din Osman, "Reform of the Legal Status of Moslem Women in the

Sudan;" paper presented at the Conference on Law and Development in Contemporary Societies of the Middle East, University of California, 1983; Athaliah Molokomme, "The Woman's Guide to the Law: An Outline of How the Law Affects Every Woman and Her Family in Botswana," prepared for the Women's Affairs Unit, Ministry of Home Affairs, Botswana; Joan Harris, "Women in Kenya: Revolution or Evolution?" *Africa Report* March/April 1985; Eddison Zvobgo, "Women in Zimbabwe: Removing Laws that Oppress Women," *Africa Report* (March/ April 1983); Rosalyn Thomas, "Women: The Laws in Southern Africa: Justice for All?," *Africa Report* (March/April 1985); A. Graham Tipple, "Ghana: Revolution in Property Rights," *West Africa* (1985); Rhoda Howard, "Human Rights and Personal Law: Women in Sub-Saharan Africa," by Rhoda Howard, *Issue: A Journal of Africanist Opinion* (vol. XII, nos. 1/2, Spring/Summer 1982).

On page 109, paragraph 1, *Zambia Daily Mail* (February 13, 1986).

On Page 109, paragraph 2, on the comparison with Europe, see Teitelbaum, "Relevance."

On page 110, paragraph 1, the Kenyan woman is quoted from Perdita Houston, *Third World Women Speak Out* (Washington, D.C., Praeger and Overseas Development Council, 1979), p. 79.

On page 112, paragraph 4, on the Mexico Conference, see Davidson R. Gwatkin, "The State of the World's Population Movement: Implications of the 1984 Mexico Conference", *World Development* (vol. 13, no. 4, 1985), pp. 557–569.

On page 116, paragraph 2, the Kenyan woman is quoted from "USAID Analogies and Strategies for Assistance in Family Planning and Fertility Reduction in Kenya," USAID-Kenya, Office of Population and Health, January 1985.

On page 117, paragraph 3, on sleeping sickness, see *The New York Times* (July 16, 1985); and on diarrheal diseases, see *The New York Times* (May 27, 1986).

On page 118, paragraph 1, on reasons for the possible rampant spread of AIDS, see Lynn W. Kitchen, "AIDS in Africa, Knowns and Unknowns," *CSIS Africa Notes* (July 17, 1987).

On page 121, paragraph 3, on the relationship of women's education to limiting fertility, see The World Bank, "Population Growth and Policies," pp. 4ff, also 38ff, 46, and 47.

On page 123, paragraphs 2 and 3, on the cost of family planning programs in Africa, see the World Bank, *Ibid,* pp. 63–65.

# 5: EDEN ERODING

For my understanding of Africa's agrarian crisis, I owe much to Carl K. Eicher (who is, however, in no way responsible for the views expressed herein). In addition to his pathbreaking *Foreign Affairs* article, "Facing up to Africa's Food Crisis" (Fall 1982), Eicher's extremely useful analyses of the problem and strategies for coping with it include: "West Africa's

Agrarian Crisis," paper prepared for the Fifth Bi-Annual Conference of the West African Association of Agricultural Economists, Abidjan, Ivory Coast, December 7–11, 1983; "Food Security Policy in Sub-Saharan Africa" with John M. Staatz; paper prepared for the XIXth Conference of the International Association of Agriculture Economists, Malaga, Spain, August 25–September 5, 1984; "Transforming African Agriculture," the *Hunger Project Papers* (no. 4, January 1986); and "Strategic Issues in Combating Hunger and Poverty in Africa," in Berg and Whitaker, *Strategies*. See also John W. Mellor, Christopher Delgado, and Malcolm Blackie, *Accelerating Food Production in Sub-Saharan Africa* (Baltimore: Johns Hopkins University Press, 1987), for an exhaustive compendium including a number of the foremost authorities on agriculture in Africa.

On Africa's environmental crisis I am greatly indebted to Lloyd Timberlake, whose *Africa in Crisis* (London: Earthscan, 1985) became a basic text; and also to Lester W. Brown and Edward C. Wolf, for "Reversing Africa's Decline," *Worldwatch Paper 65* (June, 1985). See also Jon Tinker "Africa: The Environmental Factor," *Horizons* (Spring 1985); and *Tropical Forests: A Call for Action* (Part II, Case Studies), Report of an International Task Force Convened by the World Resources Institute, the World Bank and the United Nations Development Program, 1985; and Uma Lele and Wilfred Candler, "Food Security in Developing Countries: National Issues," in Carl K. Eicher and John M. Staatz, et al, *Agricultural Development in the Third World* (Baltimore: Johns Hopkins University Press, 1984), pp. 207–221.

On page 127, paragraph 1, Monica Wilson and Leonard Thompson et al, *The Oxford History of South Africa* (vol. 1, South Africa to 1870, Oxford: Oxford University Press, 1969), p. 83.

On page 128, paragraph 2, Michael F. Lofchie, "Africa's Agrarian Malaise" in *African Independence*, pp. 164–167.

On page 128, paragraph 3, the Native Commissioner is quoted from F. W. Fox and D. Black, *A Preliminary Survey of the Agricultural and Nutritional Problems on the Ciskei and Transkeian Territories with Special Reference to their Bearing on the Recruiting of Laborers for the Mining Industry* (Johannesburg, 1938), p. 176. The contrasting quotes are found in David J. Webster, "The Political Economy of Food Production and Nutrition in Southern Africa in Historical Perspective," *The Journal of Modern African Studies* (23, 1986), pp. 447–463.

On page 129, paragraph 1, on fallow periods in the Nigerian villages, see Mohamed T. El-Ashry, "Sustainable Resource Management in Sub-Saharan Africa," *Journal '86*, World Resources Institute, Washington, D.C., p. 7.

On page 129, paragraph 2, see J. A. Binns, "The Resources of Rural Africa: The Geographical Perspective," *African Affairs*, January 1984, p. 36.

On page 129, paragraph 3, see Timberlake, *Africa in Crisis*, p. 62.

On page 130, paragraph 3, on monocrop economy, see Timberlake, *Africa in Crisis*, p. 70.

On page 132, paragraph 2, see Mette Monsted, "The Changing Division of Labor within Rural Families in Kenya," in Caldwell and Ware, *Persistence,* Chapter 7, pp. 264–266.

On page 134, paragraph 4, on the characteristics of the Sahel, see Steven Reina, "Economics and Fertility: Waiting for the Demographic Transition in the Dry Zone of Francophile West Africa," in Caldwell and Ware, *Persistence,* Chapter 11, p. 396.

On page 135, paragraph 1, on early effects on the Sahel's ecology, see "Desertification Defines Ordeal of the Sahel," *Science* (vol. 224, p. 468).

On pages 137 and 138, on Africa's climatic zones, see Timberlake, *Africa in Crisis,* p. 109.

On page 138, paragraph 3, see Kenneth Newcombe, "An Economic Justification for Rural Afforestation: The Case of Ethiopia," *Energy Department Paper,* no. 16, (Washington, DC: The World Bank, 1984).

On page 139, paragraph 2, see Brown, "Reversing Africa's Decline," p. 24; and Timberlake, *Africa in Crisis,* p. 106; see also Dennis Anderson, "Declining Tree Stocks in African Countries," *World Development* (vol. 14, no. 7, 1986) pp. 853–863.

On page 140, paragraph 1, on the use of wood as a source of energy see Brown, p. 47, and Timberlake, pp. 112–113.

On page 140, paragraph 2, on Malawi, see David French, "Confronting an Unsolvable Problem: Deforestation in Malawi," *World Development* (vol. 14, no. 4, April 1986), pp. 531–540.

On page 140, paragraph 3, on the Sudan, see Brown, p. 13.

On pages 141 and 142, on the relationship between deforestation and rainfall, see Brown, pp. 22–27; also G.O.P. Obasi, "Understanding the Drought," *Bulletin of the Atomic Scientist* (September 1985), pp. 43–45.

On page 142, paragraphs 2 and 3, on Ethiopia's erosion, see Haile Lul Tebicke, "Sustainable Agriculture: An Ethiopian View", *Bulletin of the Atomic Scientist* (September 1985), pp. 39–42.

On page 143, paragraph 1, on the opening up of African lands to cultivation, I am indebted to Ralph M. Rotty for figures on sub-Saharan Africa.

In the same paragraph, on Senegal's push for land expansion, see El-Ashry, "Sustainable Resource Management," p. 7.

On page 143, paragraph 2, Timberlake, p. 133.

On page 143, paragraph 3, Food and Agriculture Organization of the United Nations, "Potential Population-Supporting Capacities of Lands in the Developing World.".

On page 144, paragraph 2, Timberlake, p. 132.

On page 145, paragraph 1, I am indebted to Leonard Berry on the changing attitudes of African leaders on conservation.

On page 146, paragraph 2, re the "Johnny Appleseed Project," Timberlake, p. 123.

On page 146, paragraph 3, see Timberlake, pp. 134–136.

On page 149, paragraph 3, on the African farm labor shortage, see John W. Mellor, *Accelerating Food Production,* and John W. Mellor and C. G. Ranade, "Technological Change in a Low Labor Productivity, Land

Surplus Economy: The African Development Problem"; also Colin Norman "The Technological Challenge in Africa," *Science* (February 8, 1985), p. 616.

On page 150, paragraph 2, on the organization of rural labor, see Joyce Lewinger Moock, et al, *Understanding Africa's Rural Households and Farming Systems* (Boulder, Colo.: Westview Press, 1986). In the same paragraph, on the loss of crops to pests, see E. J. Kahn, Jr., *The Staffs of Life* (Boston: Little, Brown, 1985).

On page 150, paragraph 3, the relief worker in the Sahel is quoted from Timberlake, p. 5.

On page 150, and ff, valuable studies of women's lives and productivity in Africa include: Hay and Stichter, *African Women;* Paulme, *Women of Tropical Africa;* Haskin and Bay, *Women in Africa;* Jeanne Koopman Henn, "Feeding the Cities and Feeding the Peasants: What Role for Africa's Women Farmers?", *World Development*, vol. 11, no. 12, pp. 1043–1055; Achola O. Pala "A Preliminary Study of the Avenues for and Constraints on Women in the Development Process in Kenya," Institute for Development Studies, University of Nairobi, Discussion Paper no. 218, 1975; Achola O. Pala, "African Women in Rural Development: Research Trends and Priorities," Institute for Development Studies, University of Nairobi, Overseas Liaison Committee, Paper no. 12, December 1976; Jane I. Guyer, "Women's Role in Development," in Berg and Whitaker, *Strategies;* Jean M. Due and Rebecca Summary, "Constraints on Women and Development in Africa," *The Journal of Modern African Studies* (20, I, 1982), pp. 155–166; Louise Fortmann, "The Plight of the Invisible Farmer: The Effect of National Agricultural Policy on Women"; Louise Fortmann, "Women's Work in a Communal Setting: The Tanzanian Policy of Ujaama," in Edna G. Bay, ed., *Women and Work in Africa* (Boulder: Westview, 1982); Kenneth Little, *African Women in Towns*, (Cambridge: Cambridge University Press, 1973). See also *TransAfrica Forum*, special issue on women, (vol. 4, no. 3, Spring 1987).

On page 152, paragraph 1, the African woman farmer is quoted in "Africa Tomorrow: Issues in Technology, Agriculture and U.S. Farm Aid," Office of Technology Assistance, Congress of the United States, December 1984.

On page 152, paragraph 2, *The New York Times* (May 16, 1986).

On page 152, paragraph 3, on women's workload, see "African Women and Food Strategies: A Guide for Policy and Implementation Measures Relating to the Role of African Women in Food Systems," World Food Council paper in response to recommendations of the Abidjan workshop, June 1985, p. 15.

In the same paragraph, the Tanzanian man's complaint is quoted from Liz Wiley, *Women and Development: A Case Study of Ten Tanzanian Villages* (Arusha, Regional Commissioner's Office, 1981).

On page 154, paragraphs 2 and 3, on the women of Jahally and Pacharr, see Khadija Musa, "Rice from the Women of Jahally and Pacharr Lifts up Gambia," *Africa Emergency Report* (Nov.–Dec. 1985), p. 13.

On page 155, paragraph 1, on small farms, see Bruce F. Johnston, "Governmental Strategies for Agricultural Development," in Berg and Whitaker, *Strategies*.

On page 156, paragraph 1, on the technological revolution in agriculture, see Barbara Insel, "A World Awash in Grain," *Foreign Affairs* (Spring 1985); and "Scientific Advances Lead to Era of Food Surpluses Around the World," *The New York Times* (September 9, 1986).

On pages 156–158, on the differences between Africa and Asia, see John W. Mellor, "The Changing World Food Situation", *Food Policy Statement*, International Food Policy Institute, January 1985; Brown, "Reversing Africa's Decline", pp. 56–59; and Norman, "Technological Challenge in Africa," pp. 616–617. On page 156, paragraph 2, on parallels between Asian and African experience, see Carl K. Eicher, "West Africa's Agrarian Crisis," p. 47.

On page 157 and ff, for a general overview on research, see Dunstan S.C. Spencer, "Agricultural Research: Lessons of the Past, Strategies for the Future," in Berg and Whitaker, *Strategies*. On the illusion of donors that "miracle" strains were transferable, and the subsequently disappointing history of agricultural research in Africa, see Eicher, "West Africa's Agrarian Crisis," pp. 38–40. On the fragmentation of Africa's research effort see Montague Yudelman, "Sub-Saharan Agriculture Research," *Bulletin of the Atomic Scientist* (September 1985), pp. 35–38. On the need for research on African farming systems, see John W. Mellor and Bruce F. Johnston, "The World Food Equation: Interrelations among Development, Employment and Food Consumption," *Journal of Economics Literature* (vol XXII, June, 1984), pp. 558ff. On research institutions, see Chikwendu Christian Ukaegbu, "Are Nigerian Scientists and Engineers Effectively Utilized: Issues on the Deployment of Scientific and Technological Labor for National Development," *World Development* (vol. 13, no. 4, 1985), pp. 499–512.

On page 157, paragraph 3, for a graphic illustration of the fragmentation of the African environment, see William I. Jones and Roberto Egli, "Farming Systems in Africa: The Great Lakes Highlands of Zaïre, Rwanda, and Burundi," World Bank Technical Paper no. 27, (Washington, DC: The World Bank, 1984).

On page 157, paragraph 4, on irrigation in Africa, see El-Ashry, "Sustainable Resource Management," p. 9; Asit Biswas, "Irrigation in Africa," *Land Use Policy* (October 1986); and M. S. Swaminathan, "Sustainable Nutrition Security for Africa," *The Hunger Project Papers* (no. 5, October 1986), p. 5.

On page 158, paragraph 3, see Mellor, "Changing World Food Situation."

On page 158, paragraph 4, for an impressively full account of the interplay between politics and economic decision-making, see Robert H. Bates, *Markets and States in Tropical Africa: The Political Basis of Agricultural Policies* (Berkeley: University of California Press, 1981).

On page 159, paragraphs 2 and 3, on the intersection of political and economic rationality, see John Ravenhill, "Collective Self-Reliance or

Collective Self-Delusion: Is the Lagos Plan a Viable Alternative?," in Ravenhill et al, *Africa in Economic Crisis*.

On page 160, paragraph 2, on the cost of transporting food, see Mellor, "The Changing World Food Situation." On the need to decentralize the distribution of inputs, see David K. Leonard, "Putting the Farmer in Control: Building Agricultural Institutions," in Berg and Whitaker, *Strategies*. On the gaps among Africa and Asia and Latin America in training, see Eicher, "Western Science," pp. 29–33.

On page 161, paragraph 2, the story about farmer Cleophas arap Moro is from *The Washington Post* (November 18, 1982).

On page 162, paragraphs 2 and 3, on new technologies, see Carl K. Eicher and Christopher Walton, "Lessons from African Agriculture," *Finance and Development* (March 1984), pp. 13–16.

# 6: A LEARNING SOCIETY

On page 169, paragraph 1, Cheikh Hamidou Kane, *Ambiguous Adventure*, p. 10.

On page 169, paragraph 3, on the Israeli Ambassador in Cameroon, *The New York Times* (August 30, 1986).

On pages 170 and 171, Camara Laye, *The Guardian of the Word* (New York: Aventura, 1984), pp. 26 and 28.

On pages 171–173, I am indebted David D. Laitin, "Linguistic Dissociation: A Strategy for Africa," in John Gerard Ruggie, ed., *The Antinomies of Interdependence: National Welfare and the International Division of Labor* (New York: Columbia University Press, 1983), pp. 317–368, for an excellent overview of Africa's current linguistic dilemmas.

On pages 173 and 174, on Nigeria's linguistic problems, see *The Economist* (May 3, 1986).

On pages 175–180, for an excellent overview of how far African education has come and the problems it faces now, see David Court and Kabiru Kinyanjui, "African Education: Problems in a High-Growth Sector," in Berg and Whitaker, *Strategies*. See also Alain Mingat and George Psacharopoulos, "Financing Education in sub-Saharan Africa," *Finance and Development* (March 1985).

On page 176, paragraph 3, on the declines in education, see the World Bank, *Financing Adjustment With Growth*, pp. 29–30.

On page 178, paragraph 2, *Ibid*, p. 30.

On page 181, paragraph 2, the case for the priority of agricultural education in Africa has been argued most persuasively by Eicher; see studies already cited and particularly "Western Science and African Hunger," pp. 31ff; and "Transforming African Agriculture," pp. 18–22.

On pages 181 and 182, on the Côte d' Ivoire, see I. William Zartman and Christopher L. Delgado et al, *The Political Economy of Ivory Coast*, (New York: Praeger, 1984). On Senegal's experience, see Eicher, "Transforming African Agriculture," pp. 19–20.

On page 182, paragraphs 1 and 2, on donors and agricultural education see Eicher, "West Africa's Agrarian Crisis," pp. 53ff. On the SADCC experience, see Eicher, "Transforming African Agriculture," p. 20.

On page 182, paragraph 2, regarding the flow of African students to overseas universities, see Joyce Lewinger Moock, "Overseas Training and National Development Objectives in Sub-Saharan Africa," *The Comparative Education Review* (Spring 1984). On African students' thesis research, see Eicher, "Western Science," pp. 33ff.

On pages 183–186, for the discussion of the relationship between ethnicity and African styles of investment and organization, I am greatly indebted to Sara S. Berry, *Fathers Work for Their Sons,* a brilliant depiction of how people make a living and provide for the future in two Yoruba communities, showing how plausible economic strategies in the prevailing context work to constrain rather than expand productivity.

On page 184, paragraph 2, *Ibid,* p. 7.

On pages 184 and 185, regarding the mechanic's business style, see *Ibid,* pp. 139–155.

On page 185, paragraph 2, on the behavior of apprentices, *Ibid,* p. 153.

On page 186, paragraph 2, on the climate for investment, see Niles E. Helmboldt, Tina West, and Benjamin H. Hardy, "Private Investment and African Economic Policy," in Berg and Whitaker, *Strategies;* and A.N. Hawkins, "Can Africa Industrialize?" in Berg and Whitaker, *Strategies;* also Keith Marsden and Therese Belot, "Private Enterprise in Africa: Creating a Better Environment," World Bank Discussion papers, (Washington, DC: The World Bank, 1987).

On Africa's informal sector, see Helmboldt et al, "Private Investment;" Carl Liedholm and Donald C. Mead, "Small Scale Industry," in Berg and Whitaker, *Strategies;* John M. Page, Jr., and William F. Steel, "Small Enterprise Development: Economic Issues from African Experience," World Bank Technical Paper no. 26 (Washington, DC: The World Bank, 1984); and Pauline Baker, "Obstacles to Private Sector Activities in Africa."

On page 186, paragraph 3, see Sayre Schatz, "Private Capitalism and the Inert Economy of Nigeria."

On pages 189 and 190, regarding industrialization in Africa, studies include William F. Steel and Johnathan W. Evans, "Industrialization in Sub-Saharan Africa: Strategies and Performance," World Bank Technical Paper no. 25, (Washington, DC: The World Bank, 1984); Ravi Gulhati and Uday Sekhar, "Industrial Strategy for Late Starters: The Experience of Kenya, Tanzania, and Zambia," *World Development* (vol. 10, no. 11, 1982), pp. 949–972.

On page 190, paragraphs 1 and 2, data on the size of small scale enterprises comes from Liedholm, "Small Scale Industry," pp. 309–311.

On page 194, paragraph 1, for a thought-provoking exposition on the evolution of Western societies during the formation of capitalist economies, see Rosenburg and Birdzell, *The Economic Transformation of the Industrialized World.*

## 7: "SEEING IS DIFFERENT FROM BEING TOLD"

On page 197, paragraph 1, President Quett Masire is quoted in *World Development Forum* (vol. 4, no. 19, October 31, 1986).

On page 198, paragraph 3, Leopold Sédar Senghor, "West Africa in Evolution," *Foreign Affairs* (January 1961), p. 246.

On page 200, paragraph 2, Organization of African Unity, *Lagos Plan of Action for the Economic Development of Africa, 1980–2000* (Addis Ababa: OAU, 1980).

On page 200, paragraph 3, on the meeting of education ministers in Harare, Zimbabwe, see Eicher, "Transforming Africa's Agriculture," p. 21.

On page 201, paragraph 1, "Declaration on the Economic Situation in Africa Adopted by the Twenty-First Ordinary Session by the Assembly of Heads of States and Governments of the Organization of African Unity," Organization of African Unity (Addis Ababa: July 18–20, 1985); see also "Second Special Memorandum by the ECA Conference of Ministers: International Action for Relaunching the Initiative for Long Term Development and Economic Growth in Africa" (Addis Ababa: United Nations Economic Commission for Africa, April 1985).

On page 201, paragraph 2, "Consideration of the Critical Economic Situation in Africa, to Focus, in a Comprehensive and Integrated Manner, on the Rehabilitation and Medium and Long-Term Development Problems and Challenges Facing African Countries with a View to Promoting and Adopting Action-Oriented and Concerted Measures," draft report of the Ad Hoc Committee of the Thirteenth Special Session, A/S-13/AC.1-L.3 (New York: United Nations General Assembly, May 31, 1986).

On page 201, paragraph 3, the image of the African state as a cripple with no legs is quoted from Thomas M. Callaghy and Ernest J. Wilson, III, "Privatization in Africa," to be published in *The Twilight of the State-Owned Enterprise,* forthcoming from the Council on Foreign Relations, Raymond Vernon, ed.

On page 202, paragraph 1, on the July OAU session, see "Africa to Step Up Diplomacy," *Africa News* (September 1, 1986), p. 4. And on the meeting of the French West African Monetary Union, see Gerald Bourke, "Structural Adjustment Revolt," *West Africa* (March 9, 1987).

On page 202, paragraph 3, see Callaghy and Wilson, "Privatization in Africa."

On page 203, paragraph 1, N'diaye is quoted in Fiammeta Rocco, "Tensions at the ADB," *Institutional Investor,* July 1987.

On pages 203 and 204, the survey of policy reforms in Africa is drawn from "Policy Reforms in Africa: Accomplishments since 1982," USAID, 1986. See also the World Bank, "Financing Adjustment with Growth in Sub-Saharan Africa 1986–90."

On pages 205 and 206, on Nigeria's reform program, see *Financial Times* survey on Nigeria, *Financial Times* (March 2–3, 1986).

On page 208, paragraph 4, regarding alternatives to patronage, see David Leonard, "Putting the Farmer in Control," pp. 206ff.

On page 209, paragraph 4, see World Bank, *Towards Sustained Development in Sub-Saharan Africa.*

On page 211, paragraph 2, on the idea of partnership between donors and Africans see "Compact for African Development," the report on the Committee for African Development Strategies, Council on Foreign Relations and the Overseas Development Council, 1985.

On page 211, paragraph 4, on the evolution of donor-recipient relations I am indebted to conversations with Robert J. Berg.

On page 212, paragraph 1, for a description of private voluntary organizations in the United States, see *Diversity in Development: U.S. Voluntary Assistance to Africa,* (New York: Interaction, 1985).

On page 212, paragraph 3, enthusiastic endorsements of PVOs include Goran Hyden, "Business and Development in Sub-Saharan Africa," (Indianapolis: Universities Field Staff International Reports, no. 25, 1986); and *Famine, A Man-Made Disaster? A Report for the Independent Commission on International Humanitarian Issues* (London: Pan Books, 1985).

On page 213, paragraph 1, for an interesting African analysis of the dependency perspective, see S.K.B. Asante, "International Assistance and International Capitalism: Supportive or Counter-Productive?," in Carter and O'Meara, *Africa Independence: The First Twenty-Five Years,* pp. 249–273.

## 8: A FUTURE IN SHADOW

On page 219, paragraph 2, Wole Soyinka, *Ake: The Years of Childhood* (New York: Random House, 1982), pp. 156–157.

On pages 220 and 221, see *The Washington Post* (February 12–14, 1987), and *The New York Times* (February 5, 1987).

On page 222, paragraph 3, Olusegun Obasanjo, *Africa in Perspective,* p. 18; and Philip Ndegwa, *Africa's Development Crisis* (London: Heinemann Educational Books, 1985), pp. 35, 72. Other discussions of African regionalism include Carol Lancaster, "The Political Economy of Economic Integration in Sub-Saharan Africa," Colloque sur les Experiences Regionales dans Le Monde, Tunis, Tunisia, January 1987; and Vremudia P. Diejomaoh, "The Crisis in African Development and the Lagos Plan of Action," paper presented to the Temple, Bryn Mawr, Swathmore, and Haverford Colloquim on the crisis in African Development, Temple University, Philadelphia, November 1984. See also Edem Kodjo, *Africa Tomorrow* (New York: Continuum 1987) for an African view on Africa's future, emphasizing the need for continental unity.

On page 222, paragraph 4, Kojo Laing, *Search Sweet Country* (New York: William Morrow, 1986), p. 290.

On page 228, paragraph 2, for an excellent discussion of the relationship between popular arts and culture, see Karin Barber, "The Popular Arts in Africa," commissioned by the ALCS/SSRC Joint Committee on Africa Studies for presentation at the 29th Meeting of the Africa Studies Association, October 30–November 2, 1986, Madison, Wisconsin.

On pages 228 and 229, for an insightful discussion of new currents in African religion, see Goran Hyden, "Religion, Politics, and the Crisis in Africa," *Universities Field Staff International Reports* (no. 18, 1986). The quote from Laing, *Search Sweet Country,* is on p. 64. See also Thomas M. Callaghy, "Culture and Politics in Zaïre," forthcoming from Ann Arbor: ISR, University of Michigan, 1987, for a discussion of quasi-religious protest movements generated by economic decline and social instability in Zaïre, and Terence O. Ranger, "Religious Movements in Politics in Sub-Saharan Africa," *African Studies Review* (vol. 29, no. 2, June 1986). On the importance of religion to Africa's future, see also Ali A. Mazrui, *The Africans: A Triple Heritage* (Boston: Little, Brown, 1986).

On page 229, paragraph 3, on the attractions of socialism in Africa today, see William J. Foltz, Jr., "African Opinions of United States Policy," *CSIS Africa Notes* (no. 69, February 10, 1987), p. 7. In the same paragraph, on the left wing "populist" regimes in Burkina Faso and Congo, see Dov Ronen, "People's Republic of Benin: The Military, Marxist Ideology, and the Politics of Ethnicity;" and Victor T. LeVine, "Military Rule in the People's Republic of Congo;" in John Harbeson *The Military in African Politics* (New York: Praeger, 1987).

# INDEX

Abernethy, David, 52
Abidjan, 58
Abonnema people, 91
abortion, 115*n*
  data on, 111
  religion and, 102
  U.S. aid and, 124–125
  *see also* family planning
acacia trees, 144
Accra, 29
Achebe, Chinua, 15, 49, 88
acid rain, 76
adultery, 101
Africa:
  attitudes toward government in,
    199, 201
  borders in, 35–36
  children as viewed in, *see* children
  common market in, 16
  death rates in, 116
  debt of, 11, 19, 34, 84–85, 214
  democracy in, 43
  "developmental revolutions" in, 9
  disease and illness in, 116–121,
    127
  economies of, *see* African econ-
    omies; economic development
  education in, *see* education
  environmental decline in, 18,
    134–147
  explorers' views of, 127
  farm labor in, 105–106
  forests in, 139–142
  fragmentation of, 5, 22
  geography of, 137–138
  health care in, 21, 88, 101, 104,
    116, 119
  human resources of, 181–182
  international migration and, 106
  Japanese investment in, 5
  language problems of, 170–174
  Malthusian crunch in, 28
  migration within, 104
  plunder of state resources in, 50
  socialism in, *see* socialism
  soil quality in, 126–127, 137–140,
    144–147
  South, *see* South Africa
  unity needed in, 7, 225
  untapped markets in, 3–5
  West vs., 4, 5, 25–26
*African Child* (Laye), 100
African Development Bank, 202
African economies, 79–80, 82–83
  agriculture as chief priority in, 200
  business in, 184–196
  earning potential of, 38
  education and, 168
  fiscal and monetary policy in, 52,
    193–196
  foreign equity participation in, 39,
    187
  human infrastructure of, 9, 82, 86,
    160
  import choices of, 32–33
  "informal," 106
  initial common needs of, 65–66
  liquidity of, 85
  as near "economic collapse," 200
  oil shocks and, 17, 32–33
  patronage and, 52
  physical infrastructure of, 9, 80,
    86, 160
  regional conflict and, 45–46
  reliance on foreign capital, 39,
    187–189, 201–202, 211–213
  socialism and, 82
  technological infrastructure of, 9,
    86, 160
  Western advice and, 198
  *see also* economic development
African Green Revolution, 156–158,
  160–164
Agency for International Development, U.S. (AID), 69–73, 75, 78,
  181, 209
  "trickle up" approach of, 69–70
  Vietnam War and, 67
  women farmers and, 209
agriculture, 11
  African vs. Western, 128–129
  aid for, 69–70
  biology vs. politics in, 158–164
  bureaucracy and, 55–56
  competition in, 18–19
  ecology and, *see* ecology

expansion of, 105
export crop, *see* export crops
illness and, 116
industry vs., 60–61
limitations for, 138
men vs. women in, 132
"no till" cultivation in, 162
population pressure on, 139–140
in post-colonial era, 147–150
poultry, 195
slash and burn, 126, 128, 135
soil quality and, 17–19
state support for, 79–80, 81,
    158–161
suggestions for, 85–86
traditional methods of, 128–129
*see also* Green Revolution
Agriculture Department, U.S., 6
Ahidjo, Ahmadou, 41, 51, 133
Ahmadu Bello University, 65
aid to Africa, 61–86
"conditionality" and, 205
donors of, *see* donors
economic, 9–11
for education, 66–67, 77–78
effects of, 62, 71–79
expatriate staff and, 71
exports "tied" to, 76
food, 136–137, 156–158, 160, 211
grants as, 212–213
grass roots, 69–70
as impediment to progress, 77–83
military, 5, 45, 81
as "owed" to Africa, 200
Point Four Program and, 58
in postwar period, 59, 60–61
U.S. program of, 63–73
world peace tied to, 60
AID, *see* Agency for International
    Development, U.S.
AIDS (Acquired Immune Deficiency
    Syndrome), 118–120, 223
Aiken, George, 68
Ajayi, Jacob, 197
Akamba tribe, 90
Alger, Horatio, 192
Algeria, 6, 64
alleycropping, 162
alphabets, 176, 222
Amazon basin, 141
*Ambiguous Adventure* (Kane), 90,
    168–169
Amharic, 170
Amin, Idi, 30
ancestry, 91–92
Angola, 195
agriculture in, 136, 138
fertility in, 114

"Marxist," 64
South Africa and, 7, 45, 81
Angwafor, Ruben, 190, 192
apartheid, 7–8, 31
Arab Fund for African Development,
    210
Arabic, 170
Asaba people, 91
Asia, 54, 61
birth rates in, 103–104
debt of, compared with Africa's,
    19
family planning in, 103, 115
farm labor in, 105
food production in, 17–18, 31
Green Revolution in, 79, 143, 158,
    162
IMF and, 85
irrigation in, 157–158
population density in, 104
Attaturk, Kemal, 215
Australia, 142

Ba, Mariama, 98
Balewa, Abubakar Tafawa, 65
Banda, Hastings, 41, 133, 225
Banyankore people, 97
barrenness, 101–102
basic human needs, 187
bauxite, 46
beer, 95, 148
Belgium, 5, 34, 37
*Bend in the River* (Naipaul), 87, 198
Benin, 81, 139, 144, 202
Bera people, 91
Berlin Conference, 35
Berry, Sara S., 183, 184–185
Biafra, 4
biotechnology, 117, 155–157
plant genetics, 156–158
birth control:
pills, 115
*see also* abortions; contraception,
    contraceptives; family planning
Biya, Paul, 41
"Black Star" steamships, 30
black "townships," 7
Blixen, Karen, 131
blood screening, 118
border disputes, 35–37
Botswana, 41, 170
economic growth in, 42, 79–81
family planning in, 113
mineral wealth of, 42
South Africa and, 7, 45, 80
trade of, 45
Brandt Report (1978), 25
Brazil, 141

breast-feeding, 103, 111
Bretton Woods Conference (1944), 59
buccaneer capitalism, 186-192, 203
Bucharest, U.N. Conference on Population in (1974), 89, 112
Bura irrigation project, 157
bureaucracies, 51, 52-55, 106, 178, 180-181
  Western influence on, 55-56
  see also institutions
Burkina Faso, 55, 76, 94, 130, 134, 152, 202
Burundi, 49, 138

Caldwell, John C., 89-90
Cambodia, 67
Camdessus, Michel, 214
Cameroon, 41, 133, 144, 205, 216
  economic growth in, 41, 79-81
Camus, Albert, 223
capitalism, 9
  buccaneer, 186-192, 203
  socialism as precursor of, 46
  viability of, 81
CARE, 146
Carter, Jimmy, 63, 72
cassava, 149, 157
Central America, 4
certificate exams, 53, 180
Chad, 42, 114, 134
Chevron Oil Company, 44
children:
  as economic assets, 89, 93, 97-98, 105, 110-111
  in labor force, 93
  as source of prestige, 89-90
  see also families; family planning; fertility
Chiles, Lawton, 68
China, 22, 31, 61
Chogoria, Kenya, 111
cholera, 117
Chona, Mark, 164-165
Christianity, 38, 87-88, 103, 228-229
civil insurgencies, South African-supported, 7, 45, 87
civil servants, 40, 43
  protests by, 55
civil war, 4, 44-45, 49, 114
class distinctions, 173-174, 225
  see also apartheid
cocoa, 18, 30, 38, 79, 129, 130, 131, 133, 156, 207
coffee, 18, 38, 79, 129, 130, 131
  national earnings from, 130

colonialism, colonialists:
  bureaucracies and, 52, 54-56
  export crops and, 130-131
  government legitimization and, 36-38, 58
  intracontinental migration under, 107
  land acquisition under, 35-36, 126, 128, 131
  as source of economic decline, 81
  strategies of, 5-6, 25
  traditional agriculture and, 128-132, 144-149, 150-154
  tribalism under, 49
  vocational education under, 179-180
  welfare under, 39
Commonwealth Development Corporation, 210
communal land ownership, 3, 12, 126, 131, 140, 160
community boundaries, 2-3
condoms, 115n
Congo, see Zaire
Congo-Brazzaville, 39, 54, 77
Congress, U.S., 67-72, 209
Coniagui people, 98
Conrad, Joseph, 2
conservation, 144-146; see also agriculture
Constitution, U.S., 68
contraception, contraceptives, 111, 112
  availability of, 109, 111, 113, 115-116
  as immoral, 102, 110
  in rural vs. urban areas, 109-111
  social change and, 109-110
  types of, 109, 114
  as Western conspiracy, 89
  women's independence and, 110
  see also family planning
copper, 33, 39
corn, 83, 146, 157, 162-164
corporations, 148, 149
  parastatal, 23, 52, 148
Côte d'Ivoire, 18, 41, 58, 79-81, 182, 205, 207
  agriculture in, 79, 133, 139, 148, 150, 162
  economic growth in, 79-81
  Ghana's industrialization and, 133
  law changes in, 108
  wages and salaries in, 55, 153
cotton, 33, 38, 46, 80, 129, 130, 131
coups, 42-43
cow dung, 139
cowpeas, 157, 162

credentialism, 54, 168, 177–180
credit unions, 71
Cuba, 3, 45
cultural imperialism, 15–16
*Cycles of American History* (Schlesinger), 13

Dakar, 33, 75, 105
Dakar, University of, 181
debt, of Africa, 11, 19, 34, 84–85, 214
democracy, 42, 64
Deng, Francis Mading, 167
Development of Women *(Maendeleo ya Wanawake)*, 122
diamonds, 33, 38
diarrhea, infant death from, 78, 120–121, 167
Dikko, Umaru, 51
Diop, Martha, 191–192
Diouf, Abdou, 197
diphtheria, 120
disease, 117–119, 127
Doe, Samuel, 43
donors, 74, 75, 77–78
  commitment of, to reform, 83
  multiple objectives of, 73–74, 201
  planning required by, 75–76, 210
  romance of African development and, 198
  *see also* aid to Africa; *specific donors*
drought, 127, 135

ecology, 129–130
  basic elements of, 137–138
  export crops and, 129–130
  technical solutions to problems of, 144–150
  *see also* rainfall; soil erosion
economic development:
  aid planning and, 70–79
  civil war and, 44–46
  consumption vs. production in, 40
  culture and, 1–2, 47
  debt service and, 84
  defined, 59–60
  democracy and, 64
  economic culture and, 23–24, 47–48, 183–186
  ethnic loyalties and, 49
  "freeing up" economies for, 8
  future growth of, 60
  goals of, 60
  incentives for change and, 107–111
  infusion of technical assistance and training and, 78
  leadership and, 41–42, 45
  market competition and, 2–3, 6–7
  political control and, 46–48
  population growth vs., 80–81
  relief vs., 201–202
  social change and, 9, 107–111, 218–231
  stability of society and, 45
economies, *see* African economies
Edo people, 90
education, 10–11, 97, 167–196
  aid for, 65–66, 77–78
  civic, 43
  credentialism and, 53, 168, 177–180
  demand for, 168
  economic skills and, 169
  elementary, 14, 33, 39, 88, 174–177, 179
  expansion of, 53
  family planning and, 123
  institutional hierarchies and, 54
  overseas training, 182
  in post-Independence period, 39, 80–81, 168–169
  resources for, 176–180
  secondary, 88, 174, 175–177, 178, 180, 181
  tradition and, 180
  university, 39, 174, 175, 178–182
  vocational, 179–180
Egypt, 6, 63, 65
Eisenhower, Dwight D., 64
embezzlement, 50–51
Emecheta, Buchi, 100
employment, 106, 178, 190
  ethnic groups and, 53–54
end-the-war amendment, to foreign assistance bill, 68
England, 5–6, 37, 131–132
English language, 170, 172–175
entrepreneurs, African, 184–196
Equator, 14, 137
Eritrea, 44
erosion, *see* soil erosion
Ethiopia, 16–17, 170
  agriculture in, 130, 134, 136, 138, 144
  capital investment programs in, 65
  law changes in, 108
  "Marxist," 65
  military in, 43
  rains in, 16, 142
  soil erosion in, 142
  Soviet aid to, 44, 81
ethnic groups, African:
  diversity of, 5–6, 22
  economic development and, 50
  employment and, 53–54

nationalism and, 49–50
power struggles among, 48–49
*see also* tribes, tribalism
Europe, 5, 109, 127
in Middle Ages, 28
European Community, 57
Ewe people, 35, 94
exchange rates, 56, 147–148, 155, 206
expatriates, 71, 79, 181–182, 188–189
export crops, 18, 26, 33, 38, 155, 159
aid "tied" to, 77
colonial administration and, 130–131
ecology and, 129–130
oil prices and, 32
subsistence farming vs., 38, 128–133, 151–155

families, 10, 11–12
inheritance through, 92–95, 108–109, 189
land and, 92–95
nuclear, 107, 125
in urban areas, 95–96
in world outlook of children, 87
*see also* kinship bonds
family planning, 109–116
attitudes toward, 89, 109
demand for, 109–116
desired numbers of children and, 111–112, 122
education about, 114–115
feasibility of, 111
government resistance to, 123
magic vs., 114
price of, 123
private sector and, 114–115
resistance to, 113*n*
for spacing vs. limiting of children, 112
*see also* contraception, contraceptives
famine, 2, 4–5, 15–17, 25, 130, 133, 136–137
farming, *see* agriculture
fertility:
primacy of, 100–102
religion and, 90–91
in urban vs. rural areas, 95–96
*see also* population, population growth; family planning
fertilizers, 78, 129, 135, 143, 157
fishing, 74, 78, 195
food aid, 136, 156–157, 159, 209
Food and Agriculture Organization (FAO), United Nations, 78, 142–144

food imports, 18
high-yielding, 162
food production:
in post-Independence era, 132
soil quality and, 16–18
subsistence vs., 132–133
by U.N., 6
*see also* export crops
Ford Foundation, 156
Foreign Assistance Act (1973), 68–69
foreign assistance bill (1972), 68
forests, 139–141
"four freedoms," 58–59
France:
aid to Africa from, 62
colonial style of, 5–6, 37
Côte d'Ivoire and, 58
French language, 170, 171–172
French Somalia, 35
Fulbright, William, 67–68
funerals, 91–92, 108

Gambia, 109, 134, 154
genetic engineering, 117
German language, 172
Ghana, 43, 216
capital investment progressive in, 65–66
children, 93, 111–112
civil service in, 55
economic growth of, 42, 133
education in, 65–66, 77–78
law changes in 108–109, 207–209
parastatal agencies in, 52–53
trade, 29–32, 35
Gonja, 93
government:
accountability of, 50, 194–195
allocation of resources by, 37–38
control sought by, 39–40, 79, 82–83, 158–164
economic initiatives by, 193–196
expansion of educational institutions by, 53, 178–182
family groups and, 10
as fount of resources, 199
legitimacy of, 36–38, 50
tribal, 35–36
turnkey, 36–47, 148
*Grain of Wheat* (Thiong'o), 26
Grant, James, 121
Great Britain, 5–6, 37, 131–132
green beans, dry-seeded, 161
Green Revolution, 12, 79, 143–144, 156–158, 162
in Africa, 155–156, 156–158, 160–164
gross domestic product, 54

gross national products (GNPs), 4, 75
*Guardian of the Word* (Laye), 218
Guinea, 46, 81, 98, 138, 170
Guinea-Bissau, 130
Gulf of Guinea, 138
Gwembe Tonga people, 92

Habyarimona, Juvinal, 145
"Harambee," 94
Harare, 200
Hausa people, 35, 48, 173–174
health care, 21, 88, 103, 106, 117, 120
*Heart of Darkness* (Conrad), 2
hegemony, 35–38
herding, 135
hierarchies, 6, 36, 54, 220
"hotseating," 179
Houphouet-Boigny, Felix, 41, 52, 133, 225

Ibadan, 162
Ibadan, University of, 14
Ibo people, 35, 48, 164
Ibru, Michael, 194–196
Ife University, 65
Igbo people, 94, 100
illiteracy, 39, 71, 77
IMF (International Monetary Fund), 59, 73, 202, 207–210
  stabilization programs, 84–85, 207
immigration, 107
immunization, 120
imperialism:
  cultural, 15–16
  economic, 24, 64, 67
  European, 175–176
imports, 22, 38, 32–33, 147
Independence era:
  agriculture in, 147–150
  colonial institutions in, 36
  education funding and, 178–179
  industrialization in, 31
  modernization in, 132–136
  nationalism in, 64
  optimism of, 30–31
  *see also* post-Independence era
India, 31, 61, 66
Indian Ocean, 44
Indochina Postwar Reconstruction, 67–68
industrial entrepreneurship, 66, 190–193, 194–195
Industrial Revolution, 89
industry, industrialization:
  agriculture vs., 60–61
  failure of, 148
  favored through policy, 149

health care and, 106
  in Latin America and Asia, 61
  portion of workforce in, 105
  as primary objective, 132, 200–201
  privatization vs., 201–203
infant mortality, 78, 88, 120–122
"informal" economies, 106
inheritance, 108–109
institutions:
  apartheid and, 7–8
  blueprint for, 83
  colonial, in post-Independence period, 53
  corruption in, 47
  donor-supported "enclaves" for, 180–181
  education and, 168–169
  in Independence era, 36
  lack of, 26
  national, 75
  in political reform, 160
  productive, extensive reform and, 197
  structureless, 71
  viability of, 2–3
  *see also* bureaucracies
insurgencies, 7, 44–45, 81
Integrated Rural Development, 74, 181
interest rates, 34, 84
internal parasites, 117
International Bank for Reconstruction and Development, 59 *see also* World Bank
international communications network, 169
International Development Association (IDA), 63
International Fund for Agricultural Development (IFAD), 154
International Institute for Tropical Agriculture, 162
international migration, 107
International Monetary Fund, *see* IMF
International Planned Parenthood Federation, 114, 124–125
iron oxide, 128
irrigation, 70, 75, 150, 154, 157–158, 161
Islam, 103, 228–229
Israel, 63
Italian Somalia, 35
IUDs (intrauterine devices), 115n
Ivory Coast, *see* Côte d'Ivoire

"jab planters," 162
Jahally, 154

Japan, 5, 199
"jerry-building," 12
"Johnny Appleseed" project, 146
John Paul, Pope, 112
"junior service," 27

Kabwe, 153
Kaiser Aluminum, 65
Kalahari, 138
Kane, Cheikh Hamidou, 90, 168–169
Kansas State University, 65
Kapwepwe, Simon, 172
Kaunda, Kenneth, 33, 118, 164, 225
Kennedy, John F., 63, 64
Kenya, 18, 35–36, 41–42, 170, 172–173, 221
    agriculture in, 130–131, 136, 138, 144–145, 150, 162–163
    capital investment programs in, 65
    economic growth in, 79–81
    education in, 39
    family planning in, 112–113
    infant mortality in, 88, 120
    land in, 48, 74–75, 94–95, 103, 126, 153
    law changes in, 108, 153–154
    population of, 20, 58, 104
    tourism in, 79
    "tribalism" in, 48
    unemployment in, 94
    wealth in, 48, 94–95, 153
    women's opportunities in, 108, 153
Kenyan Independence, 104
Kenyatta, Jomo, 42, 48, 172, 215, 225
Keynes, John Maynard, 59
Khama, Seretse, 42
Kibaki, Ngugi, 192
Kikuyu people, 48, 131
Kilimanjaro, 112
kinship bonds, 49–50, 94–97
    unemployment and, 106
    see also families
"kleptocratic" rule, 46
Konadu, Asare, 90
Korean War, 64–65

labor, division of, 98
labor impressment, 132
labor unions, 40
Lagos, 13–14, 195
Lagos Plan of Action (1980), 200
Laing, Kojo, 222, 228
Lake Chad, 134, 138
land, 126–166
    under colonialism, 35–36, 126, 128, 131

communal, 3, 12, 126, 128, 131, 140, 160
    family and, 92–95
    patriarchal apportionment of, 10, 94
    rights to, 101, 126, 128, 131, 140, 153
    scarcity of, 89
language, 6, 22, 49, 170–174
Laos, 67
Lasswell, Harold, 60
Latin America:
    birth rates in, 104
    debt of, compared with Africa's, 19
    family planning in, 115
    farm labor in, 105
    food production in, 17–18, 31
    gross domestic products in, 54
    IMF and, 85
    industrialization of Africa vs., 61
    land ownership in, 31
Laye, Camara, 103, 170–171, 218
leadership:
    for benefit of people, 46–47
    changes in, 225
    economic development and, 45–47
    long- vs. short-term concerns of, 85
    modernization sought by, 132–133
    reform and, 197
    responsibilities of, 197, 225–226
Lesotho, 111, 153, 170
leucana trees, 146
libations to ancestors, 91–92
liberalism, economic, 226–227
Liberia, 43, 58, 65, 113, 214–216
Libya, 6, 65
life expectancy, 103, 116
locusts, 78
Lomé Agreements, 62
London School of Economics, 46
long-term loans, 82
Lusaka, Zambia, 33

McNamara, Robert S., 69
Maendeleo ya Wanawake (Development of Women), 122
maize, 80, 146, 157
Makere University, 161
malaria, 117
Malawi, 41, 113, 133, 140, 162–163
    economic growth in, 79–81
Malaysia, 133
Mali, 43, 81, 130, 134, 159, 202
Malinke people, 171
malnutrition, 116
Mangaldié, 166

"man-induced climate change," 141
Mansfield, Mike, 68
Mao Zedong, 12
Maputo, 45
markets:
  development and encouragement
    of, 3, 6–7, 79, 159–160
  regulation of, 10, 32–34, 159–160
marriage, 6, 10, 90
  childless, 100–101
  in cities vs. villages, 107
  economic responsibilities of, 98
  husband-wife bonds in, 99
  laws about, 108–109
  notions of elites about, 107
  woman-woman, 99
Marshall Plan, 59–60
Marxism, 47, 64–65
Masire, Quett, 42, 197
matrilineal societies, 98
Mauritania, 13, 43, 134, 139–140,
  195
maxim gun, 38
measles, 120
meat-packing industry, 80
media, 14, 25, 167, 169
Merell Dow Company, 117
Mexico, 156
Mexico City Conference (1984), 112,
  124
Michigan State University, 65, 182
Middle East, 7
migration, 107
military, military rule, 40, 42–43, 48
millet, 149, 157
minerals, mineral exports, 6, 15,
  32–34, 42
missionaries, 38, 87
Mobutu Sese Seko, 24, 33–34, 46,
  50, 64
Mohammed, Murtala, 43
Moi, Daniel arap, 42, 145
monogamy, 103
Moro, Cleophas arap, 161
mortality rates, 21, 89, 116–117
Mossi people, 94
Mozambique, 45, 134, 136
  civil war in, 113
  economy of, 45
  fertility in, 113
  illiteracy in, 39
  Marxist leadership in, 81
  South Africa and, 7, 45, 81
Mozambique National Resistance
  (RENAMO), 7
Mwananshiku, Fred, 196–197

Naipaul, V. S., 87, 198

Nairobi, 58, 105
  City Hall in, 49
Namib, 138
Namibia, 138
Nasser, Gamal Abdal, 31
nationalism, 40, 50, 64
National Marketing Corporation, 205
National Union for the Total Inde-
  pendence of Angola (UNITA), 7,
  45
Natural Resources Board, 143
N'diaye, Babacar, 203
Nehru, Jawaharlal, 31
Newcombe, Kenneth, 138
New International Economic Order
  (NIEO), 32, 72, 81
newspapers, 167, 169
Niger, 37, 134, 140, 202
  farming in, 78–79, 135, 146
  population growth in, 78
Nigeria, 1, 35, 66, 176, 205–206
  agriculture in, 138, 144, 162, 164
  capital of, 13–14
  civil war in, 4, 49
  conspicuous consumption in,
    50–51
  costs for public administration in,
    55
  coups in, 3, 44
  debt of, 44
  ethnic alliances and, 48
  family planning in, 110–111
  Ghanaians expelled from, 107
  Independence Day in, 1
  oil boom in, 51
  population of, 104
  rice paddies in, 75
  universities in, 65, 77
  U.S. aid to, 65–66
Niger River, 171
Nile River, 134
Nixon, Richard M., 29, 67–68
Nkrumah, Kwame, 29–31, 52, 133
No Longer at Ease (Achebe), 49
nonaligned movement, 31
Northern Rhodesia, see Zambia
"no till" cultivation, 162
Nouakchott, 135–136
Nsukka, University of Nigeria at, 65
nuclear family, 107, 125
Nuer people, 93
nutrition, 39, 116, 120, 150
Nyerere, Julius, 13, 45, 75–76, 145,
  172–173, 225

OAU (Organization of African
  Unity), 7, 197, 200–201
Obasanjo, Olusegun, 40, 164, 222

office management, 10
oil, 10, 45, 51, 80, 200
  price rise in, 32
  OPEC and, 10, 17, 32
Olympio, Sylvanus, 44
OPEC (Organization of Petroleum
  Exporting Countries), 10, 17, 32
Organization of African Unity
  (OAU), 7, 197, 200–202
Ouagadougou, 130
Out of Africa (Blixen), 131
Oxfam, 166, 212

Pacharr, 154
palm oil, 18, 88, 156, 162
Pan African confederation, 29
"pan Africanism," 222
paper mills, 76
parasites, internal, 117
parastatal organizations, 23, 52, 148
Paris Club, 19
patriotism, 48
patronage, 48, 52, 183
pay scales, 54–55
Peace Corps, 31, 78
peanuts, 33, 80, 130, 156
peas, 157
Peres, Shimon, 170
pesticides, 129, 150
Petals of Blood (Thiong'o), 87
pharmacies, 114
Philadelphia, Pa., bombing in, 169
Philippines, 156
pill, birth control, 115
plagues, 16
plant genetics revolution, 156–157
Point Four Program (1949), 58
"Policy Sciences of Development,
  The" (Lasswell), 60
polio, 120
political reform, 197–199
  agriculture, industry and, 158–164
  ethnic ties and, 50
  future of, 220–232
  organizational aspects of, 160
  past policies and, 198
polygamy, 103
polygyny, 94
population, population growth, 34,
  69, 87–125
  age and, 105, 220
  AIDS and, 118
  economic growth vs., 80
  equilibrium of, 89, 114
  family planning and, see family
    planning
  farming and, 142–143
  health improvement and, 78,
    116–125

  in South Africa, 8
  see also fertility
Port Harcourt, 195
Portugal, 5–6, 37, 45
Portuguese language, 170
post-Independence era:
  education in, 39, 77, 168–170
  expansion of public sector in, 55
  food production in, 163
  French population in colonies dur-
    ing, 58
  government in, 53, 58
  military power in, 50
  pay scales in, 56–57
  plant genetics in, 156–157
  reliance on patronage by govern-
    ments in, 48, 52, 183–185
post-partum sexual taboo, 103
poverty, attack on, see aid to Africa
pregnancy, 90, 109–110
private initiatives, 8, 72, 80
private sector, 80, 114
private voluntary organizations
  (PVOs), 212–213
privatization:
  defined, 11, 203
  industrialization vs., 200–203
  as new policy, 72
Program of Action on Population,
  112
public sector, 54, 80

radio, 45, 167, 169
rainfall, 134, 137–139
  acid, 76
  decline in, 16, 34, 141–142
  migration and, 107
  nutrients leached from soil by,
    127–128
  reforestation and, 75
Rawlings, Jerry, 207–209, 216, 229
Reagan administration, 57, 64, 72,
  230
  population planning and, 124
real estate, 189
reforestation, 75
refugee camps, 135–136
reincarnation, 91–92, 107
religion, African traditional, 6, 90
  Christianity vs., 38, 87–88, 103,
    228–229
  fertility and, 90–91
RENAMO (Mozambique National
  Resistance), 7
Rhodesia:
  Northern, see Zambia
  Southern, see Zimbabwe
rice, 75, 154, 157

Rift Valley, Kenya, 116
roads, 9, 14, 66–67, 208
Rockefeller Foundation, 156, 209
Roman alphabet, 170
Roosevelt, Franklin Delano, 58–59
Rostow, Walt Whitman, 47
rubber, 18, 38, 156
rural "homelands," 7–8
Rwanda, 49, 113, 130, 138–140

Sahara Desert, 6–7, 137–139
Sahel region, 20, 71, 78, 134–135,
    138, 144, 157–158
Sankara, Thomas, 229
schistosomiasis, 117
Schlesinger, Arthur M., Jr., 13
schooling, see education
Search Sweet Country (Laing), 222, 228
second-burial ceremonies, 91
Senegal, 202
    agriculture in, 134, 141, 159, 181,
        195
    barrier forest in, 75
    death during childbirth in, 110
    education in, 77–78
    export prices of, 33, 130
    parastatal agencies in, 52–53
    socialism in, 198
Senghor, Leopold Sédor, 171, 198,
    225
sexual customs, 6, 102–103; see also
    marriage
Shagari, Shehu, 51
Shamir, Yitzhak, 170
shantytowns, 14, 105
Sierra Leone, 58, 214
sisal, 38, 46, 156
Sisala, 93
slash and burn agriculture, 126, 128,
    135
sleeping sickness, 117
Smith, Adam, 34, 159, 198
Snow, Edgar, 12
social change, 12
    pace of, 109
    tradition vs., 107–111, 218–231
socialism, 46–47, 81–82, 198, 226
    economic problems with, 82
    viability of, 79
Society of Those Whom God Has
    Blessed, 100
soil erosion, 127–128, 145, 146, 162
    in Ethiopia, 142
So Long a Letter (Ba), 98
Somalis, Somalia, 16–17, 35, 65, 120,
    134, 204
    language and, 170
Somalian Women's Socialist Union,
    123

Sorbonne, 46
sorghum, 149, 157, 162–163
South Africa, 7–9
    air force, 45
    Botswana as economic satellite of,
        80
    civil insurgencies supported by, 7,
        44–45, 81–82
    economy of, 7–8
    military activities of, 7, 43–45,
        81–85
    population in, 7–8
    U.S. and, 7, 45
Southern Africa Development Coor-
    dination Conference (SADCC), 182
Southern Rhodesia, see Zimbabwe
South Vietnam, 67
Soviet Union, 5, 22, 44–45, 60, 81
Soyinka, Wole, 219
Spanish language, 170
State Department, U.S., 58
state-owned enterprises, 52–53
steel mills, 52, 148
sterility, 100–102
stock of debt, 83–84
Sudan, 16–17, 214
    agriculture in, 130, 134, 136, 138,
        140, 157, 162
    capital investment programs in, 62
    children in, 93
    debt of, 44
    donor competition over, 73–74
    fertility rates in, 114
    U.S. aid to, 65
    sugar, 74, 155
Sukarno, 31
supply-side economics, 73, 77
Swahili, 170, 172–174
Swaziland, 113, 170

Tanzania, 144, 152, 170, 172–173
    aid to, 76
    bureaucracies in, 55
    capital investment programs in, 65,
        133
    corruption in, 46
    education in, 39, 65, 77
    family planning in, 113
    leadership in, 45–46
    national institutions and markets
        in, 75–76
    parastatal agencies in, 52–53
    women's opportunities in, 109
taxation, 10, 34, 38, 108, 132
tax code, Zambian, 108
tea, 18, 79, 129, 155
technology:
    application of, 21–22

"appropriate," 26
biological, 118–119, 155–156
raw materials market and, 31
religion and, 87–88
in twentieth century, 8
telephone service, 13–14
television, 14
"temperate bias," 129
tetanus, 120
*Things Fall Apart* (Achebe), 15, 88
Thiong'o, Ngugi wa, 26, 87
Third World:
labor in, 15
material lives of poor in, 70
population growth in, 19–20,
103–104
Soviet Union and, 81
trade in, 18
Thomas, Lewis, 4
timber, 138–141
Timberlake, Lloyd, 146
tin, 33
tobacco, 80, 129, 156
Togo, 35, 44, 202
tools and machinery, 161
topsoil, 129, 139; *see also* soil erosion
Touré, Sékou, 81
tourism, 79
trade, 5, 45, 66
guarantees of, 62
inhibiting of, 39
international trends in, 46, 155
transSaharan, 135
trade brokers, 26
tradition:
in African vs. Western culture, 2–3
change vs., 11–12, 107–111,
218–232
education and, 180
modern aspirations and, 14
Training and Visit extension system,
154
Treasury Department, U.S., 57–58,
73, 198–199
tribes, tribalism, 2–3
under colonial rule, 49
connotations of, 48–50
control of, 21–22
government among, 35–36
in precolonial Africa, 35–36
wars of, 127, 135
Trickle Up program, 212
tropical rainforests, 137–139
Truman, Harry S., 59
tuberculosis, 120
tubers, 149, 157
Tubman, William Vacanarat Shadrach, 52

Tunisia, 6
Turkana, 74–75
turnkey governments, 37, 148

Uganda, 30, 144, 173
AIDS in, 118
children in, 97
economic growth of, 42
education in, 39
power struggles in, 49
"underdeveloped" nations, 58
UNICEF, 78, 120–121
unions, 40, 71
UNITA (National Union for the Total Independence of Angola), 7, 45
United Nations, 6
Charter, 59
conferences on population, 89,
112, 124
Food and Agriculture Organization
(FAO), 78, 142–144
Fund for Population Activities
(UNFPA), 124
influence of African states on, 31
International Fund for Agricultural Development (IFAD),
154
policy on aid to Africa, 61–62
special session on African economic crisis (1986), 112, 201
study on African work force, 105
United States:
Africa's importance to, 3–4
aid program of, 63–73
Congress, 67–72, 209
debt of, 63
domestic poverty program of, 72
economic development as viewed
by, 66, 79
international mood swings of, 63
monetary and fiscal policies of, 34,
63
South Africa and, 7, 44–45
universities, *see* education
Upper Volta, *see* Burkina Faso
urban "informal" economies, 106
urbanization, tradition and, 107
urban money economy, 89

vaccinations, 78, 117, 119
Valco aluminum smelter, 65
Vietnam War, 64–67
village councils, 35, 153
villages, 2–3, 126
vocational education, 179–180
Volkswagen, 206
Volta Dam and hydroelectric plant,
65

wages, 54–55
Walde, Pale, 51
Walter Reed Army Institute of Research, 117
Warri, 195
welfare, 39-40
Wen, Emperor, 126
West, Western cultures, 3–5, 54, 60, 199
West African School Certificate Exam, 174
wheat, 149, 157
widows, 108
witches, 101
*Woman in Her Prime* (Konadu), 90
woman-woman marriage, 99–100
women:
    children and, 97–102
    credit policies and, 193
    education of, 121–122, 132
    excessive workload of, 152
    food shortages and, 150–154
    land rights of, 153
    responsibilities of, 97–98
    tax code and, 108
wood, 138–140
workers, workforce, 7–8, 22–23, 37, 105
World Bank, 22, 26, 57, 72, 181
    on demand for wood, 139
    farming training by, 146, 154, 161
    lending commitments of, 69
    loans of, 32, 63–64, 76, 206
    personnel of, 63
    policy formulation by, 61–62
    population projections by, 104–105, 111, 113–115, 121
    projections on economic growth, 113–114
    set-up of, 59
    state-led industrialization funded by, 47
    support for education, 66–67, 76–77
    U.S. and, 63–64

yams, 149, 157, 162
*Years of Childhood* (Soyinka), 219
Yoruba people, 35, 48, 91–92, 171, 174, 183

Zablocki, Clement Jr., 68
Zaire, 24, 137, 141, 162
    communism in, 64
    economic restructuring in, 65
    education in, 39
    family planning in, 111–114
    fish farming in, 78
    "kleptocratic" rule in, 46
    leadership in, 45–46
    mineral wealth in, 33–34
    taxation in, 34, 132
    U.S. intervention in, 46
Zambia, 188–189, 204, 212–214
    agriculture in, 13, 131, 136, 163–165
    AIDS in, 118–119
    copper in, 33, 39
    economic progress in, 33, 164–165
    education in, 39, 77–78
    family bonds in, 92–93
    family planning in, 110
    foreign exchange in, 163–164
    South Africa and, 7
    tax code in, 108
*Zambian Daily News,* 109
Zende, Matthew, 165
Zimbabwe, 216
    agriculture in, 131, 136, 138, 143–144, 150, 162–163
    economic growth in, 77–80
    family planning in, 112–116
    private vs. public sector in, 80
    South Africa and, 7, 45
    trade of, 45
zinc, 33

# About the Author

Jennifer Seymour Whitaker has written extensively on southern Africa and U.S. policy, including two previous books, *Conflict in Southern Africa*, and *Africa and the United States: Vital Interests*, as well as articles and reviews on Africa, the Middle East and other areas of the Third World in *The Atlantic, Foreign Affairs, The New York Times, The Nation, The News Leader* and others. She is co-editor of *Strategies for African Development*, for which she won a 1986 World Hunger Media Award.

Ms. Whitaker is now Director of Committees on Foreign Relations at the Council on Foreign Relations. Formerly a Senior Fellow specializing in Africa, and before that, Associate Editor of *Foreign Affairs*, she recently served as co-director of the Committee on African Development Strategies (sponsored by the Council on Foreign Relations and the Overseas Development Council). She lived in Africa for several years, mostly in Nigeria.